National
5

Biology

Writing team
James Torrance
James Fullarton
Clare Marsh
James Simms
Caroline Stevenson

Diagrams by
James Torrance

HODDER
GIBSON
AN HACHETTE UK COMPANY

Cover photo: The crab has been temporarily submerged by a wave from the incoming tide. It is expelling excess sea water from its gills as two jets. Photo courtesy of James Torrance

The Publishers would like to thank the following for permission to reproduce copyright material:

Photo credits
Fotolia, p. 1 (background) and Unit 1 running head image; Lester V. Bergman/Corbis, figure 1.4; Biophoto Associates/ SPL, figure 2.16; Power and Syred/SPL, figure 3.3; Science Source/SPL, figure 4.3; Prof. K.Seddon & Dr. T.Evans, Queen's University Belfast/SPL, figure 5.1; Phototake Inc./Alamy, figure 5.2; Nigel Cattlin,/Visuals Unlimited/Corbis, figure 6.5; CNRI/SPL, figure 7.8; John Fryer/Alamy, figure 7.12; Fotolia, p. 73 (background) and Unit 2 running head image; Professor Miodrag Stojkovic/SPL, figure 10.1; Avita Medical, figure 10.4; peretzp, figure 10.5; M. I. Walker/ SPL, figure 10.8; Dr Colin Chumbley/SPL. figure 11.3; CNRI/SPL, figure 11.5; Innerspace Imaging/SPL, figure 12.3; MedicalRF.com/Corbis, figure 12.4; Martyn Chillmaid/SPL, figure 13.19; Nathan Benn/Corbis, figure 15.4; Lunagrafix/ SPL, figure 15.8; Steve Gschmeissner/SPL, figure 15.9; Anatomical Travelogue/SPL, figure 15.20; Biophoto Associates/ SPL, figure 15.23; Paolo Patrizi/Alamy, figure 16.7; Scott Camazine/Alamy, figure 16.8; Fotolia, p. 143 (background) and Unit 3 running head image; Fotolia, figure 17.2; Fotolia, figure 17.14; Tom Bean/Alamy, figure 17.15; Fotolia, figure 17.16; Fotolia, figure 17.17; blickwinkel/Alamy, figure 17.19; Fotolia, figure 17.20; david tipling/Alamy, figure 17.21; David Whitaker/Alamy, figure 17.22; mike lane/Alamy, figure 17.24; Fotolia, figure 18.14; Dale Spartas/Corbis, figure 18.15; George McCarthy/Corbis, figure 18.20; Caroline Penn/Corbis, figure 20.3; Hattie Young/SPL, figure 20.4; Mitsuhiko Imamori/Minden Pictures, figure 20.9; Michael & Patricia Fogden/Corbis, figure 20.10; Biomedical Imaging Unit/Southampton General Hospital/SPL, figure 20.15; Visuals Unlimited/Corbis, figure 20.16; Terry Fountain, figure 20.19 left; andrew tiley/Alamy, figure 20.19 right; Fotolia, figure 21.2; Dario Sabljak/Alamy, figure 21.3; Fotolia, figure 21.4; Nick Hawkes/Ecoscene/Corbis, figure 21.5; FLPA/Alamy, figure 21.15; Wayne Lawler/SPL, figure 21.16.

All other photos supplied by James Torrance.

Every effort has been made to trace all copyright holders, but if any have been inadvertently overlooked the Publishers will be pleased to make the necessary arrangements at the first opportunity.

Whilst every effort has been made to check the instructions of practical work in this book, it is still the duty and legal obligation of schools to carry out their own risk assessments.

Although every effort has been made to ensure that website addresses are correct at time of going to press, Hodder Gibson cannot be held responsible for the content of any website mentioned in this book. It is sometimes possible to find a relocated web page by typing in the address of the home page for a website in the URL window of your browser.

Hachette UK's policy is to use papers that are natural, renewable and recyclable products and made from wood grown in sustainable forests. The logging and manufacturing processes are expected to conform to the environmental regulations of the country of origin.

Orders: please contact Bookpoint Ltd, 130 Milton Park, Abingdon, Oxon OX14 4SB. Telephone: (44) 01235 827720. Fax: (44) 01235 400454. Lines are open 9.00–5.00, Monday to Saturday, with a 24-hour message answering service. Visit our website at www.hoddereducation.co.uk. Hodder Gibson can be contacted direct on: Tel: 0141 848 1609; Fax: 0141 889 6315; email: hoddergibson@hodder.co.uk

First published in 2013 by
Hodder Gibson, an imprint of Hodder Education,
An Hachette UK Company
2a Christie Street
Paisley PA1 1NB

Without Answers
Impression number   5 4
Year   2017 2016 2015 2014
ISBN: 978 1 4441 8434 1

With Answers
Impression number   5 4
Year   2017 2016 2015 2014
ISBN: 978 1 4441 8432 7

Illustrations by James Torrance

Typeset in Minion Regular 11/14 by Integra Software Services Pvt. Ltd., Pondicherry, India

Printed in Dubai

A catalogue record for this title is available from the British Library

Contents

Preface   iv

Unit 1 Cell Biology

1 Cell structure   2

2 Transport across cell membranes   6

3 Producing new cells   19

4 DNA and the production of proteins   30

5 Proteins and enzymes   35

6 Genetic engineering   43

7 Respiration   48

8 Photosynthesis   56

Unit 2 Multicellular Organisms

9 Cells, tissues and organs   74

10 Stem cells and meristems   78

11 Control and communication   83

12 Reproduction   94

13 Variation and inheritance   98

14 Transport systems in plants   111

15 Animal transport and exchange systems   120

16 Effects of lifestyle choices   129

Unit 3 Life on Earth

17 Biodiversity and the distribution of life   144

18 Energy in ecosystems   157

19 Sampling techniques and measurements   166

20 Adaptation, natural selection and evolution   176

21 Human impact on environment   189

Appendix 1

Units of measurement   204

Appendix 2

pH scale   205

Appendix 3

Size scale of plants and micro-organisms   206

Appendix 4

Variable factors   207

Index   208

Answers   213
(in With Answers edition only)

Preface

This book is designed to be a valuable resource for pupils studying SQA National 5 Biology. Each unit of the book matches a mandatory unit of the syllabus. Each chapter corresponds to a syllabus sub-topic. The text is presented in a format that allows clear differentiation between the mandatory core text and the non-mandatory learning activities suggested in the syllabus. These take the form of *Related Topics, Related Activities, Case Studies, Research Topics* and *Investigations*.

Each chapter includes one or two sets of *Testing Your Knowledge* questions to allow knowledge of core content to be assessed continuously throughout the course and to check that full understanding has been achieved.

At regular intervals throughout the book, *What You Should Know* summaries of key facts and concepts are given as 'cloze' tests accompanied by appropriate word banks. These provide an excellent source of material for consolidation and revision.

Each unit ends with a varied selection of *Applying Your Knowledge and Skills* questions to foster the development of the mandatory subject skills outlined in the course arrangements. The questions are designed to prepare students for National 5 assessment, where they will be expected to demonstrate their ability to solve problems, select relevant information, present information, process data, plan experimental procedures, evaluate experimental designs, draw valid conclusions and make predictions and generalisations.

Further problem-solving exercises are available in the associated book *National 5 Biology: Applying Knowledge and Skills*.

Unit 1

Cell Biology

1 Cell structure

Cells

Every living organism is made up of one or more **cells**. Cells are the basic units of life. Nothing smaller than a cell can lead an independent life and show all the characteristics of a living thing.

Figures 1.1 and 1.2 show examples of plant cells viewed under the microscope. Some of a plant cell's parts can be clearly seen when the cell is mounted in water. An *Elodea* leaf cell, for example, is seen to possess a **cell wall** and several green **chloroplasts**. Other cell structures that are not so obvious can often be shown up more clearly by the addition of dyes called stains. Iodine solution, for example, can be used to stain **nuclei**, as shown in Figure 1.2.

Figure 1.2 Onion leaf cells in iodine solution

Figure 1.1 *Elodea* leaf cells in water

Close examination of the four types of cell shown in Figure 1.3 reveals that they have some features in common but also differ from one another in several ways. The functions of their various cellular structures are summarised in Table 1.1 on page 4.

Organelles are tiny structures (such as chloroplasts) that are:

- present in a cell's cytoplasm as discrete units, normally surrounded by a membrane
- responsible for a specialised function (such as photosynthesis).

A bacterium does not possess membrane-bound organelles. For example, it lacks a **nucleus** containing **threadlike chromosomes**. Instead, its genetic material takes the form of a single **circular chromosome** and several smaller circular **plasmids**. The structure and composition of the **cell wall** of a bacterium, a fungal cell and a green plant cell are all different from one another.

Ultrastructure

Tiny structures such as mitochondria and ribosomes form part of a cell's **ultrastructure**. Such minute structures can only be seen in detail using an electron microscope. Figure 1.4 shows an **electron micrograph** (a photo of the image produced using an electron microscope).

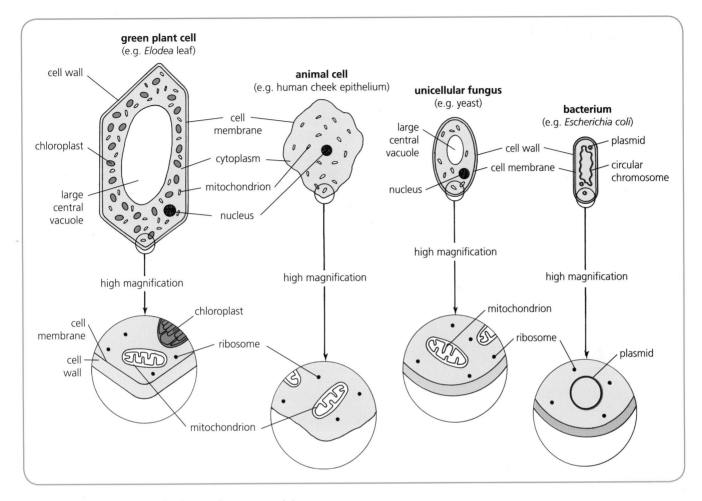

Figure 1.3 Cell structures (cells not drawn to scale)

Figure 1.4 Electron micrograph showing mitochondria and ribosomes

Location	Cell structure	Description	Function
found in cells of green plants, animals and fungi	nucleus	large, normally spherical structure containing threadlike chromosomes	controls cell's activities and passes information on from cell to cell (see chapter 3) and from generation to generation (see chapter 13)
	cell membrane	thin layer surrounding cytoplasm	controls passage of substances into and out of cell (see chapter 2)
	mitochondrion (plural mitochondria)	one of many tiny, sausage-shaped structures containing enzymes	aerobic respiration (see chapter 7)
found in cells of green plants and fungi	large central vacuole	fluid-filled sac-like structure in cytoplasm	stores water and solutes as cell sap and regulates water content by osmosis (see chapter 2)
found in cells of green plants, fungi and bacteria	cell wall	outer layer made of basket-like mesh of fibres (structure and composition of cell walls of fungi and bacteria differ from that of green plant cells)	supports the cell (see chapter 2)
found in cells of green plants only	chloroplast	one of many discus-shaped structures containing green chlorophyll	photosynthesis (see chapter 8)
found in cells of bacteria	circular chromosome	single ring of genetic material	control of cell activities and transfer of genetic information from cell to cell (see chapter 6)
	plasmid	one of several tiny rings of genetic material	
found in all cells	ribosome	one of many tiny particles lacking membrane boundary	protein synthesis (see chapter 4)

Table 1.1 Functions of cell structures

Related Activity

Measuring cell size

When a small piece of graph paper with several pinholes, 1 mm apart, is viewed under the low-power lens of a microscope, the pinholes are easily spotted because light passes up through them. Therefore the diameter of the microscope's field of view can be estimated. Figure 1.5 a), for example, shows a field of view with a diameter of 2 mm. Since **1 millimetre (mm) = 1000 micrometres (μm)**, the diameter of the field of view for this microscope lens = 2000 μm.

Next a sample of cells is viewed and the average number of cells lying end to end along the diameter of the field of view is found. Figure 1.5 b), for example, shows this number to be ten for a specimen of rhubarb epidermal cells. Since the length of ten cells = the diameter of the field of view = 2000 μm, the average length of one rhubarb epidermal cell = 2000/10 = 200 μm. Similarly, since the breadth of 20 cells = 2000 μm, the average breadth of one rhubarb epidermal cell = 2000/20 = 100 μm.

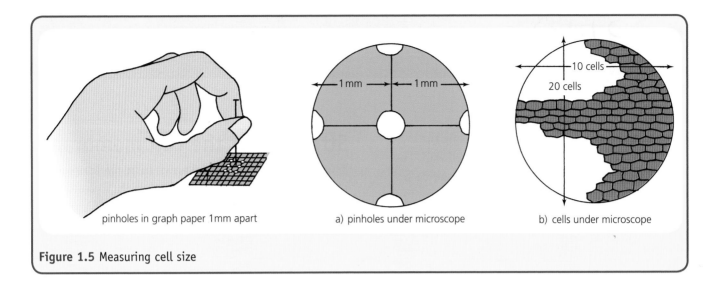

pinholes in graph paper 1mm apart   a) pinholes under microscope   b) cells under microscope

Figure 1.5 Measuring cell size

Testing Your Knowledge

1 What name is given to the basic units of life that can lead an independent existence? (1)

2 a) Name FOUR structural features that a typical plant cell and a typical animal cell have in common. (4)

  b) Identify THREE structural features present in an *Elodea* leaf cell but absent from a cheek epithelial cell. (3)

3 Give the function of each of the following structures: chloroplast, nucleus, cell membrane, mitochondrion. (4)

4 a) Express 1 millimetre in micrometres. (1)

  b) Express 1 micrometre as a decimal fraction of a millimetre. (1)

2 Transport across cell membranes

In a plant cell, the cell membrane enclosing the cytoplasm lies against the inside of the cell wall. The large central vacuole and other organelles are each surrounded by a membrane similar in structure to that of the cell membrane.

Structure of the cell membrane

The cell membrane is now known to be made up of **protein** and **lipid** molecules. It is thought to consist of a double layer of lipid molecules containing a patchy

Investigation

Structure of cell membranes

The cell sap present in the central vacuole of a beetroot cell (see Figure 2.1) contains red pigment. 'Bleeding' (the escape of this red sap from a cell) indicates that the cell membrane and vacuolar membrane have been damaged.

Figure 2.1 Beetroot cell

In the experiment shown in Figure 2.2, four identical cylinders of fresh beetroot are prepared using a cork borer. The cylinders are thoroughly washed in distilled water to remove traces of red cell sap from outer damaged cells. The

figure shows the results of subjecting the cylinders to various conditions. Bleeding is found to occur in B, C and D showing that the membranes have been destroyed.

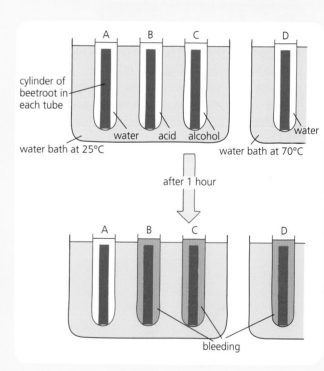

Figure 2.2 Investigating the chemical nature of the cell membrane

When molecules of protein are exposed to acid or high temperatures, they are known to become denatured (destroyed and non-functional). Molecules of lipid are known to be soluble in alcohol. It is therefore concluded that the cell membrane contains **protein** (as indicated by B and D whose denatured protein has allowed red cell sap to leak out) and **lipid** (as indicated by C whose lipid molecules have dissolved in alcohol, permitting the pigment to escape).

mosaic of protein molecules. This is known as the **fluid mosaic model** (see Figure 2.3).

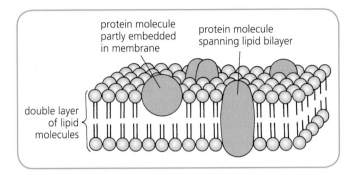

Figure 2.3 Fluid mosaic model of cell membrane

Diffusion

The molecules of a liquid (or a gas) move about freely all the time. In the experiment shown in Figure 2.4, a crystal of purple potassium permanganate is dropped into a beaker of water. The diagram illustrates the events that follow. The purple particles move from a region of **high concentration** (the dissolving crystal) to a region of **low concentration** (the surrounding water) until the concentration of purple particles (and water) is uniform throughout.

Diffusion is the name given to the movement of the molecules of a substance from a region of high concentration of that substance to a region of low concentration until the concentration becomes equal.

Concentration gradient

The difference in concentration that exists between a region of high concentration and a region of low concentration is called the **concentration gradient**. During diffusion, movement of molecules always occurs down a concentration gradient from high to low concentration. Diffusion is a **passive** process. This means that it does not require energy.

Importance of diffusion in cells

Unicellular organisms

Diffusion of oxygen and carbon dioxide

Different concentrations of substances exist inside a cell compared with outside in its environment. In a unicellular animal such as *Paramecium*, oxygen is constantly being used up by the cell contents during respiration. This results in the concentration of oxygen molecules inside the cell being lower than in the surrounding water. The cell membrane is freely permeable to the tiny oxygen molecules. Oxygen therefore **diffuses into** the cell from a higher concentration to a lower concentration (see Figure 2.5).

At the same time, the living cell contents are constantly making carbon dioxide (CO_2) by respiration. This results in the concentration of carbon dioxide inside the cell being higher than in the surrounding water.

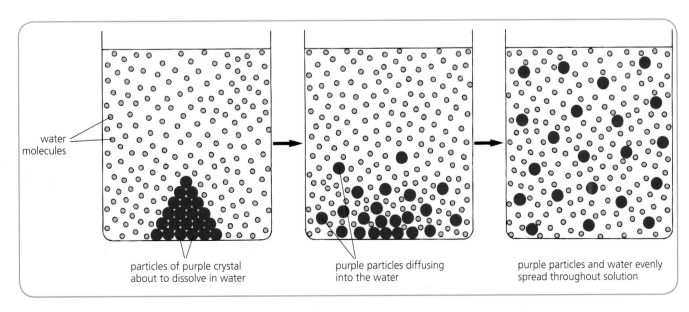

water molecules

particles of purple crystal about to dissolve in water

purple particles diffusing into the water

purple particles and water evenly spread throughout solution

Figure 2.4 Diffusion

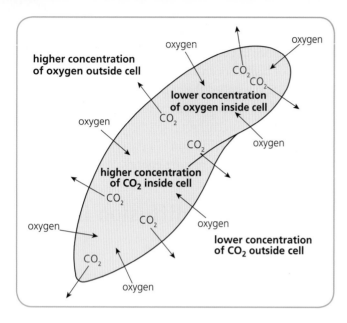

Figure 2.5 Diffusion into and out of a cell

Multicellular animals

In a multicellular animal such as a human being, diffusion also plays an important role in the exchange of respiratory gases. Blood returning to the lungs from respiring cells (see Figure 2.6) contains a higher concentration of carbon dioxide and a lower concentration of oxygen than the air in the air sac. Carbon dioxide therefore **diffuses out** of the blood and oxygen **diffuses in**. When the blood reaches living body cells, the reverse process occurs and the cells gain oxygen from the blood and lose carbon dioxide by diffusion. Similarly, diffusion is essential for the movement, along a concentration gradient, of molecules of dissolved food (such as glucose and amino acids) from the animal's bloodstream to its respiring cells.

Since the cell membrane is also freely permeable to tiny carbon dioxide molecules, these **diffuse out**, as shown in Figure 2.5.

Role of the cell membrane

Although the membrane of a cell is freely permeable to small molecules such as oxygen, carbon dioxide and water, it is not equally permeable to all substances.

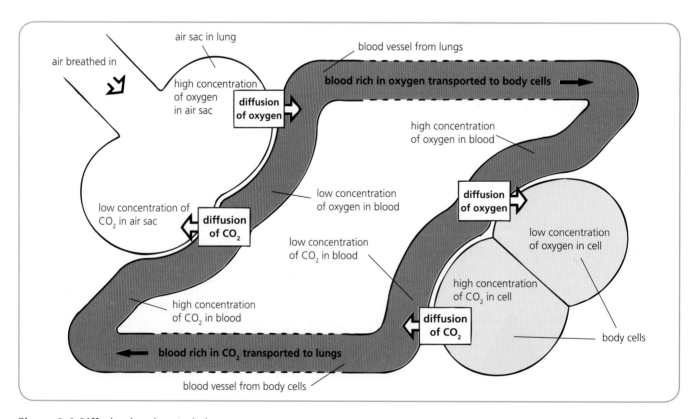

Figure 2.6 Diffusion in a human being

Larger molecules such as dissolved food can pass through the membrane slowly. Molecules that are even larger, such as starch, are unable to pass through. Thus the cell membrane controls the passage of substances into and out of a cell.

The exact means by which the cell membrane exerts this control is not fully understood. It is known that most cell membranes possess **tiny pores**. It is thought that many small molecules enter or leave by these pores. Other molecules are kept inside or outside the cell because they are too big to pass through the pores (see Figure 2.7). The cell membrane is therefore said to be **selectively permeable**.

Osmosis

In both of the investigations shown on page 10, overall movement of tiny water molecules occurred from a region of **higher water concentration (HWC)** to a region of **lower water concentration (LWC)** across a membrane. The larger sugar molecules were unable to diffuse through the membrane because the membrane was **selectively permeable**. This movement of water molecules from HWC to LWC across a selectively permeable membrane is a special case of diffusion called **osmosis**.

Water concentration gradient

The difference in water concentration that exists between two regions is called the **water concentration gradient**. At the start of the experiment shown in Figure 2.11, a water concentration gradient exists between the regions on either side of the Visking tubing membrane in cell models A and C. During osmosis, water molecules move down a water concentration gradient from high to low water concentration through the selectively permeable membrane.

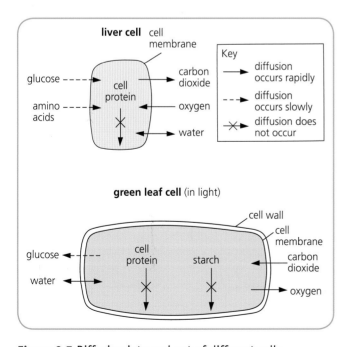

Figure 2.7 Diffusion into and out of different cells

Effect of water and concentrated sugar solution on potato cylinders

In the experiment shown in Figure 2.8, the very dilute sugar solution outside potato cylinder A has a higher water concentration (HWC) than the contents of the potato cells, which have a lower water concentration (LWC). The contents of the potato cells in cylinder B have a higher water concentration (HWC) than the surrounding sugar solution, which has a lower water concentration (LWC).

After 24 hours, cylinder A is found to have increased in volume and mass and to have become firmer (turgid) in texture. Cylinder B, on the other hand, has decreased in both volume and mass and has become softer (flaccid). It is therefore concluded that water molecules have diffused into cylinder A and out of cylinder B through the cell membranes.

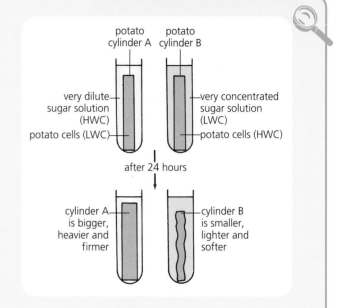

Figure 2.8 Effect of two sugar solutions on potato cells

Effect of water and concentrated sugar solution (syrup) on eggs

In the experiment shown in Figures 2.9 and 2.10, each egg is surrounded by its membrane only. Its shell has been removed by acid treatment prior to the experiment. After 2 days, egg A swells up whereas egg B shrinks. It is therefore concluded that water has diffused into egg A (from a higher water concentration to a lower water concentration) and out of egg B (from a higher water concentration to a lower water concentration).

Figure 2.9 Osmosis takes effect

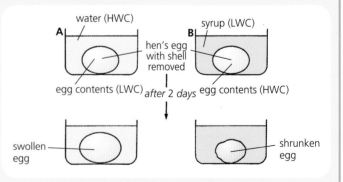

Figure 2.10 Osmosis in eggs

Constructing cell models of osmosis

Visking tubing is a synthetic material. Over a short time-scale (such as 2 hours) it acts like the selectively permeable membrane that surrounds a cell. Lengths of Visking tubing tied at both ends can therefore be used to act as models of cells.

Figure 2.11 shows three cell models (A, B and C) set up to investigate osmosis. Cell model A is found to gain mass since water has passed into the 'cell' from a region of higher water concentration (HWC) to a region of lower water concentration (LWC) by osmosis. B neither gains nor loses water since the solutions inside and outside are equal in water concentration. C is found to lose mass since water has passed out of the 'cell' from a region of HWC to a region of LWC by osmosis.

Figure 2.11 Molecular model of osmosis

Osmosis and cells

Movement of water by osmosis occurs between cells and their immediate environment. The direction depends on the water concentration of the liquid in which the cells are immersed compared with that of the cell contents.

Red blood cells

Since pure water has a higher water concentration than the contents of red blood cells, water enters by osmosis until the cells burst (see Figure 2.12). Since 0.85% salt solution has the same water concentration as the cell contents, there is no net flow of water into or out of the cells by osmosis (see Figures 2.12 and 2.13). Since 1.7% salt solution has a lower water concentration than the cells, water passes out and the cells shrink (see Figures 2.12 and 2.14).

Plant cells

Plant cells such as onion cells mounted in liquids of different water concentrations respond in different ways. Pure water has a higher water concentration than the contents of a normal plant cell, therefore water enters by osmosis. The vacuole swells up and presses the cytoplasm against the cell wall, which is made of a mesh of basket-like fibres (see Figure 2.16 on page 14). The cell wall stretches slightly and presses back, preventing the cell from bursting. Cells in this swollen condition are said to be **turgid** (see Figure 2.17 on page 14). A young plant depends on the turgor of its cells for support.

Since the dilute sugar solution used in Figure 2.17 has the same water concentration as the cell contents, no net flow of water occurs and the cell remains unchanged (also see Figure 2.18 on page 14).

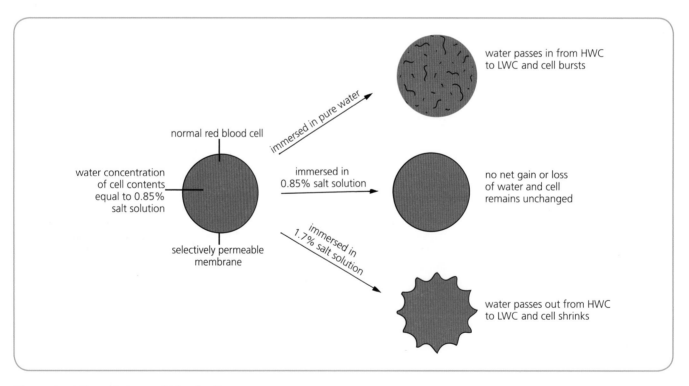

Figure 2.12 Osmosis in a red blood cell

Figure 2.13 Red blood cells in 0.85% salt solution

Figure 2.14 Red blood cells in 1.7% salt solution

Control of water balance in unicellular animals

Unicellular animals such as *Amoeba* that live in fresh water take in water continuously by osmosis. Bursting is prevented by the **contractile vacuole** (see Figure 2.15) removing excess water.

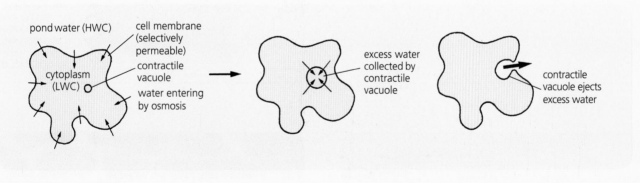

Figure 2.15 Role of contractile vacuole in *Amoeba*

Since the concentrated sugar solution used in Figure 2.17 has a lower water concentration than the cell contents, water passes out of the cell by osmosis. The living contents shrink and pull away from the fairly rigid cell wall. Cells in this state are said to be **plasmolysed** (also see Figure 2.19). However, they are not dead. When immersed in water, plasmolysed cells regain turgor by taking water in by osmosis.

Figure 2.16 Fibrous nature of cell wall

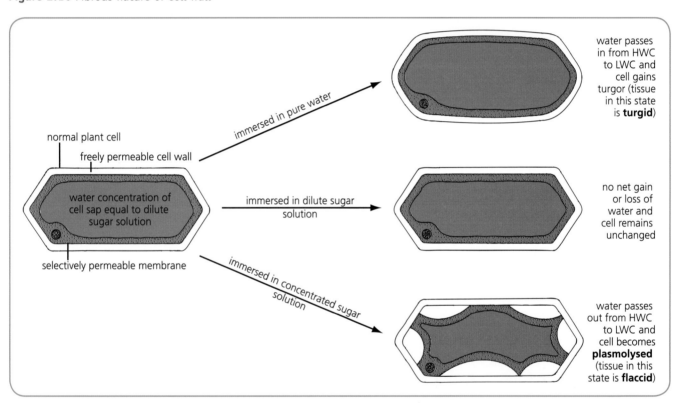

normal plant cell

freely permeable cell wall

water concentration of cell sap equal to dilute sugar solution

selectively permeable membrane

immersed in pure water

immersed in dilute sugar solution

immersed in concentrated sugar solution

water passes in from HWC to LWC and cell gains turgor (tissue in this state is **turgid**)

no net gain or loss of water and cell remains unchanged

water passes out from HWC to LWC and cell becomes **plasmolysed** (tissue in this state is **flaccid**)

Figure 2.17 Osmosis in a plant cell

Figure 2.18 Red onion cells unchanged in dilute sugar solution

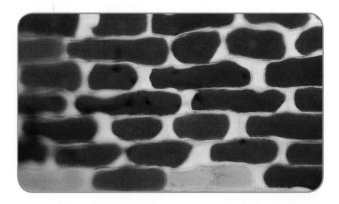

Figure 2.19 Red onion cells plasmolysed in concentrated sugar solution

Power generation by osmosis

Methods of generating power using osmosis are still in the early stages of development. One type of **osmotic power plant** (built in Norway at a location close to where a river meets the sea) is illustrated in a simple way in Figure 2.20. Its successful operation depends on the difference in water concentration between sea water and river water (both of which are readily available).

As liquid rises in the inner compartment and exerts a pressure, this is made to turn a turbine and **generate electrical energy**. The waste product of the process is dilute sea water, which is safely discharged into the surrounding waters.

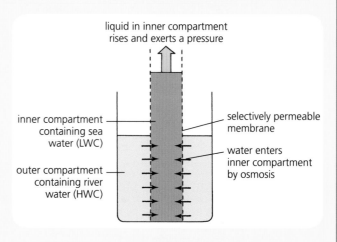

Figure 2.20 Power generation by osmosis

Research Topic **Desalination**

Desalination is the process by which the solute (salt) in sea water is separated from its solvent (water) so that the water can be used for drinking or irrigation. It is an important process in countries that have little or no natural fresh water. One method of desalination is reverse osmosis.

Reverse osmosis is the process by which water molecules are forced to pass from sea water, a region of low water concentration (LWC) through a selectively permeable membrane to a region of higher water concentration (HWC). For this to be possible, a pressure has to be applied to the sea water that is far greater than the pressure that would normally be exerted by the water molecules moving passively by osmosis from a HWC to a LWC. Reverse osmosis is shown in a simple way in Figure 2.21.

Figure 2.21 Desalination

Active transport

Active transport is the movement of ions (electrically charged particles) or molecules across the cell membrane from a low to a high concentration **against** a concentration gradient. Figure 2.22 on page 16 shows ion type A being actively transported into the cell and ion type B being actively transported out. This form of

transport is brought about by certain membrane proteins acting as **carrier molecules** that recognise specific ions or molecules and transfer them across the membrane.

Active transport works in the **opposite direction** to the passive process of diffusion and always requires **energy** for the membrane proteins to move ions or molecules against their concentration gradient.

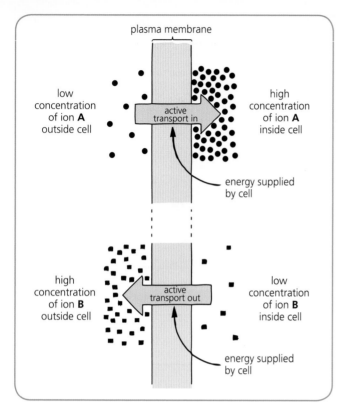

Figure 2.22 Active transport of two different ions

Sodium/potassium pump

Active transport carriers are often called **pumps**. Some of them play a **dual role** in that they exchange one type of ion for another. An example is the **sodium/potassium pump** where the same carrier molecule actively pumps sodium ions out of the cell and potassium ions into the cell, each against its own concentration gradient, as shown in Figure 2.23. Maintenance of the difference in ionic concentration by this pump is particularly important for the proper functioning of nerve cells.

Conditions required by protein pumps

A pump requires energy. Therefore factors such as temperature and availability of oxygen and food, which directly affect a cell's respiratory rate, also affect the rate of active transport.

Iodine

Sea water contains only a tiny trace of **iodine**, yet some brown seaweeds are found to have 0.4% of their

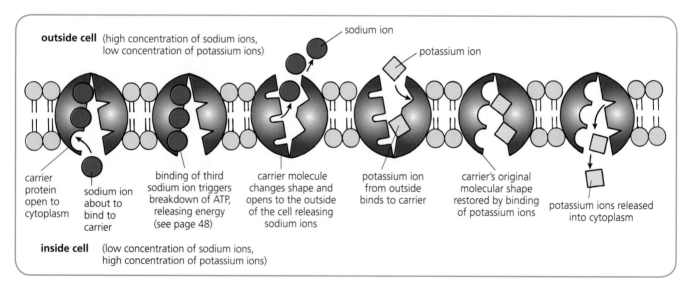

Figure 2.23 Active transport by sodium/potassium pump

dry weight as iodine. By actively transporting iodine into their cells against a concentration gradient, these seaweeds are able to concentrate iodine in their cell sap by a factor of **several thousand** times. Therefore they provide a commercial source of this element.

Investigation

Uptake of dyes by yeast cells

A small sample of yeast cells from a freshly aerated culture is placed on a slide and a drop of **methylene blue dye** is added. The procedure is repeated using a sample of yeast cells that have been boiled and cooled. After 5 minutes, cover slips are added and the cells are viewed under the microscope.

The live cells are found to contain little or no blue dye but the dead cells are found to be blue. Therefore it can be concluded that the blue dye diffuses into the yeast cells but only the live cells (that are able to respire and generate energy) are able to actively transport it back out against a concentration gradient.

Testing Your Knowledge 2

1 Rewrite the following paragraph choosing the correct answer at each underlined choice. (8)
Osmosis is a form of diffusion/ion uptake. It is an active/a passive process that requires/does not require energy. During osmosis oxygen/water molecules move across a freely/selectively permeable membrane from a higher/lower water concentration to a higher/lower water concentration along/against a concentration gradient.

2 a) With reference to the water concentrations involved, explain why a red blood cell bursts when placed in water yet an onion epidermal cell does not. (4)

b) Why does a red blood cell shrink when placed in concentrated salt solution? (1)

3 a) Describe and explain the osmotic effect of very concentrated sugar solution on an onion epidermal cell. (2)

b) What term is used to describe a cell in this state? (1)

c) How could such a cell be restored to its turgid condition? (1)

4 a) Define the term *active transport*. (2)

b) Copy and complete Table 2.1 by answering the five questions. (5)

Question	Diffusion	Active transport
What is an example of a substance that moves through the cell membrane by this process?		
Do the particles move from high to low or from low to high concentration?		
Do the particles move along or against a concentration gradient?		
Is energy required?		
Is the process passive?		

Table 2.1

What You Should Know Chapters 1–2

active	gain	permeable
against	gradient	plasmolysed
along	lipid	ribosomes
animal	lose	sap
burst	lower	selectively
cells	membrane	shrink
chloroplasts	mitochondria	supported
concentration	nucleus	useful
diffusion	osmosis	vacuole
energy	passive	walls

1 All living things are composed of one or more _____, the basic units of life.

2 The cells of green plants, animals and fungi have several structures in common including a _____, a cell _____ and mitochondria.

3 _____ cells lack a cell wall and a large central _____.

4 Only green plant cells contain _____ but all cells contain ribosomes.

5 The cell's activities are controlled by the nucleus. A plant cell is _____ by the cell wall and its cell _____ is stored in its vacuole.

6 Chloroplasts are responsible for photosynthesis, _____ for respiration and _____ for protein synthesis.

7 The cell membrane consists of protein and _____ molecules and is _____ permeable.

8 Diffusion is the movement of molecules from a high to a low concentration _____ a concentration _____. It is a _____ process and does not require a supply of energy.

9 _____ is the means by which _____ molecules enter and waste materials leave a cell.

10 _____ is a special case of diffusion during which water molecules move along a water _____ gradient from a region of higher water concentration to a region of _____ water concentration through a selectively _____ membrane.

11 When placed in a solution with a water concentration higher than that of their cell contents, cells _____ water by osmosis. Animal cells swell up and may _____; plant cells also swell up but are prevented from bursting by their cell _____.

12 When placed in a solution with a water concentration lower than that of their cell contents, cells _____ water by osmosis. Animal cells _____ and plant cells become _____.

13 Ions and molecules of some chemical substances are actively transported across the cell membrane _____ a concentration gradient.

14 _____ transport is brought about by membrane protein molecules and requires _____.

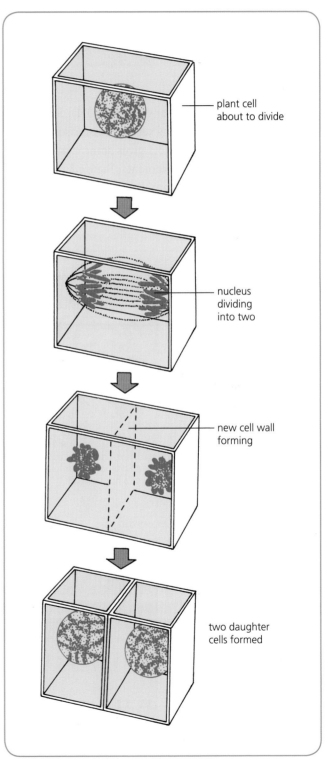

Figure 3.2 Cell division in a plant cell

Growth is the irreversible increase in the dry mass of an organism. It is normally accompanied by an increase in **cell number** as a result of repeated cell division.

Cell division

Figure 3.1 shows cell division in an animal cell. The **nucleus** divides first and the two daughter nuclei separate. Next the **cytoplasm** becomes pinched off between the two nuclei, forming two daughter cells.

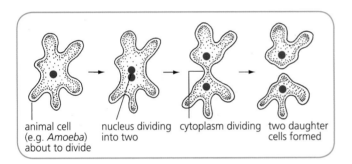

animal cell (e.g. *Amoeba*) about to divide | nucleus dividing into two | cytoplasm dividing | two daughter cells formed

Figure 3.1 Cell division in an animal cell

Division in a plant cell is shown in Figure 3.2. The cytoplasm cannot become pinched off in the middle because of the presence of the **cell wall**. Instead, nuclear division is followed by the laying down of a new cell wall between the daughter cells.

Chromosomes

Chromosomes (see Figure 3.3) are threadlike structures found inside the nucleus of plant and animal cells. Each chromosome carries information that is necessary for the development of the cell and the survival of the living organism to which it belongs.

Chromosome complement

Each species of plant and animal has a definite and characteristic number of chromosomes called its **chromosome complement** present in each cell. Every normal human body cell, for example, contains

Figure 3.3 Chromosomes

Species of living thing	Diploid chromosome complement
onion	16
cabbage	18
rice	24
fruit fly	8
frog	24
cat	38
human	46
horse	66

Table 3.1 Diploid chromosome complements

46 chromosomes as 23 pairs (see Figure 3.4). Such a cell, which has two matching sets of chromosomes, is described as **diploid**. Table 3.1 gives some examples of diploid chromosome complements. Figure 3.5 shows the diploid chromosome complement of the fruit fly, which is composed of two identical matching sets of four chromosomes.

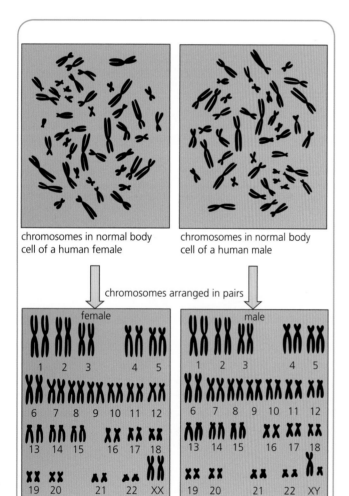

Figure 3.4 Matching sets of chromosomes

Figure 3.5 Diploid chromosome complement of fruit fly

Every normal human sex cell such as a sperm contains 23 unpaired chromosomes. Such a cell, which has a single set of chromosomes, is described as **haploid**. Diploid cells are often represented by the symbol $2n$ because they have two sets of chromosomes. Haploid cells, which have a single set of chromosomes, are represented by the symbol n (where n equals the number of different chromosomes).

Mitosis

Mitosis is the process by which the **nucleus** divides into two daughter nuclei, each of which receives exactly the same number of chromosomes as were present in the original nucleus. Figure 3.6 shows the sequence of events that occurs during mitosis. Figure 3.7 shows a microscopic view of some of the stages in root tip cells that are dividing.

Figure 3.6 Mitosis

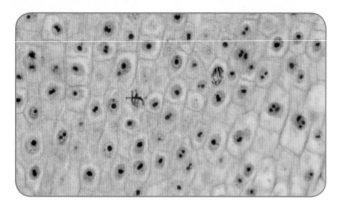

Figure 3.7 Mitosis in root tip cells

As each chromosome becomes shorter and thicker, it is seen to be a double thread. Each thread is called a **chromatid**. The two chromatids of a chromosome are joined together by a **centromere**. The nuclear membrane disappears and a spindle made of **spindle fibres** forms. Each chromosome becomes attached by its centromere to one of the spindle fibres at the 'equator'. Next, each centromere splits and one chromatid from each pair moves to the 'north pole' and one to the 'south pole'. Finally a nuclear membrane forms around each group of chromatids (now regarded as chromosomes) and nuclear division (mitosis) is complete.

Mitosis is followed by division of the cytoplasm to form **two identical daughter cells**. Since each of the two cells produced has received a complete set of chromosomes, each new cell contains a copy of exactly the same information. Each cell now undergoes a period of cell growth. During this time the chromosomes in each nucleus cannot be seen and sometimes this stage (called interphase) is referred to as the resting period. However, the chromosomes are not resting. During this time, each is completely uncoiled and undergoing **replication**. By this means, an exact copy of each chromosome (a chromatid) is formed in preparation for the next nuclear division.

Maintenance of diploid chromosome complement

Chromosomes provide the main source of genetic information typical of a particular species of living thing. It is essential that each cell formed as a result of mitosis receives a full complement of chromosomes so that during growth and development, the cells of the multicellular organism will be able to provide the animal or plant with the characteristics of its species. This **continuity of diploid chromosome complement** from cell to cell is maintained by **mitosis**.

Related Topic

Length of time

The time taken by a cell to go through the entire cycle of cell division from interphase to interphase varies from species to species. An onion root tip cell takes 22 hours to complete the full cycle at room temperature. Of this time, mitosis (nuclear division) only takes 90 minutes. The remainder of the time is spent on cell growth and formation of chromatids.

Related Topic

Growth curves

Measuring growth

Growth is usually investigated by measuring changes in an organism's fresh mass, height or cell number over a period of time.

Growth curve

Table 3.2 records the height of a plant shoot measured over a period of 16 days. When graphed, the results for total height of shoot give a **growth curve** as shown in Figure 3.8.

Careful study of Figure 3.8 and the data in Table 3.2 reveals that during the first 4 days of growth, each daily increase in height was greater than that of the previous day. This phase is called the period of **accelerating growth**. During days 4 to 8, the daily increase in height remained constant. This phase is called the period of **steady rapid growth**. During days 8 to 12, growth continued but each day's increase in height was less than that of the previous day. This phase is called the **period of decelerating growth**. During days 12 to 16, the shoot failed to gain further height. It had entered the **period of no growth**. This pattern of growth, with minor variations, is common to almost all living things. Figure 3.9 shows a generalised version of the growth curve and its four phases.

Time from start (days)	Total height of shoot (mm)	Daily increase in height of shoot (mm)	Growth phase
start	0	-	period of accelerating growth
1	1	1	
2	3	2	
3	7	4	
4	15	8	
5	23	8	period of steady rapid growth
6	31	8	
7	39	8	
8	47	8	
9	51	4	period of decelerating growth
10	53	2	
11	54	1	
12	54	0	
13	54	0	period of no growth
14	54	0	
15	54	0	
16	54	0	

Table 3.2 Growth of a plant shoot

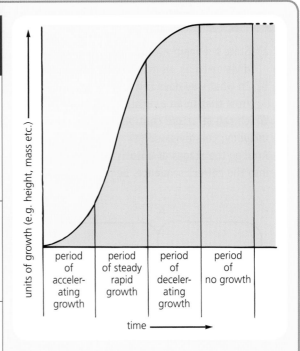

Figure 3.9 Growth curve

Human growth curve

Growth in humans, as indicated by change in body mass, gives a similar curve but it has two phases of rapid growth (called **growth spurts**) instead of one (see Figure 3.10). The first occurs during the 2 years following birth; the second occurs at puberty after a long period of steady growth. On average, a human male reaches puberty later and attains a larger adult size than a human female.

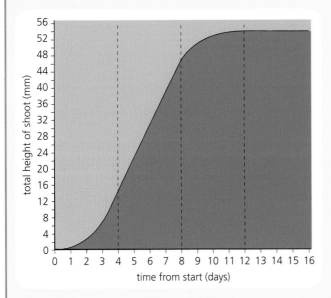

Figure 3.8 Graph of growth of height of plant shoot

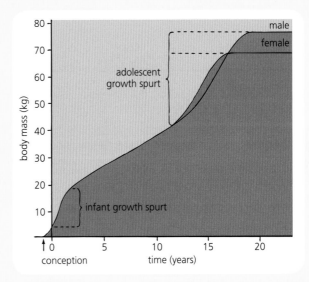

Figure 3.10 Human growth curves

Testing Your Knowledge 1

1 a) State the main events that occur during cell division in an animal cell. (2)
   b) In what way does cell division in a plant differ from that in an animal? (1)
2 Which cell structure controls all cell activities including cell division? (1)
3 Arrange the stages of mitosis shown in Figure 3.11 into the correct sequence, beginning with B. (1)

4 Briefly describe the process of mitosis using all of the following terms: *centromere*, *chromatid*, *equator*, *spindle fibre*. (4)
5 Why is it important that the diploid chromosome complement of daughter cells in a multicellular organism is maintained? (2)

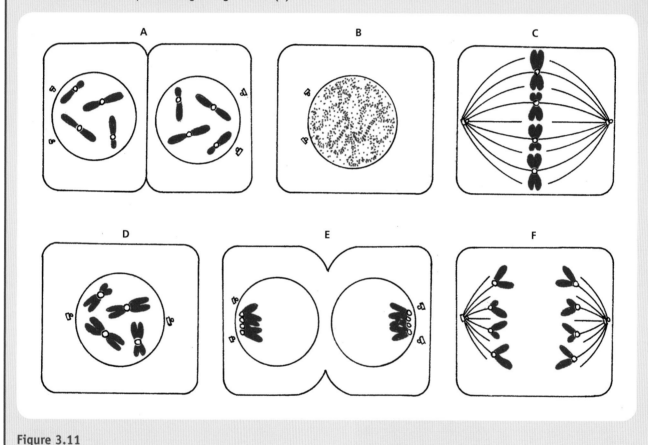

Figure 3.11

Culturing cells

Airborne micro-organisms

In the experiment shown in Figure 3.12, the nutrient agar in plate A is exposed to air for 30 minutes and then the plate is incubated. After 2 days, many micro-organisms are found to be growing on the nutrient agar (see Figure 3.13). Since plate B, the control, shows no microbial growth, it is concluded that air contains many types of micro-organism. Many of these are present in dust as **airborne spores** and are constantly landing on all surfaces and entering open containers.

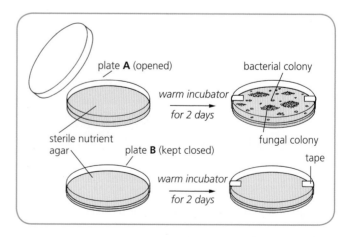

Figure 3.12 Micro-organisms from the air

Figure 3.13 Airborne micro-organisms

Cultures

When a supply of a certain type of cell (such as yeast, bacteria or human stem cells) is required, **cultures** of the cell may be grown. During this type of laboratory work with micro-organisms (or cultures of mammalian cells), certain precautions are taken to try to create **aseptic** (**sterile**) conditions in which to carry out the investigation and prevent unwanted microbes from gaining access to the growth medium.

Precautions and aseptic techniques

Work surface

In a microbiology laboratory all surfaces should be made of a hard, non-absorbent material such as glass or plastic and be cleaned with **disinfectant** before starting an experiment.

Microbiologist

To prevent contamination (and risk of infection), hands should be washed, any cuts should be covered with waterproof **dressings** and **lab coats** should be worn. There should be no eating or drinking in the laboratory.

Sterile equipment and materials

An **autoclave** is a special container used to **sterilise** equipment and materials before a microbiological investigation is carried out. When it is sealed up and its heating element turned on, an autoclave can be heated up under pressure to temperatures well above the boiling point of water. Normally it is used to heat up equipment to 121 °C for 20 minutes. Whereas boiling water kills *most* microbes, autoclave treatment kills *all* micro-organisms.

Preparation of sterile nutrient agar

Agar powder and nutrients such as sugar are added to distilled water in McCartney bottles and the caps replaced but not screwed on tightly. The bottles and their contents are then sterilised in an autoclave as shown in Figure 3.14.

Sterile Petri dish

Micro-organisms are often cultured in containers called **Petri dishes**. These are also referred to as plates and may be made of plastic or glass. Glass Petri dishes can be sterilised in an autoclave. Plastic Petri dishes have already been sterilised during their manufacture.

Figure 3.14 Use of an autoclave

Their insides stay sterile as long as they are not opened. A marker pen is normally used to write important information on the **base** of an unopened Petri dish.

Preparing a plate of nutrient agar

Once a bottle of nutrient agar has been sterilised in the autoclave, it has to be poured into a sterile Petri dish to prepare a plate of nutrient agar. To reduce the chance of a stray microbe from the air entering the nutrient agar at this stage, further precautions must be taken as follows:

- The work is carried out close to a Bunsen flame so that the upward flow of warm air will carry any spores in the air up and away from the experiment.
- The cap of the McCartney bottle is removed and the bottle held in one hand while its neck is flamed for 2–3 seconds (see Figure 3.15).
- The other hand is used to lift the lid of the Petri dish just enough to allow the nutrient agar to be quickly poured into the dish.
- The lid is immediately replaced and the dish is gently swirled once to spread out the molten agar before it sets.

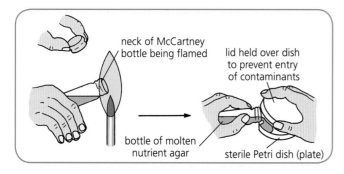

Figure 3.15 Preparing a plate of nutrient agar

Inoculating loop

An instrument is needed to transfer a sample of the micro-organisms from the bottle containing the pure culture (see Figure 3.16) to another site such as a Petri dish containing nutrient agar. This instrument is called an **inoculating loop**. The wire part of the loop is sterilised by heating it to **red heat** in a Bunsen flame to kill all microbes (see Figure 3.17). This is done by heating the shaft near the handle first and then drawing the rest of the wire through the flame until all parts have been red hot. After this **flaming** process, the loop is allowed to cool for a few seconds before use (but it must not be laid down on a non-sterile surface).

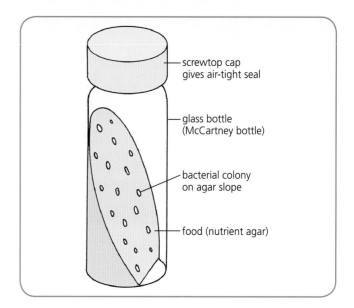

Figure 3.16 Culture bottle of a micro-organism

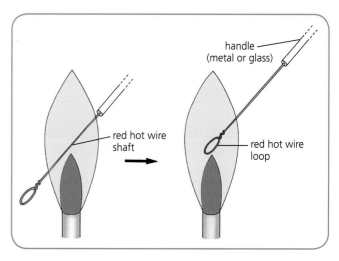

Figure 3.17 Sterilising a wire inoculating loop

Culturing the micro-organism

Figures 3.18 and 3.19 show examples of experiments that involve culturing fungi and bacteria. From these experiments, it is concluded that micro-organisms need to be given **nutrients** in their medium to grow. They do not grow on plain agar or in distilled water. At the start of each of these experiments, when the agar or broth is being **inoculated** with the particular micro-organism to be cultured, aseptic techniques are adopted to stop foreign microbes entering and contaminating the plate or culture bottle. Preventing **contaminants** from entering and growing in a culture is important to ensure that only the desired micro-organism is being cultured.

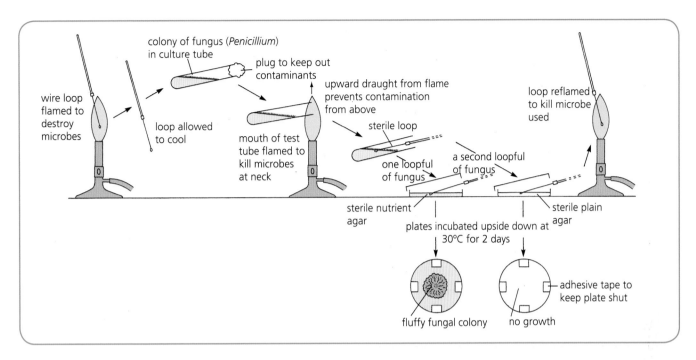

Figure 3.18 Growth of a fungal culture

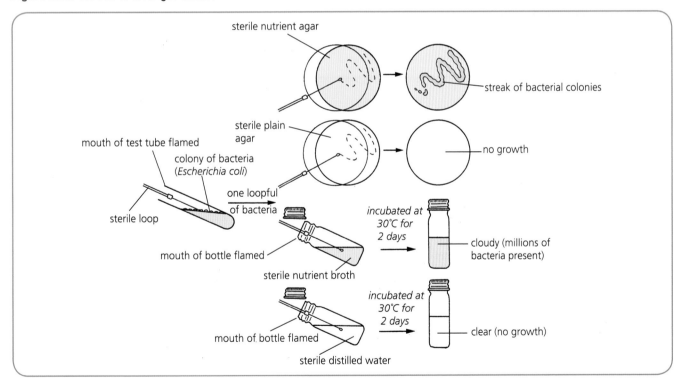

Figure 3.19 Growth of a bacterial culture

Cell culture requirements

When cells are being cultured, they require:

- a **sterile** environment free from contaminants that might act as competitors
- an appropriate **growth medium** that contains an energy source such as glucose and nutrients for

building new cells (in the case of micro-organisms, this may take the form of nutrient agar or broth whereas in the case of mammalian cells, a complex culture medium is required)

- an environment that is **controlled** to provide optimum levels of factors such as oxygen concentration, pH and temperature.

27

Factors affecting growth of bacteria

Temperature

The effect of **temperature** on the growth of bacteria is investigated in the experiment shown in Figure 3.20. From the results, it is concluded that bacteria grow best in warm conditions but do not grow in extremes of temperature. The results are explained by the fact that the activity of essential **enzymes** (see chapter 5) is closely related to temperature.

pH

When the experiment is redesigned with **pH** as the variable factor and temperature kept constant throughout at 30 °C, the bacteria are found to grow well in neutral conditions (pH 7) but fail to grow in acidic conditions (pH 4) or in alkaline conditions (pH 10). These results are explained by the fact that a cell's enzymes normally function best in conditions of neutral pH.

state of broth	clear	clear	cloudy	very cloudy	clear
reason	no growth of bacteria	no growth of bacteria	some growth of bacteria	much growth of bacteria	no growth of bacteria

Figure 3.20 Effect of temperature on bacterial growth

Related Topic

Fermenter

Biotechnological industries culture cells on a vast scale in order to produce huge quantities of cells or obtain useful products such as vaccines and antibiotics from the cells. These activities are made possible by the use of enormous industrial **fermenters** (often able to hold thousands of litres of nutrient liquid).

Figure 3.21 shows a simplified version of an industrial fermenter being used to grow a micro-organism. The system is controlled automatically by **computers**. Sensors (not shown in the diagram) are in contact with the nutrient solution and monitor the various conditions that are needed for the best growth of the micro-organism. If any one of these factors varies from the **optimum** level, the sensor picks up the change and sends information to the computer. The computer responds by communicating with the source of supply of the essential factor. The supply is then adjusted accordingly until the required level is restored.

When given constant optimum conditions, the micro-organism grows rapidly and produces the useful end product, which it normally releases into the surrounding medium. Computer-controlled technology also monitors this release and brings the process to a halt when the required level has been reached.

Figure 3.21 Fermenter

Testing Your Knowledge 2

1 a) Match precautions and aseptic techniques 1–9 in
       Figure 3.22 with the following answers. (9)

Figure 3.22 Summary of precautions

A sterile Petri dishes of nutrient agar kept closed
   until required to prevent entry of contaminants
B inoculated dish sealed with tape to prevent
   entry and exit of microbes
C lab coat worn to protect clothing and prevent
   contamination
D smooth, non-absorbent work surface
   disinfected before and after experiment to kill
   microbes
E wire loop has been flamed to destroy unwanted
   microbes
F bin lined with plastic bag for safe disposal of
   used plates

G hands washed before and after experiment to
   remove micro-organisms
H autoclave used to sterilise glassware
I lid held over Petri dish during inoculation to
   prevent entry of contaminants
   b) Explain the meaning of the notices displayed on
       the lab wall. (1)
   c) What is the meaning of the sign on the bin? (1)
2 Name TWO types of growth medium suitable for
   culturing bacteria. (2)
3 Identify TWO environmental factors that should be
   controlled to promote optimum growth of cells during
   culturing. (2)

DNA and the production of proteins

Structure of DNA

Chromosomes are threadlike structures composed of genes found inside the nucleus of plant and animal cells. They contain **DNA** (deoxyribonucleic acid). A molecule of DNA consists of two strands twisted together into a **double helix**. Each strand has a 'chain' of **base** molecules (see Figure 4.1).

Normally the two strands are held together by weak bonds between pairs of bases. Each base's molecular structure is such that it can only fit one other type of base. A fits T and G fits C. **A-T** and **G-C** are called **complementary base pairs**.

Sequence of DNA bases

The DNA of one member of a species differs from that of another member by the order in which the bases occur in their chromosomes. It is this **sequence** of bases along the DNA strands that is unique to an organism. The sequence contains the **genetic instructions** that control the organism's inherited characteristics.

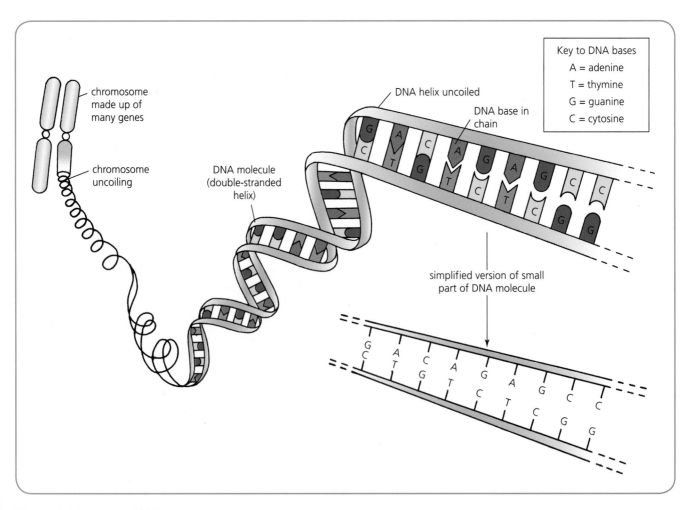

Figure 4.1 Structure of DNA

Genetic code

A region of DNA on a chromosome that codes for a protein is called a **gene** and normally it is hundreds or even thousands of bases long. The information present in the DNA takes the form of a molecular language called the **genetic code**. Amino acid molecules are the building blocks of proteins. Each group of three bases along a DNA strand represents a 'codeword' for one of the 20 types of amino acid that make up proteins.

Research Topic	**Establishing the structure of DNA**

Chemical analysis

In the late 1940s, Chargaff analysed the base composition of DNA extracted from a number of different species. He found that the quantities of the four bases were not all equal but that they always occurred in a **characteristic ratio** regardless of the source of the DNA.

These findings, called **Chargaff's rules**, are summarised as follows:

- The number of A bases = the number of T bases (in other words A:T = 1:1).
- The number of G bases = the number of C bases (in other words G:C = 1:1).

X-ray crystallography

At around the same time, Wilkins and Franklin were using **X-ray crystallography** to investigate the structure of DNA. They found that when X-rays are passed through a crystal of DNA, they become deflected into a **scatter pattern** (see Figure 4.2). The form this pattern takes is determined by the arrangement of the atoms in the DNA molecule.

When the scatter pattern is recorded using a photographic plate (see Figure 4.3), it reveals information that can be used to build up a **three-dimensional picture** of the molecules in the crystal. Wilkins and Franklin found that the X-ray scatter patterns of DNA from different species were identical.

From the X-ray scatter patterns produced by Wilkins and Franklin, Watson and Crick figured out that the DNA must be a long, thin molecule of constant diameter coiled in the form of a **helix**. From Chargaff's rules they figured out that base A must be paired with T and base G with C. They realised that this could only be possible if DNA consisted of two strands held together by specific **pairing of bases**. Watson and Crick then set about building a wire model of DNA and in 1953 were first to establish the three-dimensional **double helix** structure of DNA.

Figure 4.3 X-ray scatter pattern of DNA

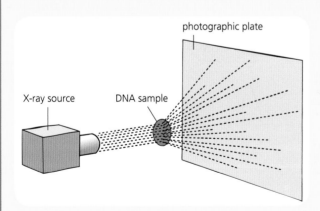

Figure 4.2 X-ray crystallography

Messenger RNA (mRNA)

A gene codes for a particular protein by making a messenger molecule that is complementary to one of its DNA strands (see Figure 4.4). This molecule is called **messenger RNA (mRNA)**. It carries the copy of the genetic code from the gene's DNA in the nucleus out into the cytoplasm. When mRNA meets a **ribosome**, amino acid molecules become assembled into a molecule of protein.

The sequence of amino acids that are joined together into the protein is determined by the information in the sequence of the mRNA's codewords and (indirectly) by the order of the bases on the DNA. By this means, DNA encodes the information for a particular **sequence** of amino acids in a protein, which in turn dictates the **structure** and **function** of that protein (see chapter 5).

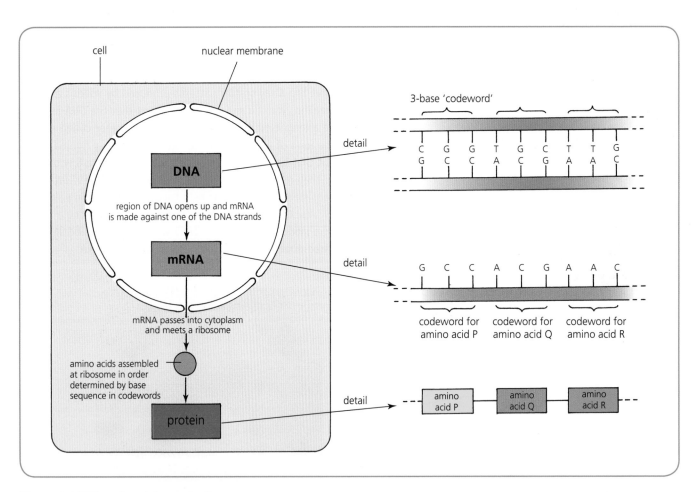

Figure 4.4 DNA and protein production

| **Research Topic** | **Locating a gene on a chromosome** |

Figure 4.5 shows the diploid chromosome complement of a fruit fly. These chromosomes (extracted from cells of larvae) are found to take up stain and produce a **banding pattern** that is a **constant characteristic** of each type of chromosome. This banding pattern is shown for chromosome 1.

It is possible to relate the **location of individual genes** to particular bands on chromosomes. For example, when chromosome 1 from white-eyed flies is compared with chromosome 1 from red-eyed flies (see Figure 4.6), the former is found to lack one of the characteristic bands. Since the chromosome complement of the two types of fly is identical in every other way, it is concluded that the gene that controls red eye colour must be located at the position of the missing band on chromosome 1.

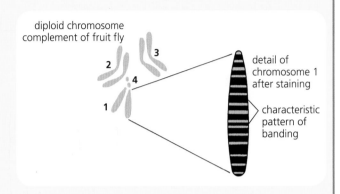

Figure 4.5 Pattern of banding on chromosome

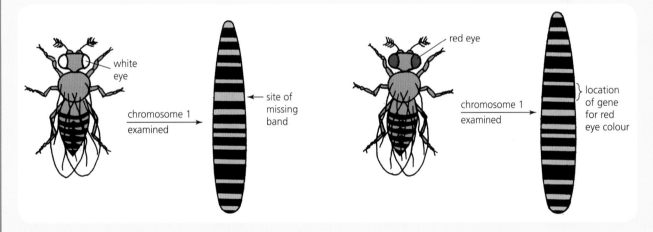

Figure 4.6 Location of gene on chromosome

| **Testing Your Knowledge** |

1 What are chromosomes and where are they located in a cell? (2)

2 a) What do the letters DNA stand for? (1)
  b) How many strands are present in a DNA molecule? (1)
  c) i) How many different types of base molecule are found in DNA?
    ii) Describe the base-pair rule. (2)

3 a) By what means is the genetic code present in the DNA of a gene transported from the nucleus to the cytoplasm of a cell? (1)

b) i) What subunits make up a protein?
  ii) Where in the cytoplasm are these subunits assembled into proteins?
  iii) What determines the sequence in which these subunits are joined together?
  iv) Why is the sequence of these subunits in a protein molecule important? (4)

What You Should Know Chapters 3–4

amino	contaminating	mitosis
aseptic	diploid	nucleus
base	DNA	optimum
centromere	energy	protein
chromatids	equator	ribosome
chromosome	fibre	RNA
code	helix	sequence
complement	medium	wall

1 During cell division, the _____ divides first, followed by the cytoplasm. In a plant cell, a new cell _____ is laid down between the two daughter cells formed.

2 Every species has a characteristic number of chromosomes called its chromosome _____. Normally this takes the form of two matching sets of chromosomes and the cell that contains them is said to be _____.

3 The process by which the nucleus of a diploid cell divides into two nuclei, each of which receives a copy of the diploid _____ complement, is called _____.

4 During mitosis each chromosome, consisting of two identical _____, becomes attached by its _____ to a spindle _____ at the cell's _____. One chromatid from each chromosome moves to the north pole and one to the south pole, forming two nuclei.

5 During culturing of cells, _____ techniques are employed to prevent unwanted spores _____ the cultures.

6 In order to grow, cells in a culture need an appropriate _____ containing nutrients that provide _____ and a supply of cell-building materials. They also require an environment where all factors are controlled and maintained at _____ levels.

7 Chromosomes contain DNA. A molecule of _____ consists of two strands coiled into a double-stranded _____. The two strands are held together by weak bonds between their bases. There are four types of base. A pairs with T and G pairs with C to form complementary _____ pairs.

8 Information called the genetic _____ is present in DNA. It takes the form of codewords of bases that correspond to _____ acids, the building blocks of proteins.

9 The sequence of bases in DNA determines the _____ in which amino acids are assembled in a _____.

10 The genetic code for a protein, present on DNA, is carried by messenger _____ from the nucleus to a _____ in the cytoplasm where the appropriate amino acids become joined together into the protein.

Proteins and enzymes

Amino acids

Each **protein** is built up from a large number of subunits called **amino acids** of which there are **20** different types. These are joined together into chains. Each chain normally consists of hundreds of amino acid molecules linked together. Depending on which amino acids are in the chain, further bonds between certain amino acids form. These make the chain coil up and become folded in a **characteristic way**. The exact nature of the coiling and folding depends on the **sequence** of the amino acids present in the chain. It determines the final **structure** of the protein, which in turn determines the function it will carry out.

Molecular shape

The **shape** of protein molecules shows wide variation. For example, an enzyme molecule has a roughly spherical shape (see Figure 5.1) whereas the protein molecules that make up structures such as bone and connective tissues often take the form of rope-like fibres. The proteins that form part of the cell membrane (see Figure 2.3) tend to be spherical or ovoid and those that make up antibodies are Y-shaped (see Figure 5.2).

Figure 5.1 Computer-generated model of an enzyme molecule

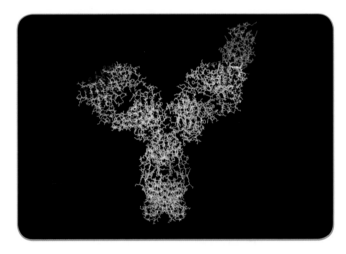

Figure 5.2 Antibody molecule

Variety of functions

Proteins as a group perform a wider range of **functions** than any other type of molecule present in the human body. Some are found in bone and muscle where their strong fibres provide support or allow movement. Others play a variety of essential roles as follows.

Enzymes

Figure 5.3 shows an **enzyme** molecule. It is made up of several chains of amino acids folded and coiled in a particular way that exposes an **active site**. This site is able to combine readily with a substrate (see page 38) and speed up a biochemical reaction such as respiration.

Structural proteins

Protein is an essential **structural component** of the cell membrane and of the membrane that encloses each of the cell's organelles.

Hormones

Hormones are chemical messengers transported in an animal's blood to 'target' tissues where they bring about a particular effect. Many hormones are made of protein and **regulate** processes such as growth and metabolism.

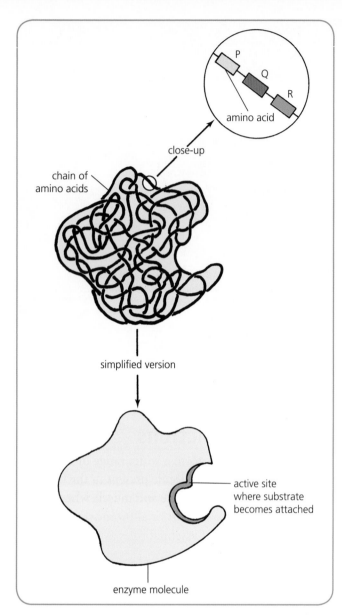

Figure 5.3 An enzyme's molecular structure

Antibodies

Antibodies are protein molecules made by white blood cells to **defend** the body against micro-organisms that could cause disease.

Biological catalysts

Since living things cannot tolerate the high temperatures needed to make chemical reactions proceed at a rapid rate, they employ catalysts. **Biological catalysts** are called **enzymes**. Enzymes are made by all living cells.

Importance of enzymes

Enzymes **speed up** the rate of all biochemical reactions yet remain **unchanged** by the process. They allow biochemical reactions to proceed rapidly at the relatively low temperatures (such as 5–40 °C) needed by living cells to function properly. In the absence of enzymes, biochemical pathways such as respiration and photosynthesis would proceed so slowly that life as we know it could not exist.

Importance of a control

A **control** is a copy of the experiment in which all factors are kept exactly the same except for the one being investigated in the original experiment. When the results are compared, any difference found between the two must be due to that **one factor**. For example, in the experiments shown on page 37, we can conclude that in the first one a catalyst and in the second one an enzyme increased the rate of breakdown of hydrogen peroxide. If controls had not been set up it would be valid to suggest that the breakdown of hydrogen peroxide would have proceeded rapidly whether a catalyst or an enzyme had been present or not.

Active site

At some point on the surface of the protein molecule that makes up an enzyme, there is an **active site** (see Figure 5.6). The shape of the active site is determined by its chemical structure, which results from the **sequence of**, and **bonding between**, **amino acids** in the enzyme molecule.

Mechanism of action

An enzyme is able to act on only one type of substance (its **substrate**) since this is the only substance whose molecules exactly fit the enzyme's active site. The enzyme is therefore said to be **specific** to its substrate and the shape of the enzyme's active site is said to be **complementary** to the substrate's molecular shape.

When a molecule of substrate enters the active site, the shape of the enzyme molecule and its active site change slightly, making the active site **fit closely** round the substrate molecule. This close contact increases the chance of the chemical reaction taking place (see Figure 5.6 on page 38).

Effect of a catalyst on the breakdown of hydrogen peroxide

In the experiment shown in Figure 5.4, the bubbles forming the froth in tube A are found to relight a glowing splint. This shows that oxygen is being released during the breakdown of hydrogen peroxide. In tube B, the control, the breakdown process is so slow that no oxygen can be detected.

It is concluded therefore that manganese dioxide (which remains chemically unaltered at the end of the reaction) has increased the rate of this chemical reaction, which would otherwise have only proceeded very slowly. A substance that has this effect on a chemical reaction is called a **catalyst**.

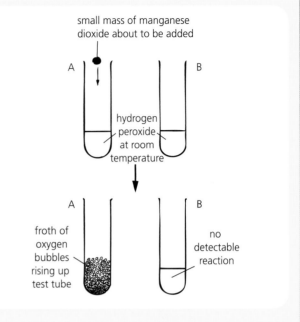

Figure 5.4 Effect of a catalyst

Effect of catalase on the breakdown of hydrogen peroxide

Catalase is an enzyme made by living cells. It is especially abundant in fresh liver cells. In the experiment shown in Figure 5.5, the bubbles produced in tube C are found to relight a glowing splint. This shows that oxygen is being released during the breakdown of hydrogen peroxide. In tube D (the control), boiling the liver has destroyed the catalase with the result that the breakdown process is too slow for any oxygen to be detected.

It is concluded that the enzyme catalase has increased the rate of the chemical reaction shown in the following equation, which would otherwise have proceeded only very slowly.

$$\text{hydrogen peroxide} \xrightarrow{\text{catalase}} \text{oxygen} + \text{water}$$
$$\text{(substrate)} \qquad\qquad\qquad \text{(end products)}$$

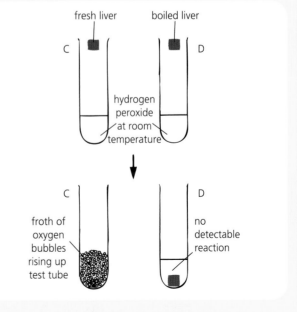

Figure 5.5 Effect of catalase

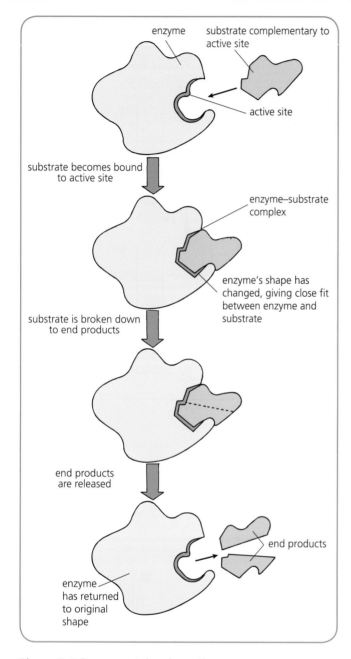

enzyme   substrate complementary to active site

active site

substrate becomes bound to active site

enzyme–substrate complex

enzyme's shape has changed, giving close fit between enzyme and substrate

substrate is broken down to end products

end products are released

end products

enzyme has returned to original shape

Figure 5.6 Enzyme-catalysed reaction

Factors affecting enzyme activity

To function efficiently an enzyme requires a suitable **temperature** and a suitable **pH**.

One variable factor

An investigation is a fair test if at each stage only one difference (**variable factor**) is studied at a time. If several differences were involved at the same time then it would be impossible to know which one was responsible for the results obtained. The experiment shown in the Related Activity on page 39 is **valid** and **fair** because it tests only one variable factor (temperature). (Also see Appendix 4.)

Effect of temperature

The graph in Figure 5.8 summarises the general effect of **temperature** on enzyme activity. At very low temperatures, enzyme molecules are **inactive** but **undamaged**. At low temperatures, enzyme and substrate molecules move around **slowly** in their surrounding medium. They meet only rarely and the rate of enzyme activity remains low. As the temperature increases, the two types of molecule move about at a **faster rate** and the rate of the reaction increases.

Optimum temperature

The temperature at which **most enzyme-substrate molecular activity** occurs (without any molecular damage taking place) is a value within the range of 35–40 °C. This temperature at which the reaction works best is called the enzyme's **optimum** temperature.

Testing Your Knowledge 1

1 Copy the following sentences and complete the blanks. The amino acids in a protein are built into a particular order that is determined by the sequence of the _____ on a portion of DNA in a _____. The sequence of amino acids determines the protein's _____ and _____. (4)

2 a) What general name is given to biological catalysts? (1)
   b) State TWO properties of a biological catalyst. (2)

3 a) Where are enzymes found in a living organism? (1)
   b) Of what type of substance are enzyme molecules composed? (1)

   c) Briefly explain why enzymes are needed for the functioning of all living cells. (2)

4 a) What determines the shape of an enzyme's active site? (1)
   b) What term is used to refer to the substance upon which an enzyme acts? (1)
   c) Why is an enzyme said to be *specific* in its relationship with its substrate? (1)

Investigating the effect of temperature on amylase activity

Amylase is an enzyme that promotes the breakdown of **starch** (its substrate) to simple sugar. In the experiment shown in Figure 5.7, a test tube containing amylase and a test tube containing starch suspension are placed in each of four water baths at **different temperatures**. The test tubes are left for 30 minutes to allow their contents to equilibrate (become equal with) the temperature of the surrounding water.

During this time, two spotting tiles are set up with a drop of **iodine solution** in every cavity. Following equilibration, the enzyme in each tube is added to the tube of starch at each temperature. Separate droppers are

immediately used to add a small sample of each tube's **enzyme-substrate mixture** to iodine on the spotting tile. This procedure is repeated at the time intervals indicated in Figure 5.7, which also shows a typical set of results after 20 minutes.

Failure by a sample to produce a blue-black colour with iodine solution is regarded as evidence that the starch in that tube has been broken down by amylase. Since failure to produce the blue-black colour occurs first with the samples from the tube at 35 °C, it is concluded that the amylase is most active at 35 °C. At the higher temperature of 60 °C, no breakdown of starch is found to occur. At the lower temperature of 2 °C, breakdown of starch takes a long time.

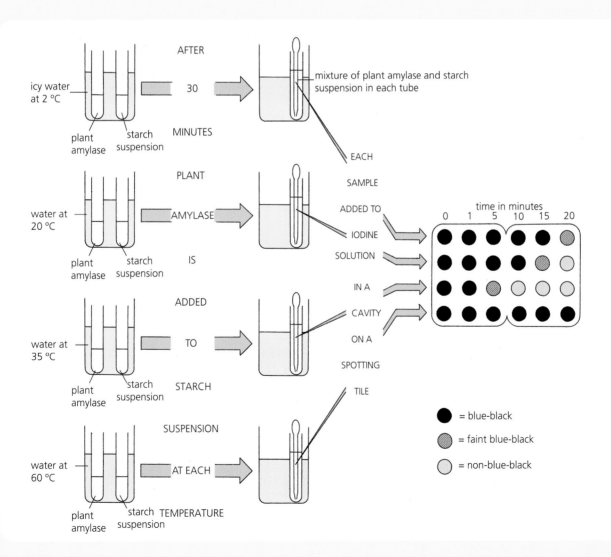

Figure 5.7 Effect of temperature on plant amylase activity

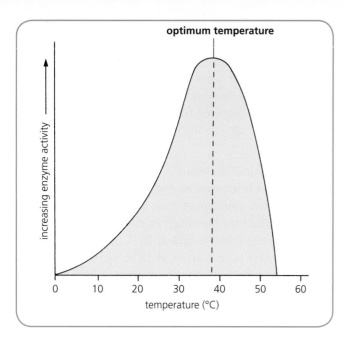

Figure 5.8 Effect of temperature on enzyme activity

Denaturation

At temperatures above 40 °C, an enzyme's atoms vibrate so much that some of the chemical bonds holding its amino acids together break and the molecule begins to come apart. Soon the shape of its active site becomes **altered** and the enzyme is unable to fit with its substrate. An enzyme in this damaged state is said to be **denatured**. It is permanently inactive.

Beyond 40 °C, as more and more molecules of enzyme become denatured and inactive, the rate of the reaction **decreases rapidly**. At temperatures of about 55–60 °C enzyme activity is often found to have come to a complete halt. This is because all the enzyme molecules have become denatured.

Related Activity

Investigating the effect of pH on catalase activity

In the experiment shown in Figure 5.9, the action of **catalase** on hydrogen peroxide is investigated. The one variable factor is the **pH** of the hydrogen peroxide solution. Each of the different pH conditions is maintained by adding a suitable **buffer solution** (a special chemical that keeps a solution at a required pH).

When an equal-sized piece of fresh liver was added to each cylinder, the results shown in the diagram were produced. This is because liver contains the enzyme catalase, which promotes the breakdown of hydrogen peroxide to oxygen and water. As oxygen is released, it produces a **froth of bubbles**. The height of the froth formed indicates the activity of the enzyme at each pH.

From the results it can be seen that this catalase was most active at around pH 9 and worked fairly well over a range of about pH 7 to 11. This is called its **working range** of pH. This catalase does not work well outside this range.

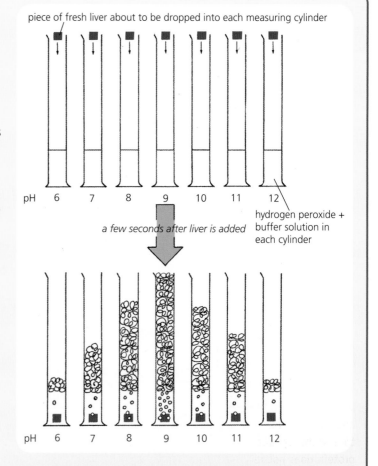

Figure 5.9 Effect of pH on catalase activity

Investigating the effect of pH on the activity of pepsin

Pepsin is an enzyme secreted by glands in the stomach wall. It digests **protein** to soluble end products. The protein used in the experiment shown in Figure 5.10 is egg white. It has been heated in advance to form a cloudy suspension of insoluble particles ready for use. The three test tubes are set up as shown in the diagram and maintained at 37 °C, the optimum temperature for pepsin activity.

After 30 minutes, the contents of tube A (acidic conditions) are found to be **clear** whereas those of B (neutral conditions) and C (alkaline conditions) remain **cloudy** and unchanged. It is therefore concluded that pepsin digests large particles of insoluble protein to soluble end products in **acidic** conditions only.

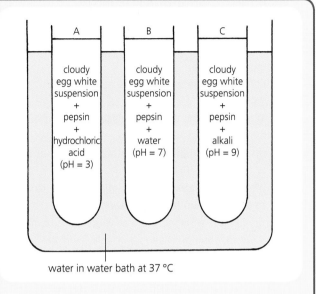

Figure 5.10 Effect of pH on pepsin

Optimum pH

Each enzyme is found to work best at a particular pH (its **optimum** pH), as shown in Figure 5.11. Most enzymes function within a working pH range of about 5–9 with an optimum of around pH 7 (neutral). However, there are exceptions. Pepsin works best in strongly acidic conditions of pH 2.5; alkaline phosphatase (which plays a role in bone formation) works best at pH 10.

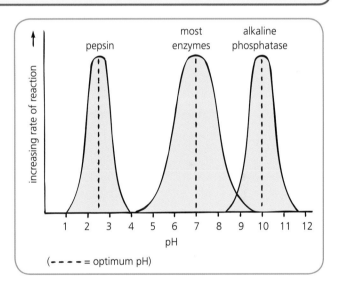

Figure 5.11 Effect of pH on enzymes

Effect of temperature and pH on egg white

Egg white is made of a protein called albumin. In this activity, the albumin acts as a **model** for the effect of temperature and pH on proteins in general, including **enzymes**.

Temperature

When raw egg white is heated, the albumin coagulates and changes from a colourless, transparent liquid to a white, opaque solid. On cooling, the egg white protein does not return to its original state. Its molecular structure has been altered irreversibly (denatured).

pH

When acid is added to raw egg white to reduce its pH value to a low level, the albumen coagulates. When the pH is returned to neutral by the addition of an alkali, the egg white protein does not resume its original transparent state. The change in its molecular structure is irreversible and it is in a denatured state.

Similarly, most enzymes are irreversibly altered in molecular structure by high temperatures and extremes of pH and therefore become non-functional following exposure to these adverse conditions.

Testing Your Knowledge 2

1 Salivary amylase is an enzyme that digests starch in the human mouth.

   a) Compare the rate of amylase activity at 5 °C and 25 °C. (1)

   b) i) Compare the rate of amylase activity at 40 °C and 70 °C.

     ii) Explain the difference in rate in terms of the molecules. (3)

2 a) Which temperature given in question 1 is closest to the optimum for most enzymes? (1)

   b) i) Suggest a temperature at which an enzyme is inactive but capable of activity if the temperature changes.

     ii) Explain your answer. (2)

   c) Why does exposure to concentrated acid normally result in an enzyme becoming inactive? (1)

3 a) Explain the meaning of the term *optimum condition* as applied to the activity of an enzyme. (1)

   b) Which of the following is the optimum range of pH for the human enzyme pepsin? (1)

    A 2–3

    B 4–5

    C 6–7

    D 8–9

6 Genetic engineering

Chromosomal material of a bacterium

A bacterium has one **chromosome** in the form of a complete circle and one or more small circular **plasmids**, as shown in Figure 6.1. The chromosome and plasmids are composed of DNA and are made up of many genes. Each gene carries the information necessary to make a certain protein such as an enzyme.

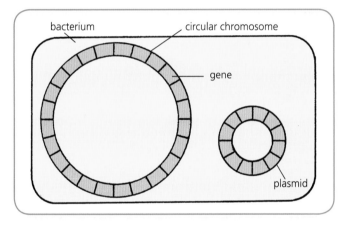

Figure 6.1 Genetic material of a bacterium

Transfer of genetic material

Genetic information in the form of DNA can be transferred from one cell to another by **natural** means. For example, a copy of a bacterial plasmid can be passed from one bacterium to another and the DNA in a virus can be inserted into a host cell that is being attacked by the virus. DNA can also be transferred from one cell to another **artificially** by genetic engineering.

Genetic engineering

In recent years, scientists have developed technology that enables them to transfer pieces of chromosome containing sections of DNA from one organism such as a human being to another organism such as a bacterium. This process is called **genetic engineering**

and the organism that has been 'reprogrammed' is described as a **genetically modified (GM)** organism. This transformed organism now possesses some characteristic that makes it useful to humans.

For example, a GM bacterium may act as a chemical factory and produce a useful product, as shown in Figure 6.2. This diagram shows a simplified version of genetic engineering involving the following stages:

1 identification of the section of DNA that contains the required gene (such as the gene for human insulin) on the source chromosome
2 cutting of the source chromosome using a special enzyme (acting as biochemical 'scissors') to release the required gene
3 extraction of a plasmid from a bacterial cell
4 opening up of a plasmid using the same enzyme used in stage 2
5 sealing of the required gene into the plasmid using a different type of enzyme
6 insertion of the plasmid into the bacterial host cell
7 growth and multiplication of the transformed bacterial cell
8 formation of many duplicate plasmids that express the 'foreign' gene and make the desired useful product (such as insulin), which is then extracted and purified.

In this example the plasmid containing the required gene acts as a **vector** (a carrier) between the two different organisms.

Advantage of using micro-organisms

Whereas isolated cells of an advanced multicellular organism such as a human being are often difficult to mass-produce in culture, micro-organisms can be grown quickly and easily, often at low cost. Given suitable conditions, GM bacteria multiply at a rapid rate and manufacture large quantities of a **useful product** that can then be extracted, concentrated, purified and put to use.

Figure 6.2 Genetic engineering

Multicellular organisms

The production of GM organisms by genetic engineering is not restricted to micro-organisms such as bacteria and yeast. In recent years many applications have been successfully carried out involving multicellular organisms. For example, scientists have found ways of injecting a plasmid containing a required gene into the cells of a multicellular organism. These transformed cells then grow into a **multicellular GM organism**. By this means, genetic engineers have produced:

- plants with improved nutritional value, such as golden rice (see Related Topic)
- plants that are resistant to pests, such as blight-resistant potatoes (see Related Topic)
- fruit with a longer shelf life, such as tomatoes (see Related Topic).

Related Topic

Products of medical value

Many products of genetic engineering have important **medical applications**. In each of the examples given in Table 6.1, a particular gene has successfully been inserted into a bacterium, which is then allowed to multiply and make the product of medical value.

Scientists have also managed to reprogramme yeast cells to produce **human serum albumin** (used in blood replacements), **epidermal growth factor** (which speeds up the healing of wounds) and **hepatitis B antigens** (used in the manufacture of hepatitis B vaccine).

Figure 6.3 Insulin pen

Product of genetic engineering	Normal source and function of substance	Medical application of gene product made by GM bacteria
insulin	Made by pancreas cells. Controls the level of glucose in the blood.	Given to people who are diabetic and do not make enough insulin naturally. (An insulin pen is shown in Figure 6.3.)
human growth hormone (HGH)	Made by cells in the pituitary gland. Essential during childhood and adolescence to control growth and development.	Given by regular injection to children who do not make enough of their own. Prevents severely reduced growth.

Table 6.1 Medical applications of gene products

Related Topic

Golden rice

Vitamin A is a chemical needed in small quantities in the diet for good health and, in particular, for healthy eyesight. Normal cultivated rice contains very little vitamin A in its grains. In regions of the world where this type of rice is the main part of the staple diet and where people fail to obtain enough vitamin A from other food sources, vitamin A deficiency is common. Shortage of this vitamin leads to **vision problems** and even blindness and may cause premature death.

Genetic engineers have now succeeded in transferring two genes from other plants into traditional rice to create a new variety called **golden rice** (see Figure 6.4). This new strain of rice plant makes a yellow chemical that accumulates in the rice grains giving them a golden appearance. When the rice grains are eaten, the yellow chemical is changed into vitamin A by the body. It then acts in the normal way and prevents vision problems.

Golden rice's nutritional value is further increased by the presence of a higher concentration of **iron** in its grains compared with those of normal varieties. Iron is needed for the production of new red blood cells.

Figure 6.4 Golden rice

Related Topic

Blight-resistant potatoes

A fungal parasite attacks potato plants and causes a disease called **blight** (see Figure 6.5) that ruins the potatoes and makes them inedible. It was this devastating disease that led to the Irish potato famine in 1845–6 and the Scottish Highland potato famine in 1846.

In recent years, genetic engineers managed to identify and extract from a wild potato plant a gene that gave **blight resistance**. They then introduced it into other varieties of potato plant, making them resistant. However, new strains of the fungus soon evolved that were able to break down the potato plants' resistance.

Disease resistance is now known to be a complex feature of a potato plant's genetic makeup. It involves **several interacting genes**. Some Scottish scientists are using a technique that enables them to locate several genes (some for disease resistance, others for quality traits) and transfer them as a group. On being introduced to potato plants, these act together and significantly increase the plant's resistance to blight.

The production of GM crops that are resistant to pests is of benefit to the environment because little or no chemical pesticide needs to be used to keep the crops healthy.

Figure 6.5 Potato leaf infected with blight

Related Topic

Tomatoes with longer shelf life

Genetic engineers are now able to insert into an organism a gene that **switches off** (silences) the activity of another gene. This process has been developed commercially to extend the **shelf life** of tomatoes. Under normal circumstances, a certain gene controls the production of an enzyme that breaks down a chemical in the cell walls of a tomato, making the fruit become soft.

By switching off the gene that codes for this enzyme (but not the genes that control colour or flavour), scientists have made it possible to **delay the softening** of tomatoes while allowing their colour and flavour to develop as normal. Therefore the fruit has a much longer shelf life before it becomes over-ripe and spoiled. The two groups of tomatoes shown in Figure 6.6 are the same age and are genetically identical except that those on the top have been genetically modified to silence the 'fruit-softening' gene.

Figure 6.6 GM tomatoes (top) and their non-GM relatives

Testing Your Knowledge

1 a) What is meant by the term *genetic engineering*? (2)
   b) An agent that acts as a carrier between two species is often called a vector. Which part of a bacterium's genetic material could this term be used to describe? (1)
2 Arrange the following steps involved in the process of genetic engineering into the correct order. (1)
   A cutting of source chromosome to release required gene
   B insertion of required gene into plasmid and plasmid into host cell
   C growth of transformed host cell into GM organism
   D extraction of a plasmid from a bacterial cell
   E identification of section of DNA that contains required gene
3 a) Give an example of a product of genetic engineering. (1)
   b) Explain why this product is of benefit to human beings. (1)

What You Should Know Chapters 5–6

active	enzymes	products
antibodies	function	protein
benefit	gene	sequence
catalyst	genetic	shape
chromosome	host	site
complementary	inserted	structural
denatured	modified	substrate
DNA	optimum	temperature
engineering	plasmid	unaltered

1 Both the shape and _____ of a protein molecule are determined by the particular _____ of amino acids that make up the _____.

2 Some proteins have a _____ function; others act as hormones, _____ or enzymes.

3 A _____ is a substance that speeds up the rate of a chemical reaction but remains _____ by the reaction. _____ are biological catalysts produced by all living cells.

4 The shape of the _____ site on an enzyme molecule is _____ to the molecular structure of its _____, allowing them to combine together closely.

5 Following catalytic activity, the end _____ become detached from the active _____, leaving the enzyme unchanged.

6 To function efficiently, an enzyme needs an appropriate pH and a suitable _____. Each enzyme works best in its _____ conditions. At temperatures above 55 °C, most enzyme molecules are inactive because their molecular _____ has been irreversibly altered. They are described as being _____.

7 _____ can be transferred naturally from one cell to another. DNA can also be transferred by genetic _____.

8 During _____ engineering, the section of DNA that contains the required _____ is identified and cut out of the source _____. Then the gene is inserted into a vector such as a bacterial _____.

9 The reprogrammed plasmid is _____ into a _____ cell such as a bacterium.

10 The transformed host cell (now a genetically _____ organism) grows and multiplies and provides humans with some _____.

7 Respiration

Glucose

Glucose, a type of sugar, is an energy-rich substance. It is the most common end product from the digestion of complex carbohydrates such as starch. Glucose is the main source of **energy** in a living cell.

Release of chemical energy

When a food is burned in air or in oxygen, its **chemical energy** is released rapidly as heat and light (see the Related Activity on page 49). However, in a living cell, the chemical energy stored in food is not released as rapidly. Instead an orderly release of energy takes place relatively slowly through a series of enzyme-controlled reactions called **respiration**. Respiration occurs in all living cells.

Adenosine triphosphate (ATP)

Adenosine triphosphate (ATP) is an energy-rich chemical compound. A molecule of ATP is made of adenosine and three inorganic phosphate (Pi) groups, as shown in Figure 7.1. Energy stored in an ATP molecule is released when the bond attached to the terminal phosphate is broken down by enzyme action. This results in the formation of adenosine diphosphate (ADP) and Pi. On the other hand, energy is required to regenerate ATP from ADP and Pi. This reversible reaction is summarised by the equation:

ATP
(high energy state)
$\xrightarrow{\text{breakdown releasing energy}}$
$\xleftarrow{\text{build-up requiring energy}}$
ADP + Pi
(low energy state)

Role of ATP

When an energy-rich substance such as glucose is gradually broken down during respiration in a living cell, it releases energy that is used to **regenerate** ATP. As a result, many molecules of ATP are present in every living cell. ATP can rapidly revert to ADP and Pi. This makes energy immediately available for **energy-requiring processes** such as:

- muscular contraction
- cell division
- synthesis of proteins
- transmission of nerve impulses
- active uptake of ions and molecules (see page 16)
- carbon fixation during photosynthesis (see page 58).

ATP is therefore important because it acts as the **link** between energy-releasing reactions and energy-consuming reactions. It provides the means by which chemical energy is **transferred** from one type of reaction to the other in a living cell, as shown in Figure 7.2.

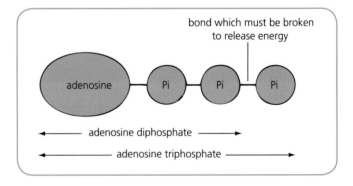

Figure 7.1 Structure of ATP

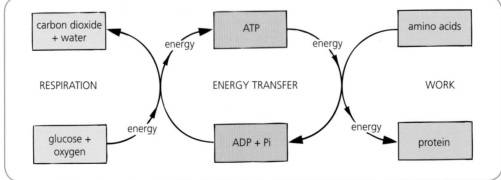

Figure 7.2 Transfer of chemical energy by ATP

Measuring the energy content of food

Energy is measured in **kilojoules (kJ)**. 4.2 kJ is the quantity of energy required to raise the temperature of 1000 g of water by 1 °C. The chemical energy contained in food can be changed into heat energy and measured. In the experiment shown in Figure 7.3, 1 g of peanut is ignited and held under a beaker containing 1000 g water. The temperature of the water is found to rise by 2 °C. Therefore 1 g of peanut has released 8.4 kJ of energy.

Sources of error

The experiment in Figure 7.3 contains the following sources of error:

- much of the heat energy released by the burning peanut is lost to the surroundings
- the heat energy that does reach the water is not evenly spread out
- the peanut is not completely burned to ashes.

Food calorimeter

The energy content of a food can be measured accurately using a **food calorimeter** (see Figure 7.4). This equipment overcomes the limitations of the simple apparatus shown in Figure 7.3 in the following ways:

- the food sample is **enclosed**, therefore loss of heat energy is reduced to a minimum
- the **stirrer** and **coiled chimney** bring about even distribution of the heat energy released during burning
- the **oxygen** supply ensures that the peanut burns completely.

This time the temperature of the water is found to rise by 6 °C, showing that 1 g of peanut has released 25.2 kJ of energy.

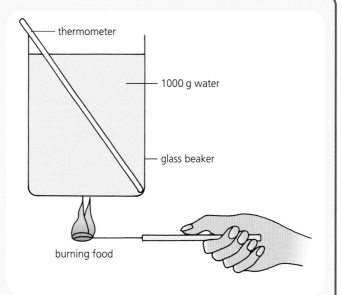

Figure 7.3 Measuring energy in food

Figure 7.4 Food calorimeter

Related Activity

Investigating respiration in a green plant

Hydrogen carbonate indicator solution is a chemical that varies in colour depending on the concentration of carbon dioxide (CO_2) that it contains. Table 7.1 shows the relative CO_2 concentrations indicated by the various colours.

In the experiment shown in Figure 7.5, the hydrogen carbonate indicator in tube A changes from red to yellow, whereas the indicator in tube B, the control, remains unchanged. It is therefore concluded that the green plant, *Cabomba*, has released CO_2 formed in its cells by respiration. The dark cover is used to prevent photosynthesis (see chapter 8) from occurring.

If the experiment is repeated in bright light without covers over the tubes, the indicator in tube A is found to change from red to purple while that in tube B remains unchanged. It is therefore concluded that in bright light, the quantity of CO_2 taken in by the plant for photosynthesis exceeds the quantity of CO_2 given out as a result of respiration.

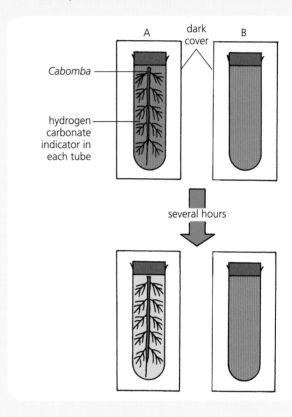

Figure 7.5 Respiration in a green plant

Relative CO_2 concentration	Colour of hydrogen carbonate indicator
high (above atmospheric)	yellow
medium (atmospheric)	red
low (below atmospheric)	purple

Table 7.1 Hydrogen carbonate indicator range

Testing Your Knowledge 1

1 Which sugar is the most common source of energy in living cells? (1)

2 a) What name is given to the series of enzyme-controlled reactions by which energy stored in sugar is released? (1)

   b) Where does this process occur in living organisms? (1)

3 a) Draw a simple labelled diagram of an ATP molecule. (2)

   b) In the two-way equation that follows, which numbered arrow represents:

   i) energy release?

   ii) energy uptake? (1)

$$ADP + Pi \underset{2}{\overset{1}{\rightleftharpoons}} ATP$$

   c) Identify the source of energy needed to drive this process of energy uptake. (1)

   d) The energy released during the process is put to many uses by living cells. Name THREE of these uses. (3)

Biochemistry of respiration

Respiration is the process by which chemical energy is released during the breakdown of a food such as glucose. It occurs in every living cell and involves the regeneration of the high-energy compound ATP by a complex series of biochemical reactions.

Breakdown of glucose

Within a cell, the first stage of respiration is the breakdown of each molecule of glucose by a series of enzyme-controlled steps to form two molecules of **pyruvate** (pyruvic acid), as shown in Figure 7.6. This respiratory pathway also results in the production of **two molecules of ATP** per molecule of glucose. It takes place in the cell's **cytoplasm** and does not need oxygen to be present.

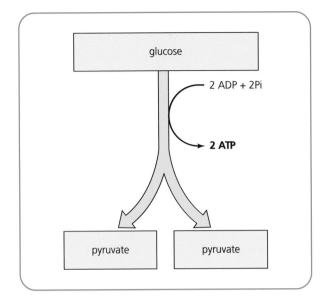

Figure 7.6 Breakdown of glucose

Aerobic respiration

When oxygen is present, aerobic respiration occurs in the cell's **mitochondria** (see Figures 7.7 and 7.8). The inner membrane of each mitochondrion is folded into many extensions that present a **large surface area** upon which the respiratory processes can take place. The extensions project into the central cavity, which contains essential enzymes. Cells such as sperm, liver, muscle and neurons in animals and companion cells (see page 117) in green plants that require much energy contain a relatively high number of mitochondria.

Fate of pyruvate

The respiratory pathway that takes place in mitochondria is illustrated in a simplified form in Figure 7.9. Each molecule of pyruvate (which diffuses into the mitochondrion from the cytoplasm) is broken down by many enzyme-controlled steps. This results in the formation of carbon dioxide, water and **18 molecules of ATP per molecule of pyruvate**. Therefore the complete breakdown of **one molecule of glucose** by aerobic respiration generates **38** (2 + 18 + 18) **molecules of ATP**. These high-energy ATP molecules make energy available for use by the cell. Aerobic respiration of glucose can be summarised as follows:

glucose + oxygen $\longrightarrow$ carbon dioxide + water

Figure 7.7 Mitochondrion

Figure 7.8 Electron micrograph of mitochondrion

51

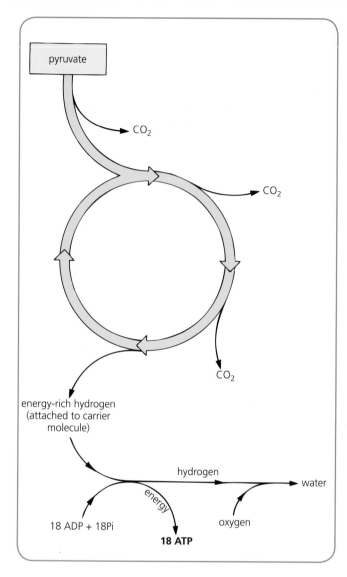

Figure 7.9 Aerobic breakdown of pyruvate

Fermentation pathway

This is the process by which a little energy is derived from the partial breakdown of glucose in the absence of oxygen. Breakdown of glucose begins as normal in the cell and **2 molecules of ATP** are formed per molecule of glucose. However, the pathway involving the complete breakdown of pyruvate to carbon dioxide and water cannot proceed in the absence of oxygen. Instead the pyruvate undergoes one of the following pathways.

Animal cells

During vigorous muscular activity when oxygen supply cannot meet demand, animal cells continue to respire in these anaerobic conditions by fermentation and **lactic acid** is formed as in the following equation:

$$\text{glucose} \longrightarrow \text{pyruvate} \longrightarrow \text{lactic acid}$$

Figure 7.11 represents this form of respiration in muscle cells in the human body when they are short of oxygen. As concentration of lactic acid builds up, it reduces the efficiency of the muscles. They may also suffer **muscle fatigue**. During this time, an **oxygen debt** builds up. The debt is repaid when oxygen becomes available during a rest period (see Figure 7.12) and energy, generated by aerobic respiration, is used to convert lactic acid back to pyruvate. The conversion of pyruvate to lactic acid in respiring animal cells is therefore described as a **reversible** process.

Related Activity

Investigating the effect of exercise on breathing rate

Breathing rate is the number of breaths taken per minute. Each breath involves breathing in and breathing out. With the aid of a stopwatch, the person times him/herself sitting quietly for 2 minutes to allow their breathing rate to settle at a steady pace. Then they measure their breathing rate for 1 minute while continuing to sit quietly.

Next the person exercises vigorously by running on the spot for 3 minutes. Then they measure their breathing rate immediately after stopping exercising. The person pools their results with other students and calculates **mean values** for breathing rate before and immediately

after exercise. This procedure makes the results more **reliable**.

Exercise is found to make breathing rate increase. The person takes **more breaths** per minute than they do at rest. They also take **deeper** breaths. These changes to breathing help to ventilate the lungs more thoroughly during and after exercise. This increases the rate of gas exchange between the air in the air sacs and the blood flowing through the lungs. As a result, the person is able to gain the **oxygen** needed by respiring muscle cells to generate energy for movement. The increased breathing rate also enables the person to exhale more of the **carbon dioxide** formed by respiring muscle cells during exercise.

Measuring rate of respiration in yeast

The experiment is shown in Figure 7.10. Table 7.2 gives the purpose of each piece of equipment. Live yeast cells, immobilised in gel pellets, are added to glucose solution in the conical flask at room temperature. Air is pumped through the system and the experiment is run for a set length of time (such as 30 minutes).

The computer software monitors the data from the sensors and displays the information on-screen. From these data the yeast's rate of respiration (for example, measured as **volume of oxygen consumed per unit time**) can be determined.

The immobilised yeast pellets are then rinsed and placed in a second conical flask of glucose solution in a water bath at 35 °C. This flask is given time to acclimatise to the temperature of the water bath. When the experiment is repeated at the higher temperature, the yeast's rate of respiration is found to increase.

Equipment	Purpose
soda lime tube (containing sodium hydroxide)	to absorb all carbon dioxide from incoming air so that its initial concentration is not a variable factor
air pump	to pump a continuous flow of air through the system
flow meter	to maintain the flow of air at a steady rate that is low enough for the carbon dioxide sensor to work
condensing bath and drying column	to remove water vapour from passing air since the sensors need air to be dry
oxygen probe (sensor)	to measure percentage oxygen concentration and send data to computer
carbon dioxide probe (sensor) and analyser	to measure carbon dioxide in parts per million and send data to computer

Table 7.2 Purposes of respirometer equipment

Figure 7.10 Measuring respiration rate

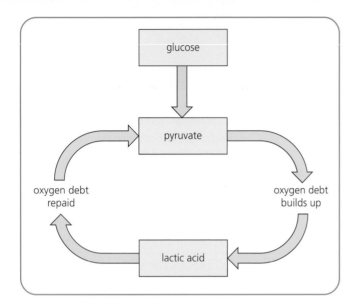

Figure 7.11 Fermentation in animal cells

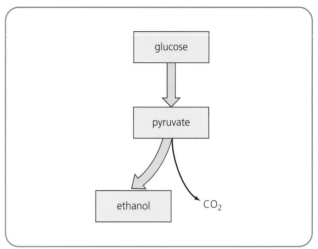

Figure 7.13 Fermentation in plant cells

Figure 7.12 Repayment of oxygen debt

Plant cells

Root cells of plants in waterlogged soil and yeast cells deprived of oxygen, for example during wine-making, are unable to respire aerobically. Such plant cells are dependent on **fermentation** (respiration in anaerobic conditions), as shown in Figure 7.13.

Since a molecule of carbon dioxide is lost each time a molecule of pyruvate is broken down to **ethanol** (alcohol), fermentation in plant cells is an **irreversible** process. It is summarised by the following equation:

glucose $\longrightarrow$ pyruvate $\longrightarrow$ ethanol + carbon dioxide

Comparison of aerobic respiration and fermentation

Table 7.3 compares the two forms of respiration with reference to one molecule of glucose.

	Aerobic respiration	Fermentation
Need for oxygen	oxygen always required	oxygen never required
Energy yield	efficient method releasing 38 ATP per molecule of glucose	inefficient method releasing 2 ATP per molecule of glucose
Degree of breakdown of glucose	glucose completely broken down	glucose partially broken down
End products	carbon dioxide and water	lactic acid in animal cells; ethanol and carbon dioxide in plant cells
Location of process in cell	begins in cytoplasm and is completed in mitochondria	occurs in cytoplasm

Table 7.3 Comparison of aerobic respiration and fermentation

Testing Your Knowledge 2

1   Write a word equation to summarise the complete breakdown of one molecule of glucose by aerobic respiration. (1)

2   a) Give the word equation that summarises anaerobic respiration in animal cells. (1)

   b) The following four statements refer to fermentation in human muscle tissue. Arrange them into the correct order. (1)
      A lactic acid builds up
      B oxygen supply becomes limited
      C muscles become less efficient
      D lactic acid is produced

   c) i) Is fermentation in animal cells reversible?
      ii) Justify your answer to i). (2)

3   a) Give the word equation that summarises fermentation in yeast cells. (1)

   b) i) Is this process reversible?
      ii) Justify your answer to i). (2)

4   Using the letters A and F, indicate whether each of the following statements refers to A (aerobic respiration) or F (fermentation). Some statements may need the use of both letters. (8)

   a) It involves the splitting of glucose into pyruvate.

   b) It yields 38 ATP from one molecule of glucose.

   c) It only yields 2 ATP from one molecule of glucose.

   d) It takes place in the cytoplasm only.

   e) It starts in the cytoplasm and is completed in the mitochondria.

   f) Its end products are CO_2 and water.

   g) Its end products are CO_2 and ethanol.

   h) It creates an oxygen debt in muscle cells.

8 Photosynthesis

Capture of light energy

Photosynthesis consists of a series of enzyme-controlled reactions that allow green plants to make their own food. This process involves the capture of **light energy** from the sun. Light energy is trapped by the green pigment **chlorophyll**. Chlorophyll is found in discus-shaped structures called **chloroplasts** present in green leaf cells (see Figure 1.1 on page 2).

Production of carbohydrate

A **carbohydrate** is a compound containing the chemical elements carbon (C), hydrogen (H) and oxygen (O) combined together using energy. The production of a carbohydrate food (such as **glucose**, a type of sugar) requires a supply of the raw materials **water** and **carbon dioxide** to be available to supply the necessary chemicals. During photosynthesis, molecules of carbon dioxide combine with hydrogen from water in the presence of chlorophyll and light energy to form sugar. Oxygen is released as a by-product of the process.

Figure 8.1 Photosynthesis in a leaf of a land plant

Summary

The process of photosynthesis is summarised in Figure 8.1 and by the following equation:

carbon dioxide   +   water   +   light energy (absorbed by chlorophyll) ⟶ sugar   +   oxygen

raw materials   food product   by-product

Biochemistry of photosynthesis

Photosynthesis consists of two distinct stages:

- the light-dependent stage consisting of several **light reactions**
- the temperature-dependent stage called **carbon fixation**.

Light-dependent stage

During this series of light reactions, **light** energy is trapped by chlorophyll and converted to **chemical** energy in the form of energy-rich **ATP**, which has been regenerated from ADP + Pi (also see page 48). Some energy is also used during this stage to **split water** into hydrogen and oxygen (see Figure 8.2). The oxygen is released as a by-product and diffuses out of the plant. The hydrogen and the ATP are used during the carbon

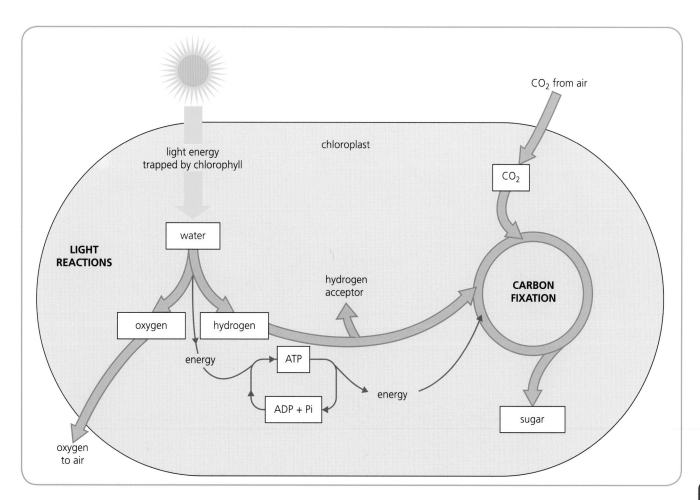

Figure 8.2 Biochemistry of photosynthesis

fixation stage of photosynthesis. It cannot proceed without them.

Carbon fixation

This second stage of photosynthesis also occurs in chloroplasts (see Figure 8.2). It consists of several **enzyme-controlled reactions** in the form of a cycle that result in **carbon** (from carbon dioxide) becoming 'fixed' into a **sugar** (such as glucose) by combining with the hydrogen from the light-dependent stage. ATP supplies the energy needed to drive this process.

Conversion of glucose into plant products

Carbohydrates

As a plant grows, it continues to make glucose by photosynthesis. Some of this sugar is broken down again by **respiration** to supply the plant with energy for vital processes such as cell division and reproduction. Some of the remaining glucose molecules become linked into long chains and packed together into **starch** grains found in the cell's cytoplasm (see Figures 8.3, 8.4 and 8.5). This plant product is the plant's store of food and can be converted back to sugar when energy is required. Starch is therefore called a **storage** carbohydrate.

Other glucose molecules are built into long chains of **cellulose**. These are gathered together to form the fibres needed to build cell walls (see Figure 8.3 and Figure 2.16 on page 14). Cellulose is therefore called a **structural** carbohydrate.

Fats and proteins

Carbohydrates produced during photosynthesis can also be converted into **fats** and **proteins**. (Additional chemicals such as nitrate are required to make proteins. These chemicals are absorbed from the soil solution by the plant's root hairs.)

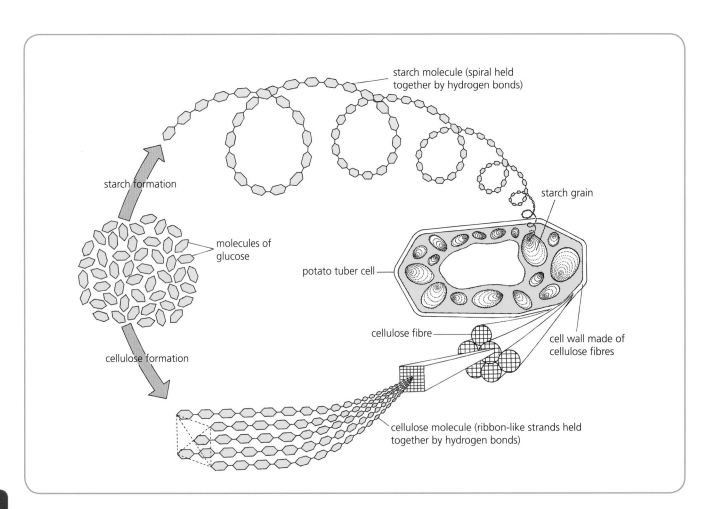

Figure 8.3 Formation of storage and structural carbohydrate

Figure 8.4 Potato tuber cells in water

Figure 8.5 Potato tuber cells in iodine solution

Investigation

Effect of light on starch production

A green plant is set up as shown in Figure 8.6 and left in bright light for 2 days. With the aid of a cork borer, a disc is then cut from a leaf that has been in light. When the disc is tested by following the procedure shown in Figure 8.7, it is found to turn **blue-black**, showing that it contains starch. When the experiment is repeated using a disc from the leaf that has been in darkness, it does not turn blue-black, showing that it lacks starch. Therefore it is concluded that **light** is necessary for starch production (and photosynthesis).

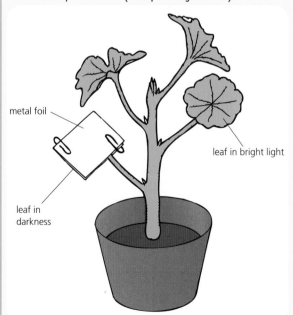

Figure 8.6 Investigating the need for light

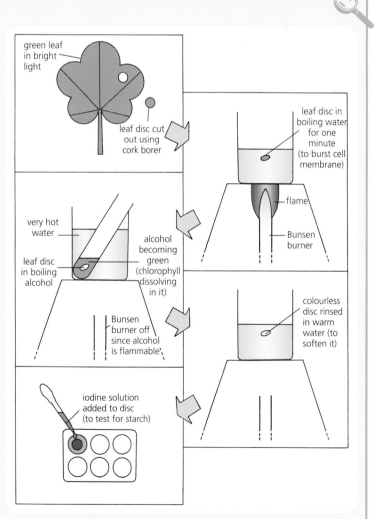

Figure 8.7 Testing a leaf disc for starch

Investigation

Effect of carbon dioxide on starch production

Two destarched green plants are set up as shown in Figure 8.8 and left in bright light for 2 days. A leaf disc from each plant is then tested for starch by following the procedure shown in Figure 8.7. The disc from plant A is found to contain starch whereas the disc from plant B is found to lack starch. Therefore it is concluded that **carbon dioxide** is necessary for starch production (and photosynthesis).

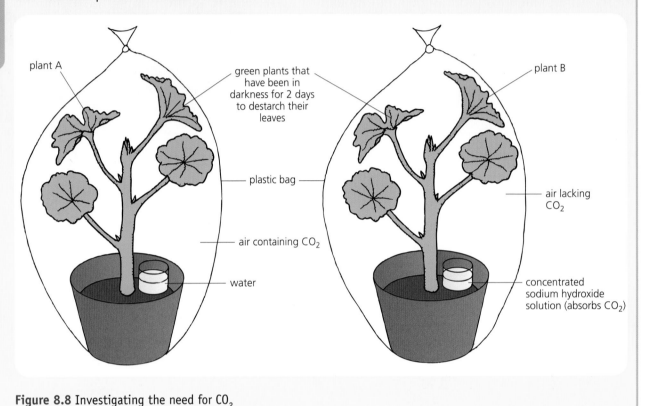

plant A

green plants that have been in darkness for 2 days to destarch their leaves

plant B

plastic bag

air lacking CO_2

air containing CO_2

water

concentrated sodium hydroxide solution (absorbs CO_2)

Figure 8.8 Investigating the need for CO_2

Investigation

Effect of chlorophyll on starch production

When the starch test is applied to a leaf that is **variegated** (has two colours, one of which is green, as shown in Figure 8.9), only the green regions react positively with iodine solution (see Figure 8.10). Therefore it is concluded that **chlorophyll** is necessary for starch production (and photosynthesis).

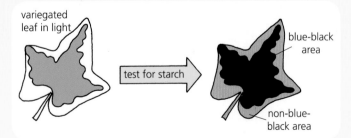

variegated leaf in light

test for starch

blue-black area

non-blue-black area

Figure 8.10 Investigating the need for chlorophyll

Figure 8.9 Plant with variegated leaves

Testing Your Knowledge 1

1 Figure 8.11 gives an illustrated summary of the biochemistry of photosynthesis.

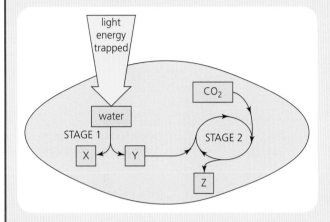

Figure 8.11

a) i) Name the discus-shaped organelle within which photosynthesis takes place.
   ii) Give the colour and name of the chemical substance responsible for trapping light energy. (3)
b) i) Identify substances X, Y and Z.
   ii) Which of these is the carbohydrate end product?
   iii) Which of these is a by-product that diffuses out of the plant? (5)
c) i) Name stages 1 and 2.
   ii) Which high-energy substance needed to drive stage 2 has been omitted from the diagram? (3)
2 Name:
   a) the structural and
   b) the storage carbohydrate formed in plant cells using glucose molecules made by photosynthesis. (2)

Factors affecting photosynthetic rate

Several environmental factors affect the rate of photosynthesis. These include light intensity, carbon dioxide concentration and temperature.

Effect of varying light intensity

Elodea bubbler experiment

The number of oxygen bubbles released per minute by the cut end of an *Elodea* stem (see Figure 8.12) indicates the rate at which photosynthesis is proceeding. At first the lamp (see Figure 8.13) is placed exactly 100 cm from the plant and the number of bubbles released per minute is counted. The lamp is then moved to a new position (say 60 cm from the plant) and the rate of bubbling noted (once the plant has had a short time to become acclimatised to this new higher light intensity).

The process is repeated for lamp positions even nearer the plant, as recorded in Table 8.1. When this typical set of results is displayed as a graph (Figure 8.14), it can be concluded that as light intensity increases, photosynthetic rate also increases until it reaches a maximum, in this case of 25 bubbles per minute at around 64 units of light.

Figure 8.12 Release of oxygen from cut stem of *Elodea*

Distance from plant (cm)	Units of light (calculated using a mathematical formula)	Number of oxygen bubbles released per minute
100	4	4
60	11	10
40	25	19
30	45	24
25	64	25
20	100	25

Table 8.1 *Elodea* bubbler results

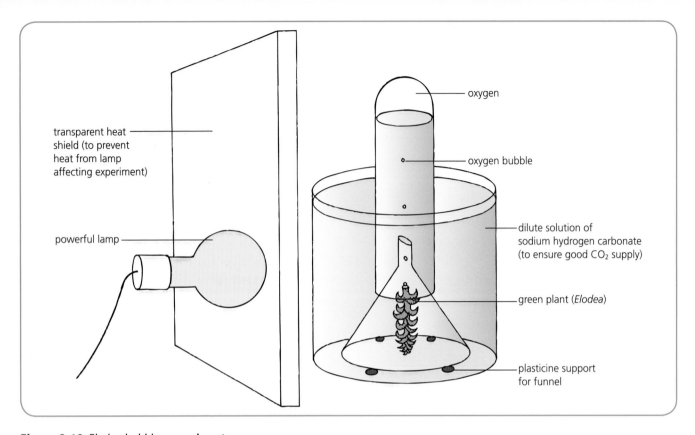

Figure 8.13 *Elodea* bubbler experiment

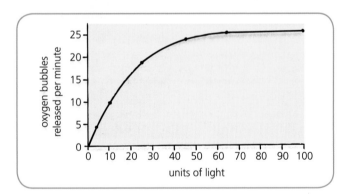

Figure 8.14 Graph of *Elodea* bubbler experiment results

Ingredients needed to make one loaf	Baker A's stock	Baker B's stock
500 g flour	5 kg flour	5 kg flour
30 g fat	60 g fat	300 g fat
10 g yeast	50 g yeast	50 g yeast
5 g sugar	40 g sugar	15 g sugar

Table 8.2 Factors limiting bread making

Limiting factors

Consider the information in Table 8.2. Although Baker A has plenty of flour, yeast and sugar, he can only make two loaves because he has a limited supply of fat. Baker B has plenty of fat but she can only make three loaves because her stock of sugar limits production. A **limiting factor** is a factor that holds up a process because it is in short supply.

Similarly, limiting factors such as light intensity, carbon dioxide concentration and temperature can hold up photosynthesis. In the *Elodea* bubbler

experiment described above, further increase in light intensity beyond 64 units does not increase photosynthetic rate. It remains at 25 bubbles per minute. This is because some other factor such as shortage of carbon dioxide is now holding up the process and acting as a limiting factor.

Impact of limiting factors

If one of the factors that affect the rate of photosynthesis is limiting then the plant makes less sugar than it would under optimum conditions. Cell growth slows down and less food is stored as starch.

Related Activity

Investigating the effect of varying carbon dioxide concentration

In this experiment the concentration of carbon dioxide made available to the *Elodea* plant is gradually increased by adding appropriate masses of sodium hydrogen carbonate to the water. The number of oxygen bubbles released is counted as before. The lamp is kept in one position to give uniform light of medium intensity.

The graph of a set of results (see Figure 8.15) shows that when the plant is supplied with a carbon dioxide concentration of only 1 unit, the rate of photosynthesis is **limited** by this low concentration of carbon dioxide to 3 oxygen bubbles per minute. When the carbon dioxide concentration is increased to 2 units, rate of photosynthesis increases to 6 bubbles per minute but no further, since carbon dioxide concentration becomes limiting again.

A further increase in carbon dioxide concentration to 3 units brings about a further increase in photosynthetic

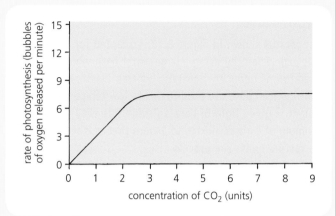

Figure 8.15 Variation in CO_2 concentration at one light intensity

rate. However, beyond this point the graph levels out and any further increase in carbon dioxide concentration does not affect photosynthetic rate. This is because some other factor (such as light intensity) is now limiting the process.

Related Activity

Analysing the effect of carbon dioxide concentration at different light intensities

In Figure 8.16, graph ABC represents a repeat of Figure 8.15 and graph ADE represents the results from a further *Elodea* bubbler experiment using the same plant in conditions of constant high light intensity. In this second experiment, an increase in carbon dioxide concentration to 4 and then to 5 units brings about a corresponding increase in photosynthetic rate in each case. This is because carbon dioxide concentration is still the **limiting factor** up to 5 units of carbon dioxide when the light intensity is high. However, beyond 5 units of carbon dioxide, the graph levels off again since some other factor (such as light intensity or temperature) has become limiting.

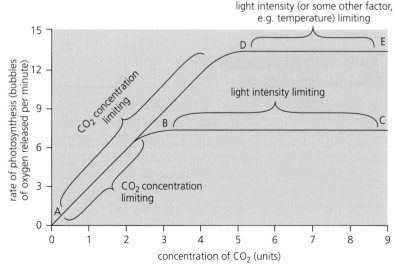

Figure 8.16 Variation in CO_2 concentration at two light intensities

Investigating the effect of varying temperature

The apparatus shown in Figure 8.13 is adapted for use in this experiment by using a large water bath whose temperature is under thermostatic control. Plastic bags containing ice cubes are used to create low temperatures. The plant is given light of constant high intensity and a rich supply of carbon dioxide to ensure that neither of these factors limits the process.

The graph in Figure 8.17 shows that the photosynthetic rate, in this case, rises to its maximum level at around 35 °C, the **optimum** temperature for this type of plant. (The optimum temperature varies from species to species and is often lower than 35 °C). At values below the optimum, temperature is acting as the limiting factor. At values above the optimum temperature, the photosynthetic rate drops rapidly. This is because photosynthesis consists of many reactions controlled by enzymes that are denatured at higher temperatures.

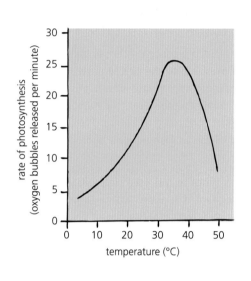

Figure 8.17 Effect of temperature on photosynthetic rate

If a crop plant in a field is affected in this way there is little that the farmer can do to solve the problem. However, if some factor is limiting the rate of photosynthesis by a crop of plants such as tomatoes in a glasshouse, steps can be taken to improve the situation.

If **temperature** is the only limiting factor then on cold, bright winter days, for example, the temperature of the glasshouse can be increased using a heating system. When **light intensity** is the only limiting factor then on dull winter days, for example, the horticulturist can employ electric lighting to increase light intensity. When **carbon dioxide concentration** is the limiting factor, extra supplies can be added to the air in a glasshouse. This creates a **carbon dioxide enriched environment**, which increases the yield of photosynthetic product. By using a combination of these techniques, the horticulturist can produce early crops and maximise photosynthetic yield.

1 a) Identify TWO environmental factors that can be demonstrated by the experiment in Figure 8.13 to affect the rate of photosynthesis. (2)
   b) As the distance between the powerful lamp and the *Elodea* plant is gradually decreased, what effect does this have on:
      i) the intensity of the light reaching the plant?
      ii) the number of bubbles of oxygen released by the plant per minute? (2)
2 a) What is meant by the term *limiting factor*? (1)
   b) When no other factors are limiting the process of photosynthesis, what effect on photosynthetic rate is brought about by raising the temperature of the plant from:
      i) 15 °C to 35 °C?
      ii) 35 °C to 55 °C? (2)
3 a) Explain why it is economically viable to supply tomato plants but not wheat plants with a carbon dioxide enriched environment. (2)
   b) What benefit would a horticulturist gain by providing a crop of plants in a glasshouse with supplementary heating and lighting during the winter? (1)

What You Should Know Chapters 7–8

ADP	ethanol	oxygen
aerobic	fermentation	photosynthesis
ATP	fixation	pyruvate
cellular	glucose	regenerate
cellulose	hydrogen	respiration
chlorophyll	intensity	split
cytoplasm	lactic	temperature
dioxide	light	thirty-eight
energy	limited	two
enzymes	mitochondria	water

1 The chemical _____ stored in glucose is released by a series of reactions controlled by _____. This biochemical process is called _____.

2 _____ is a high-energy compound that can be broken down to ADP and phosphate. This process releases the energy required for _____ processes.

3 ATP is regenerated from _____ and phosphate using energy released during respiration.

4 The first stage of the respiratory pathway is common to both _____ respiration and fermentation (anaerobic respiration). It involves the breakdown of glucose to _____.

5 In the presence of _____, aerobic respiration occurs. _____ and carbon dioxide are formed and _____ molecules of ATP are produced per molecule of glucose.

6 In the absence of oxygen, _____ occurs. In animal cells, pyruvate is reversibly converted to _____ acid. In plant cells, pyruvate is irreversibly converted to _____ and carbon dioxide. In each case only _____ molecules of ATP are produced per molecule of glucose.

7 Aerobic respiration begins in a cell's cytoplasm and is completed in its _____. Fermentation occurs in the _____ only.

8 Green plants use _____ as their source of energy to make food. This process is called _____. It is a two-stage process.

9 During the first stage, which is made up of light reactions, light energy is captured by green _____ in chloroplasts. Some energy is used to _____ ATP from ADP and phosphate. Some energy is used to _____ water into oxygen and _____.

10 During the second stage of photosynthesis, called carbon _____, hydrogen produced during the first stage is combined with carbon _____ to form glucose. This process requires energy, which is supplied by ATP.

11 Some _____ molecules produced by photosynthesis are used in cellular respiration; others are converted to products such as starch and _____.

12 Photosynthesis is affected by environmental factors such as light _____, carbon dioxide concentration and _____. Its rate is therefore _____ by whichever one of these factors is in short supply.

Applying Your Knowledge and Skills Chapters 1–8

1 The rows in Table KS1.1 give triplets of features characteristic of certain cells.

Row	Triplet of features characteristic of cell		
1	mitochondria	nucleus	plasmids
2	cytoplasm	nucleus	mitochondria
3	large central vacuole	cell wall	mitochondria
4	cell wall	chloroplasts	circular chromosomes
5	plasmid	circular chromosome	cell wall
6	ribosomes	plasmids	mitochondria

Table KS1.1

a) Which row refers correctly to both plant and animal cells? (1)
b) Which row is correct for plant cells only? (1)
c) Which row refers correctly to a bacterial cell? (1)

2 a) Figure KS1.1 shows three cells under the high power of a microscope. The diameter of the field of view is 0.03 mm. What is the average diameter of a cheek cell in micrometres? (1 millimetre = 1000 micrometres) (1)

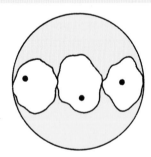

Figure KS1.1

b) A human red blood cell is 7 micrometres in diameter. Express this as a decimal fraction of a millimetre. (1)
c) If a cell is 0.008 millimetres long, what is its length in micrometres? (1)

3 Three identical cylinders of fresh turnip were immersed in the liquids shown in Figure KS1.2 for 24 hours. Each was then removed and held between forefinger and thumb as shown in Figure KS1.3.

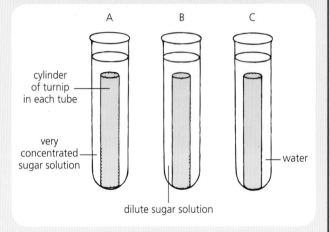

cylinder of turnip in each tube

very concentrated sugar solution

dilute sugar solution

water

Figure KS1.2

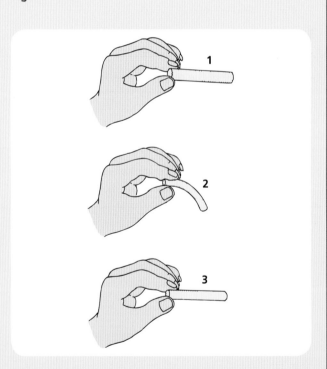

Figure KS1.3

a) Match numbers 1, 2 and 3 with letters A, B and C. (3)
b) Justify your choice in each case. (3)

4 Figure KS1.4 shows the direction of movement of two different substances through the cell membrane of an animal cell.

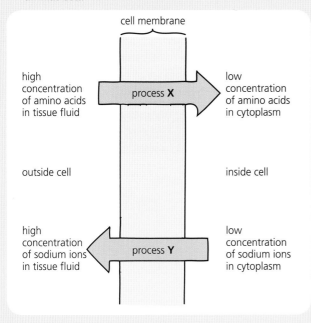

Figure KS1.4

a) i) Name processes X and Y.
   ii) Which of these processes requires energy?
   iii) Which process will be unaffected by a decrease in oxygen concentration in the animal's environment? (4)
b) i) Predict what will happen to the rate of process Y if the temperature of the cell is reduced to 4 °C for several hours.
   ii) Give a reason for your answer. (2)

5 Figure KS1.5 shows a complete cycle of the stages that occur before, during and after mitosis in a certain type of animal cell.

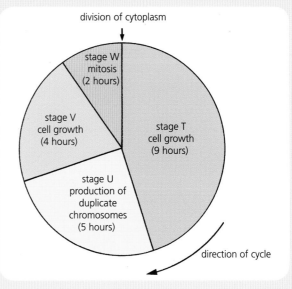

Figure KS1.5

a) Which of the bar graphs in Figure KS1.6 best represents the information in the pie chart? (1)

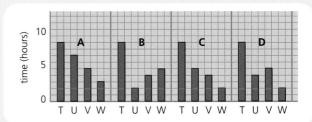

Figure KS1.6

b) How much time was spent on cell growth in one complete cycle? (1)
c) Express your answer to b) as a percentage of the total time required for one cycle. (1)

6   The graph in Figure KS1.7 shows the number of
    bacteria growing in nutrient broth kept at constant
    optimum temperature over a period of 30 hours.

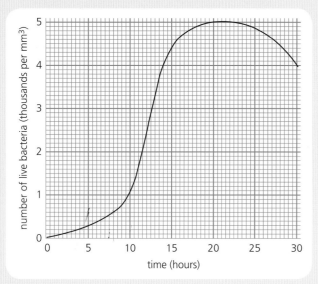

Figure KS1.7

a) i) How many bacteria were present per mm³ at
        5 hours?
    ii) From this point in time onwards, how many
        more hours passed before the bacteria had
        doubled in number? (2)
b) During which of the following periods of time was
    the growth rate greatest? (1)
    A   0–5 hours
    B   5–10 hours
    C   10–15 hours
    D   15–20 hours

c) For how many hours was the number of live
    bacteria found to be above 4000 per mm³? (1)
d) Give TWO possible reasons why the number of
    bacteria began to decrease after 23 hours. (2)

7   Table KS1.2 shows a sample of Chargaff's data follow-
    ing the analysis of DNA extracted from several species.

Species	%G	%A	%C	%T
maize	22.9	27.1	22.9	27.1
wheat	22.7	27.3	**box P**	27.3
chicken	21.6	28.4	21.6	28.4
human	20.2	**box Q**	20.2	29.8

Table KS1.2

a) Study the data and calculate the figures that
    should have been entered in boxes P and Q. (2)
b) i) State Chargaff's rules.
    ii) Do the data in the table support these rules?
    iii) Explain your answer to ii). (3)

8   Table KS1.3 gives the results from an experiment set
    up to investigate the effect of temperature on the
    action of a digestive enzyme.

Temperature (°C)	Mass of substrate broken down (mg/h)
0	0
5	1
10	4
15	8
20	14
25	22
30	28
35	31
40	32
45	29
50	18
55	0

Table KS1.3

a) Present the data as a line graph. (3)
b) i) Explain what is meant by the term *optimum
        temperature*.
    ii) State the optimum temperature for the action
        of this enzyme. (2)
c) i) By how many times was the rate of enzyme
        activity greater at 30 °C than at 20 °C?
    ii) Explain the difference in terms of rate
        of molecular movement and frequency of
        collisions between enzyme and substrate
        molecules at these two temperatures. (3)
d) Which rise in temperature of 5 °C brought about
    the biggest increase in rate of enzyme activity? (1)
e) At the temperature range 50–55 °C, the molecules
    are still gaining energy, so why does the reaction
    come to a halt at 55 °C? (1)
f) Predict the mass of substrate that would be
    broken down at 75 °C. (1)

9 The graph in Figure KS1.8 shows the effect of pH on the activity of three enzymes, X, Y and Z.

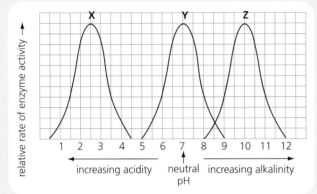

Figure KS1.8

a) State the working range of pH for each of the enzymes. (3)

b) What generalisation can be drawn about:
   i) the breadth of working range of pH of each of the enzymes?
   ii) the extent to which they all share the same actual pH working range? (2)

c) State the optimum pH for each of the enzymes. (3)

d) Suggest which of the enzymes would show optimum activity in:
   i) the human mouth
   ii) the human stomach. (2)

10 A transgenic animal is one that has had its genetic material modified deliberately by humans. This is often done by microinjecting the required gene(s) from one organism into the nuclei of the eggs of another species. Some people support this line of work and point out its potential benefits; others oppose it and claim that it is ethically wrong.

a) Find out what *ethics* means and try to describe it in your own words. (2)

b) Group the eight conversation bubbles shown in Figure KS1.9 into:
   i) those for the production of transgenic animals
   ii) those against the practice. (2)

c) i) Are you in favour of the development of transgenic animals?
   ii) Justify your answer to **i)**.

A Blood anti-clotting factors needed by haemophiliacs can be obtained from the milk of transgenic cows, sheep and goats.

B The development of transgenic animals could change the direction of evolution for the worse.

C Flocks of transgenic sheep that produce more meat and more wool than normal would benefit the economy.

D Transgenic animals such as pigs could provide a reliable source of hearts needed for transplant surgery.

E If transgenic animals escaped into the wild, they could upset the balance of nature.

F The use of transgenic animals only considers the welfare of humans and not that of the animals involved.

G Transgenic animals are unnatural and could harbour some unknown diseases in the future.

H Transgenic animals that show disease symptoms can be used as disease models to find out which new treatments work.

Figure KS1.9

11 Read the passage and answer the questions that follow it.

During normal growth, plants produce ammonia as a by-product of their metabolism. This is normally rendered harmless as follows:

$$\text{ammonia} \xrightarrow{\text{enzyme action}} \text{end products}$$
$$\text{(toxic)} \qquad\qquad\qquad \text{(non-toxic)}$$

Glufosinate is an active ingredient in several brands of herbicide. It works by disrupting the enzyme action referred to in the above equation. As ammonia builds up, it destroys the plant's chloroplasts.

Some plants have been genetically modified for resistance to glufosinate in the following way.

A gene that deactivates glufosinate was found to occur in species of *Streptomyces* bacteria. This gene was transferred to a type of soil bacterium that normally infects plant roots and injects its DNA into the plants. The genetically modified (GM) version of this bacterium was used to deliberately infect certain crop plants and introduce the gene for resistance to glufosinate into them. By this means, some of the crop plants were successfully transformed into GM plants resistant to herbicide containing glufosinate. When a crop of these resistant plants is sprayed with weedkiller, the crop survives but the weeds growing beside it die. This has led to a reduction in use of herbicide from a mass of 7 kg/ha to as little as 0.7 kg/ha in many cases. (ha = 1 hectare = 100 acres)

a) Give the meaning of the term *herbicide*. (1)
b) Explain why the destruction of chloroplasts is fatal to a plant. (1)
c) Describe the means by which a crop plant resistant to herbicide is produced. (3)
d) Calculate the percentage reduction in mass of herbicide used as a result of growing GM crops. (1)

e) 'Resistance to herbicide occurs naturally in the environment.' Justify this statement using information from the passage. (1)

12 Figure KS1.10 shows six versions of the apparatus set up during an investigation to compare the energy content of two different foods.

a) Explain fully why a valid comparison cannot be made between set-ups:
  i) A and B
  ii) A and C
  iii) A and E. (6)
b) Describe THREE changes that would need to be made to set-up C so that a valid comparison could be made between it and D. (3)
c) The experiment was carried out using set-ups B and F and the results in Table KS1.4 were obtained.

Food	Water temperature (°C)		Temperature rise (°C)	Energy content (kJ)
	at start	at finish		
peanut	25	47		
glucose	26	38		

Table KS1.4

i) Calculate the energy content of the two foodstuffs in kilojoules per gram using the formula:

energy released (kJ) = $4.2MT/1000$

where M = mass of water (g) and T = rise in temperature (°C)
(Note: 1 cm^3 of water has a mass of 1 g.)

ii) A data book was found to give the energy content per gram for peanut as 25 kJ and for glucose as 17 kJ, measured using a food calorimeter. The fact that the results in Table KS1.4 are much lower than these is accounted for by the fact that food burned in air under a beaker loses heat to the surroundings and does not burn completely to ashes. Study the diagram of the food calorimeter on page 49 and explain how use of it largely overcomes these two shortcomings. (4)

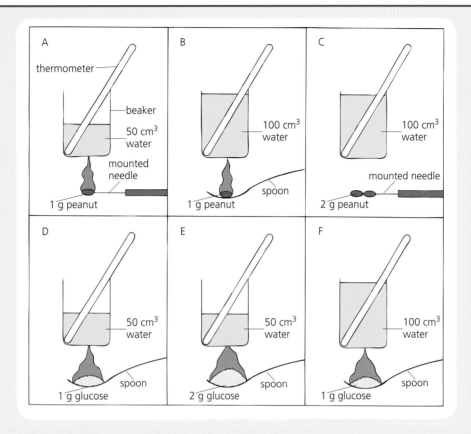

Figure KS1.10

13 The information in Table KS1.5 refers to hydrogen carbonate indicator. The experiment in Figure KS1.11 was run for 24 hours using green cells of a fast-growing alga.

Figure KS1.11

Relative carbon dioxide concentration of indicator	Colour of indicator	pH of indicator
very high	yellow	7.6
high	orange	8.0
medium	red	8.4
low	reddish-purple	8.8
very low	purple	9.2

Table KS1.5

a) What relationship exists between the pH of hydrogen carbonate indicator and its relative concentration of carbon dioxide? (1)

b) Account fully for the final colour of the indicator in each of bottles A, B and C. (6)

c) i) If the same mass of algae immobilised in smaller gel pellets was used, what effect would this have on the time required for the colour change to occur in A?

ii) Explain your answer to i). (2)

14 The graph in Figure KS1.12 shows the results from two experiments set up to investigate the rate of photosynthesis of a water plant exposed to different environmental conditions. The CO_2 concentration of the pond water was maintained at a very high level throughout the two experiments.

Figure KS1.12

a) In experiment 1, the temperature was kept constant at 20 °C.
   i) Name the environmental factor that was varied.
   ii) Name a second environmental factor that was kept constant. (2)

b) In the second experiment, the temperature was kept constant at 30 °C. Suggest how this was done. (1)

c) What factor was limiting the rate of photosynthesis at region X in the graph? (1)

d) State the light intensity at which a temperature of 20 °C first began to limit the photosynthetic rate. (1)

e) State the factor that limited the photosynthetic rate:
   i) in region Y
   ii) at point Z on the graph for experiment 2. (2)

Unit 2

Multicellular Organisms

9   Cells, tissues and organs

Levels of organisation

Cell

A **cell** is often described as the basic unit of life because it is the smallest unit that can lead an independent life. The body of a multicellular organism consists of a large number of cells. It would be inefficient for every one of these cells to carry out every function essential for the maintenance of life. Instead, a **division of labour** is achieved by the cells being organised into tissues and the tissues being united to form organs.

Tissue

A **tissue** is a group of cells specialised to perform a particular function (or functions). Figures 9.1

and 9.2 illustrate a selection of tissues from two multicellular organisms. Tables 9.1 and 9.2 describe how the structure of each of the cells is related to its function.

Organ

An **organ** is a structure composed of several different tissues coordinated to perform one or more functions. Tables 9.3 and 9.4 give some examples of organs in the human body and in a flowering plant.

System

A group of related tissues and organs (such as blood, heart, arteries, capillaries and veins) make up a **system** (such as the circulatory system).

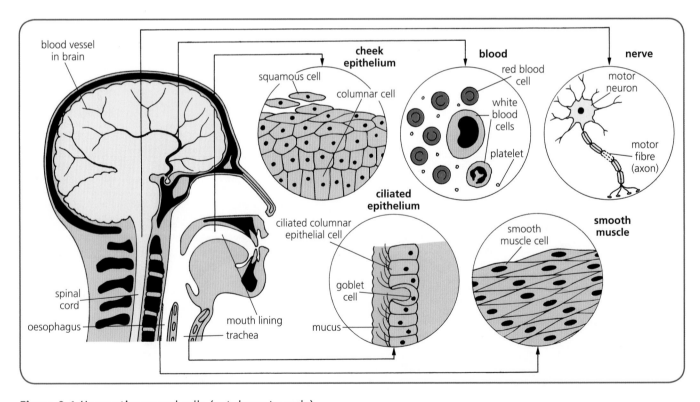

Figure 9.1 Human tissues and cells (not drawn to scale)

Figure 9.2 Plant tissues and cells (not drawn to scale)

Tissue	Cell type	Specialised structural features	Function
cheek epithelium	epithelial cell	flat, irregular shape (allowing cells to form a loose covering layer constantly replaced during wear and tear)	protection of mouth lining
blood	red blood cell	small size and biconcave shape present a relatively large surface area; rich supply of haemoglobin present	uptake and transport of oxygen to living cells
	white blood cell	able to change shape; sacs of microbe-digesting enzymes present in some types	destruction of invading microbes
nerve	motor neuron	axon (long insulated extension of cytoplasm)	transmission of nerve impulses
ciliated epithelium	goblet cell	cup shape; able to produce mucus	secretion of mucus, which traps dirt and germs
	ciliated epithelial cell	hair-like cilia that beat upwards	sweeping of dirty mucus up and away from lungs
smooth muscle	smooth muscle cell	spindle shape (allowing cells to form sheets capable of contraction)	movement of food down oesophagus by peristalsis

Table 9.1 Structure of animal cells in relation to function

Tissue	Cell type	Specialised structural features	Function
lower leaf epidermis	epidermal cell	irregular shape (allowing cells to fit like a jigsaw into a strong layer)	protection
	guard cell	sausage shape; thick inner cell wall facing stoma; chloroplasts present	control of gaseous exchange by changing shape resulting in opening and closing of stomata
mesophyll	palisade mesophyll	chloroplasts present; columnar shape (allows densely packed green layer to be presented to light)	primary region of light absorption and photosynthesis
	spongy mesophyll	'round' shape allows loose arrangement in contact with moist air spaces for absorption of carbon dioxide	secondary region of photosynthesis
phloem	sieve tube	sieve plates and continuous stream of cytoplasmic strands (but no nucleus)	transport of soluble carbohydrates up and down the plant
	companion cell	large nucleus in relation to cell size	control of sieve tube functions
xylem	vessel	hollow tube; wall strengthened by lignin; lignin deposited as rings or spirals allowing expansion and contraction	support and water transport up the plant
root epidermis	epidermal cell	box-like shape allowing cells to fit together like a brick wall	protection
	root hair cell	long extension of an epidermal cell presenting a large surface area in contact with soil solution	absorption of water and mineral salts

Table 9.2 Structure of plant cells in relation to function

Organ	Function(s)
stomach	churning and partial digestion of food
heart	pumping of blood
kidney	maintenance of water balance and removal of soluble wastes
lung	exchange of respiratory gases
skin	protection, temperature regulation and sensitivity

Table 9.3 Organs in the human body

Organ	Function(s)
root	anchorage and absorption of water
stem	support and transport of water and soluble food
leaf	photosynthesis and gaseous exchange
flower	production of seeds

Table 9.4 Organs in a flowering plant

Related Information

Organism as an integrated whole

For a complex multicellular organism to lead an independent life, all of its cells, tissues, organs and systems must operate in close coordination with each playing its particular role harmoniously as part of an **integrated whole**.

In the rat shown in Figure 9.3, for example, the chest cavity contains organs such as the lungs and trachea (parts of the **respiratory** system) and the heart and blood vessels (parts of the **circulatory** system). The chest cavity is protected by ribs made of bony tissue and moved during breathing by intercostal muscles.

The abdominal cavity contains the stomach and intestines (organs belonging to the **digestive** system), the kidneys and bladder (**excretory** system) and, in females, the ovaries, oviducts and uterus (**reproductive** system). In the male, the testes are found outside the cavity in the scrotal sac. The animal's whole body is moved by skeletal muscles supported by the bony skeleton and coordinated by the **nervous** system.

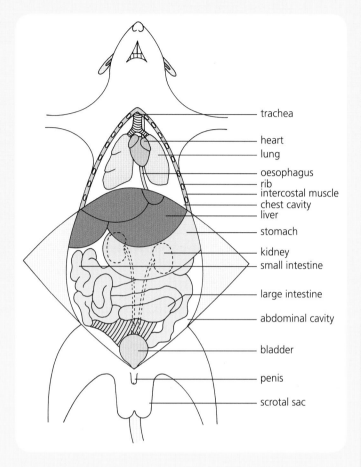

Figure 9.3 Organism as an integrated whole

Testing Your Knowledge

1 Describe a structural feature possessed by some white blood cells that enables them to destroy disease-causing bacteria. (1)

2 a) i) State the function of cheek epithelial cells.
  ii) Explain how these cells are suited to perform this function. (2)
 b) What role is played by the axon of a motor neuron? (1)

3 a) Make a simple diagram of a small sample of the tissue that covers the inner surface of the human trachea as it would be seen in longitudinal section under the microscope. (2)

 b) Name both types of cell that you have drawn and describe how each is ideally suited to the function that it performs. (4)

4 a) i) State TWO functions of xylem tissue.
  ii) Choose one of these functions and describe how a xylem vessel is structurally suited to perform it. (3)
 b) Identify TWO types of leaf cell capable of photosynthesis. (2)
 c) In what way are a leaf's epidermal cells well suited to their role of protection? (1)

5 Define the terms *tissue* and *organ*. (2)

10 Stem cells and meristems

Stem cells

Stem cells (see Figure 10.1) are unspecialised animal cells involved in growth and repair. They are able to:

- reproduce themselves indefinitely by repeated mitosis and cell division while remaining unspecialised
- develop into various types of specialised cell when required, for example, to replace cells that have come to the end of their life or have been damaged or lost.

Two types of stem cell

An early human embryo (see Figure 10.2) contains **embryonic stem cells**. These are capable of developing into all cell types found in the human body. They even have the potential to regenerate an entire organ from a few cells.

Figure 10.1 Stem cells

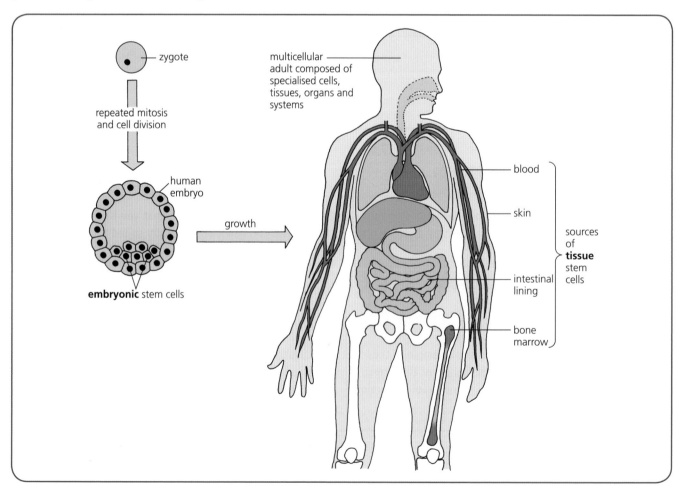

Figure 10.2 Two types of stem cell

Related Topic

Potential uses of stem cells

Human stem cells can be grown in cultures provided that they are given optimum conditions and a supply of certain key growth factors. In recent times, stem cells have been successfully put to use in a variety of ways, as in the following examples.

Bone marrow transplantation

Some forms of cancer of the blood such as leukaemia result from the uncontrolled increase in number of white blood cells. One form of treatment involves destruction of the patient's cancerous bone marrow cells and their replacement with a transplant of normal, blood-forming stem cells from a suitable donor (see Figure 10.3).

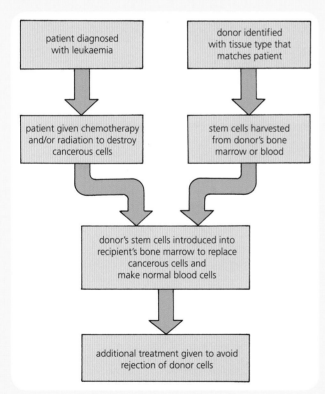

Figure 10.3 Bone marrow transplantation

Skin graft

In a traditional skin graft, a relatively large section of skin is removed from a region of the person's body and grafted to the site of injury. This means that the person has two parts of their body that need careful treatment and time to heal.

A skin graft using stem cells only requires a **small sample** of skin to be taken to obtain stem cells. Therefore the site needs much less healing time and suffers minimum scarring. The sample is normally taken from an area close to, and similar in structure to, the site of injury. Enzymes are used to isolate and loosen the stem cells, which are then cultured. Once a **suspension of new stem cells** has developed, they are sprayed over the damaged area (see Figure 10.4) to bring about regeneration of the missing skin.

Figure 10.4 Spray-on stem cell skin graft

Cornea repair

In recent years scientists have shown that **corneal damage** by chemical burning can be successfully treated using stem cell tissue. This can be grown from the patient's own stem cells located at the edge of the cornea. In many cases the person's eyesight can be restored following grafting of the stem cell tissue from the healthy eye to the surface of the damaged eye (see Figure 10.5). Since the skin graft and cornea repair techniques use the affected individual's own cells, there is no risk of the transplanted tissue being rejected.

Figure 10.5 Repair of cornea using stem cells

Future therapeutic potential of stem cells

Embryonic stem cells are able to differentiate into any type of cell in the body. Therefore they are believed to have the potential to provide treatments in the future for a wide range of disorders and degenerative conditions such as **diabetes, Parkinson's disease** and **Alzheimer's disease** that traditional medicine has been unable to cure. Already scientists have managed to generate nerve cells from embryonic stem cells in culture. It is hoped that this work will eventually be translated into effective therapies to treat disorders such as multiple sclerosis. However, the use of embryonic stem cells raises questions of **ethics** (see below).

Related Topic

Ethical issues associated with use of stem cells

Ethics refers to the moral values and rules that ought to govern human conduct. The use of stem cells raises several **ethical issues**.

Embryonic stem cells

At present, the creation of a continuous culture of embryonic stem cells (a **stem line**) for research purposes makes use of cells taken from a human embryo of no more than 14 days' growth and development. Some people consider this practice to be unethical because it results in the destruction of the embryo. It is interesting to note that normally the embryos used to obtain stem cells were generated for *in vitro* (IV) fertilisation but were additional to requirements. They would have been destroyed eventually as a matter of course.

People on one side of the debate believe that an embryo is a human *person* and that fatally extracting stem cells from it is equivalent to committing murder. People on the other side of the debate believe that the ball of cells that makes up a 14-day-old embryo is not yet a person and that removing stem cells from it for research purposes is morally acceptable.

Nuclear transfer technique

One form of this technique (see Figure 10.6) involves removing the nucleus from an egg cell (e.g. from a cow) and replacing it with a nucleus from a donor cell (e.g.

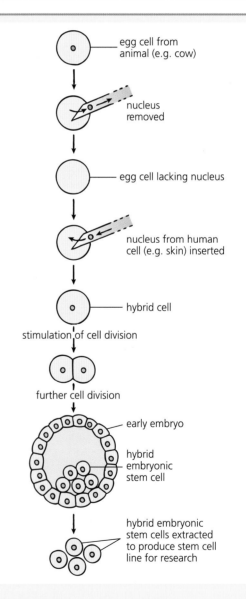

egg cell from animal (e.g. cow)

nucleus removed

egg cell lacking nucleus

nucleus from human cell (e.g. skin) inserted

hybrid cell

stimulation of cell division

further cell division

early embryo

hybrid embryonic stem cell

hybrid embryonic stem cells extracted to produce stem cell line for research

Figure 10.6 Nuclear transfer technique

a skin cell from a human). Once the hybrid cell formed begins to divide, stem cells are extracted from it after 5 days and these are used for research. However, these cells are not 100% human and are only allowed to be used for research.

Some people feel that it is unethical to mix materials from human cells with those of another species even if guarantees are given that use of the hybrid cells will be carefully restricted. Other people support the production of these hybrid cells because it helps to relieve the shortage of human embryonic cells available for research purposes.

Tissue stem cells

The use of tissue stem cells is not normally regarded as unethical because the cells have been obtained, with permission, from the tissue of an adult and their use does not cause the destruction of a human embryo.

A fully formed human possesses **tissue stem cells** at various locations such as bone marrow, blood and skin. These cells have a more limited potential than embryonic stem cells. Under natural conditions, tissue stem cells are only able to replenish the supply of one or more types of specialised cell closely related to the tissue in which they are found. Tissue stem cells in red bone marrow, for example, can only give rise to new blood cells while those in skin can only produce more skin cells.

Meristems

Whereas most multicellular animals stop growing on reaching maturity, multicellular plants continue to grow throughout their life. Production of new cells takes place only at areas called **meristems**. Meristems are found at the tips of shoots (see Figure 10.7) and at the tips of roots (see Figure 10.8). They are composed of non-specialised cells that undergo continuous cell division. Some of the cells formed remain meristematic and go on to divide again, producing more cells; others become elongated and then develop into specialised cells and tissues. Meristematic cells have the potential to become any type of plant cell.

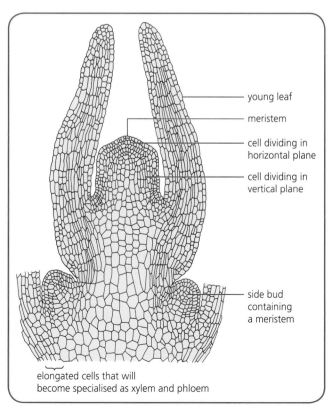

young leaf

meristem

cell dividing in horizontal plane

cell dividing in vertical plane

side bud containing a meristem

elongated cells that will become specialised as xylem and phloem

Figure 10.7 Meristem at a shoot tip

meristem

root cap

Figure 10.8 Meristem at a root tip

Related Activity

Examining a stained root tip meristem

The root tip to be examined is normally taken from a plant such as an onion or a germinating broad bean seed. About 5 mm of root tip is **fixed** in a chemical (such as warm hydrochloric acid) to preserve the internal structure of the cells. The root tip is then placed on a slide and **stained** by adding a few drops of an appropriate chemical (such as purple acetic orcein, which stains chromosomes). The specimen is covered using a cover slip and **squashed** by tapping the cover slip gently with the end of a pencil.

When viewed under the microscope at low-power magnification, the meristem is found to be located behind the protective root cap (see Figures 10.8 and 10.9). It consists of many small, densely packed cells. The relative amount of space occupied by the nucleus in each of these cells is much greater than that of the cells further back in the root tip. The older cells are no longer dividing and have undergone elongation.

When the root tip's meristem is viewed at high-power magnification, various stages of **mitosis** (see page 22) can be seen occurring in some of the stained meristematic cells.

Spread of ink marks

Figure 10.9 shows the outcome of marking the root of a germinating broad bean seed with ink at 1 mm intervals and then allowing it to grow for a few days. The space between the root tip and mark 1 remains unaltered because this region consists of the root cap and the meristem (the site of mitosis and cell division). Marks 2, 3 and 4, however, do become spread out because the cells in this region are undergoing elongation. Above mark 4 there is no change in the spacing of the ink marks because here the cells are becoming specialised to suit their future function. For example, some are becoming long, hollow xylem vessels for the transport of water.

Figure 10.9 Cell division and growth at a root tip

Testing Your Knowledge

1 a) i) What is a *stem cell*?
    ii) Identify TWO places in the human body where stem cells are found. (3)
   b) Name TWO features of a stem cell that are not exhibited by a ciliated epithelial cell. (2)

2 a) What is a *meristem*? (1)
   b) Identify TWO locations in a plant where a meristem would be found. (2)
   c) Give TWO differences between a meristematic cell and a xylem vessel. (2)

Control and communication

Nervous control

The body of a multicellular animal such as a human is composed of many different types of cells, tissues and organs. The majority of these structures are specialised to perform particular functions but they do not operate independently of one another. The body can survive and function effectively only if all of its parts work in close cooperation with one another. The internal communication needed to bring this about is provided by the **nervous system**.

In humans, the nervous system (see Figure 11.1) is composed of three parts – the **brain**, the **spinal cord** and the **nerves**. The brain and spinal cord make up the **central nervous system (CNS)**. The CNS is connected to all parts of the body by the nerves, which lead to and from all organs and systems. This arrangement ensures that all parts work together as a **coordinated whole** with the brain exerting overall control.

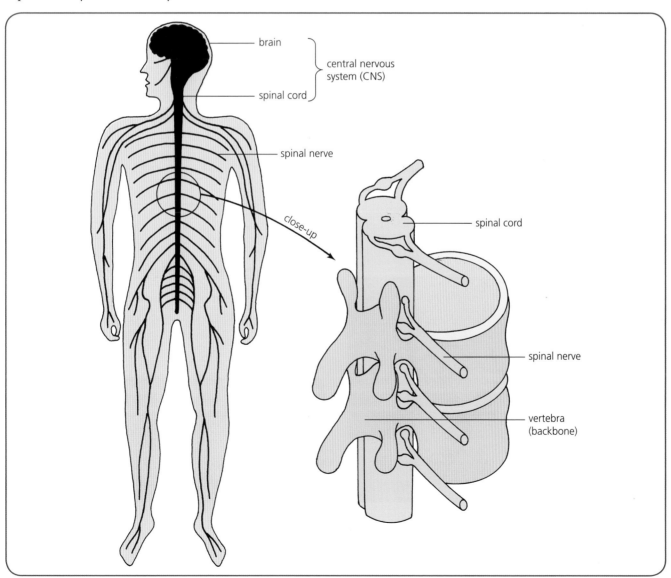

Figure 11.1 Human nervous system

Brain

The brain consists of several different regions, as shown in Figures 11.2 and 11.3. The **medulla** controls the rate of breathing and heart beat. The **cerebellum** controls balance and muscular coordination. The largest part of the brain is called the **cerebrum**. It is responsible for mental processes such as memory, reasoning, imagination, conscious thought and intelligence.

Flow of information

Figure 11.4 shows how one set of nerves (sensory) carries information from the body's **receptors** to the CNS and another set of nerves (motor) carries nerve impulses from the CNS to the body's **effectors**. Nerve messages arriving from receptors in the sense organs keep the CNS (particularly the brain) informed about all aspects of the body and its surroundings. The CNS sorts out all of this information and stores some of it. When the body is required to make a response, the CNS sends out nerve messages to the appropriate effector, such as a muscle or a gland.

Figure 11.2 Human brain

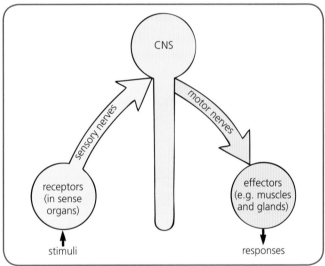

Figure 11.4 Flow of information

Neurons and reflex arc

The nervous system is made up of nerve cells called **neurons**. A neuron consists of a cell body attached to nerve fibres (see Figures 11.5 and 11.6). An electrical

Figure 11.3 Human brain in longitudinal section

Figure 11.5 Neuron

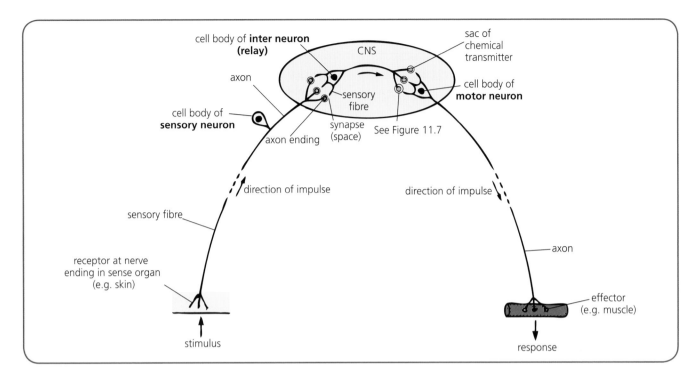

Figure 11.6 Reflex arc

impulse is carried towards the cell body of a neuron by a **sensory fibre** and away from it by an **axon fibre**. The simple arrangement of three different types of neuron shown in Figure 11.6 is called a **reflex arc**.

A tiny space called a **synapse** occurs between the axon ending of one neuron and the sensory fibre of the next. When a nerve impulse arrives, the ending of the axon branch (see Figure 11.7) releases a chemical. This diffuses across the space between the two neurons and triggers off an impulse in the sensory fibre of the next neuron in the arc.

Information collected by receptors is passed by sensory neurons to the CNS to be processed. Nerve impulses are then transmitted via inter (relay) neurons to motor neurons, which enable a response to be made by an effector. This may take the form of a slow response by a gland or a more rapid response by a muscle.

Figure 11.7 Synapse

Pain receptors

The human body has many receptors that detect information about the body's internal and external environments. This information is normally sent to the brain as electrical impulses via the nervous system, which functions as a vast collection of interrelated pathways of communication. Receptors are present in all sense organs. The skin, for example, contains receptors for touch, heat, cold, pressure and pain (see Figure 11.8).

When the brain receives nerve impulses from **pain receptors**, the affected person perceives the **sensation of pain**. Pain is of survival value because it makes the person aware of the danger. It gives them an opportunity to adopt some corrective method of behaviour such as moving a hand away from a source of intense heat before it becomes seriously injured.

People who are born without the ability to perceive pain are more vulnerable to injury because they lack this essential warning system. Such a person could even die from a severe condition such as a ruptured appendix because they would be unaware that it had taken place.

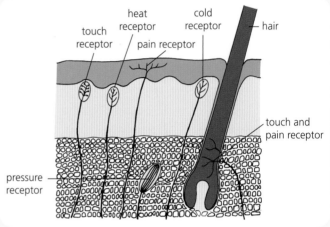

Figure 11.8 Receptors in human skin

---

1 a) i) Name THREE parts of the human nervous system.
       ii) Which of these make up the CNS (central nervous system)? (2)
    b) Briefly describe the role played by the nervous system. (1)
2 a) Which region of the brain is concerned with learning and memory? (1)
    b) Name TWO other parts of the human brain and for each state its function. (4)
3   The following structures are involved in the transmission of a nerve impulse. Arrange them in the correct order: *motor nerve, sense organ, muscle, CNS, sensory nerve*. (1)

Reflex action

The transmission of a nerve impulse through a reflex arc results in a **reflex action**. A reflex action is a rapid, automatic, involuntary response to a stimulus. Figure 11.9 shows an example of a reflex action called limb withdrawal. When the back of the hand accidentally comes in contact with intense heat, this **stimulus** is picked up by pain receptors in the skin (1) and an electrical impulse is immediately sent up the fibre of the sensory neuron (2). In the grey matter of the spinal cord, the impulse crosses the first synapse (3) and passes through the inter (relay) neuron (4). Once across the second synapse, the nerve impulse is picked up by the motor neuron (5) and quickly conducted to the axon endings (6), which are in close contact with the flexor muscle of the arm. Here a chemical is released that brings about muscular contraction (the **response**) making the arm bend and move out of harm's way.

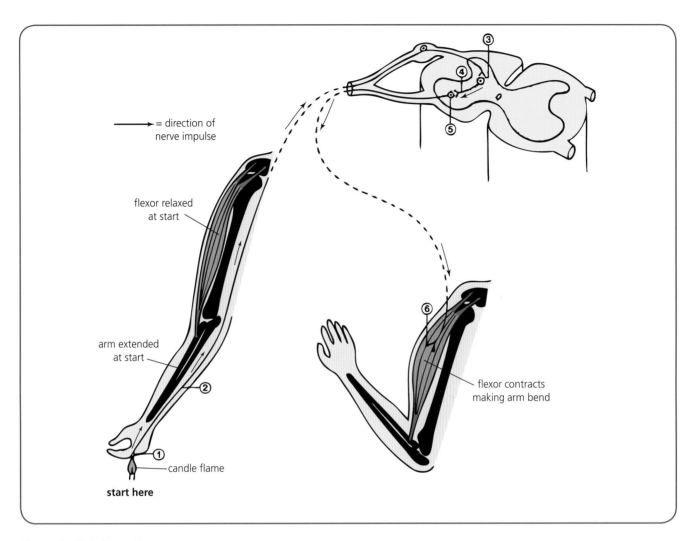

Figure 11.9 Reflex action

Knee jerk reflex action

Some reflex arcs, such as the one responsible for the **knee jerk reflex** shown in Figure 11.10, lack the inter neuron and have only one synapse between the sensory neuron and the motor neuron. This simple arrangement reduces the time delay between the stimulus and the response to a minimum.

The knee jerk reflex occurs in response to tapping the tendon that is located beneath the knee cap and connected to the extensor muscle in the thigh. Following tapping, stretch receptors in the muscle are stimulated. Sensory receptors transmit this information as nerve impulses to the CNS. Motor neurons convey impulses to the extensor muscle, which contracts, jerking the lower leg forward.

On some occasions when a person stumbles and is about to lose their balance and fall, the jarring movement of the stumble stimulates the stretch receptors in the thigh muscle. This triggers the knee jerk reflex action, making the person kick out their lower leg, which prevents them from falling and suffering an injury.

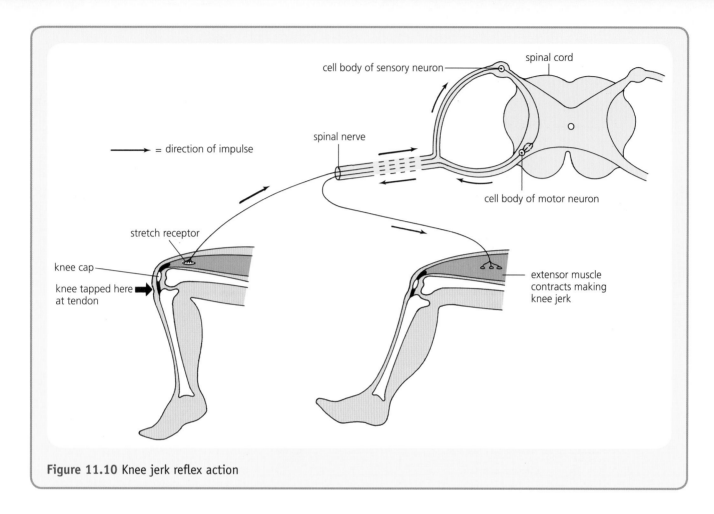

cell body of sensory neuron

spinal cord

= direction of impulse

spinal nerve

cell body of motor neuron

stretch receptor

knee cap

knee tapped here
at tendon

extensor muscle
contracts making
knee jerk

Figure 11.10 Knee jerk reflex action

Protective role

Reflex actions **protect** the body from damage. Since
they do not need conscious thought by the brain,
many reflex actions may still be performed for a
short period by an animal whose brain has been
destroyed.

Hormonal control

In addition to the control exerted by the nervous
system, further coordination of the workings of
the human body is brought about by **hormones**.
Hormones are chemical messengers secreted directly
into the bloodstream by **endocrine** (ductless) glands
(see Figure 11.11).

Hormones stimulate specific **target tissues**. The cells
on the surface of a target tissue in contact with the
bloodstream bear **specific receptors** for a particular
hormone. Therefore, when a hormone reaches its target
tissue, it evokes a specific response whilst other tissues
lacking the receptor molecules remain unaffected.

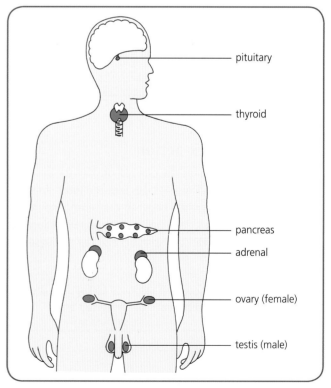

pituitary

thyroid

pancreas

adrenal

ovary (female)

testis (male)

Figure 11.11 Endocrine glands

Research Topic — Role of hormones in the human body

Table 11.1 gives a summary of some hormones that play a variety of important roles in the human body.

Endocrine gland	Hormone	Effect	Notes
pituitary	growth hormone	stimulates growth during development	over-secretion results in 'gigantism'; under-secretion leads to 'dwarfism'
pituitary	thyroid-stimulating hormone	controls thyroid gland and stimulates thyroxin production	one of many pituitary hormones that regulate the other endocrine glands
thyroid	thyroxin	a) controls rate of growth and development b) controls rate of metabolism	over-secretion in adults causes over-activity and thinness; under-secretion in adults leads to sluggishness and becoming overweight
pituitary	follicle-stimulating hormone (FSH)	a) stimulates development of follicle in ovary b) stimulates ovary tissue to produce oestrogen	Pieced together, these events make up the menstrual cycle, which involves the regular alternation of ovulation (egg release) and menstruation (break-down and release of uterus lining and unfertilised egg). If fertilisation occurs, the corpus luteum persists and continues to secrete progesterone, which sustains the uterus wall during early pregnancy.
ovary	oestrogen	a) repairs uterus lining following menstruation b) stimulates pituitary to make luteinising hormone	
pituitary	luteinising hormone (LH)	a) brings about ovulation b) causes follicle to become corpus luteum, which secretes progesterone	
ovary (corpus luteum)	progesterone	promotes thickening of uterus lining	
testis	testosterone	controls growth and development of male sex organs and secondary sexual characteristics	testis is in turn controlled by a pituitary hormone (LH)
islets of Langerhans in pancreas	insulin	controls conversion of excess glucose in bloodstream to glycogen (stored in liver)	deficiency leads to diabetes (glucose not stored as glycogen but instead lost in urine)
adrenal	adrenaline (epinephrine)	a) increases rate of heart beat and breathing b) diverts blood to skeletal muscles c) causes conversion of stored glycogen to glucose	prepares the body for energy-demanding 'fight-or-flight' during an emergency
pituitary	anti-diuretic hormone (ADH)	brings about osmoregulation by controlling the quantity of water reabsorbed into blood from kidney tubules	see Figure 11.12

Table 11.1 Hormones and their effects

START HERE

osmoreceptors in brain stimulated

excess salt in food or sweating causes decrease in blood's water concentration

nerve impulses

increased secretion of ADH into blood

pituitary gland

blood's water concentration returns to normal

blood vessel

extra water in blood

high concentration of ADH in blood makes kidney tubule more permeable

much water reabsorbed into blood stream from kidney tubule

kidney tubule

Figure 11.12 Osmoregulation in human body

Blood glucose regulation

The body employs the control mechanism described below to guarantee that a regular supply of blood glucose is available for use by cells, regardless of when and how often food is eaten.

Liver as a storehouse

About 100 grams of glucose are stored as **glycogen** in the liver. Glucose can be added to or removed from this store depending on shifts of supply and demand.

Insulin and glucagon

A rise in blood glucose level to above its optimum concentration after a meal is detected by cells in the **pancreas**, which produce **insulin**. This hormone is

transported in the bloodstream to the **liver** where it activates an enzyme that catalyses the reaction:

$$\text{glucose} \longrightarrow \text{glycogen}$$

This brings the blood glucose concentration back down to around its normal level. If the blood glucose level drops below its optimum concentration between meals or during the night, different cells in the pancreas detect this change and release **glucagon**. This second hormone is transported to the liver and activates a different enzyme, which catalyses the reaction:

$$\text{glycogen} \longrightarrow \text{glucose}$$

The blood glucose concentration therefore rises to around the optimum concentration. Figure 11.13 gives a summary of these events.

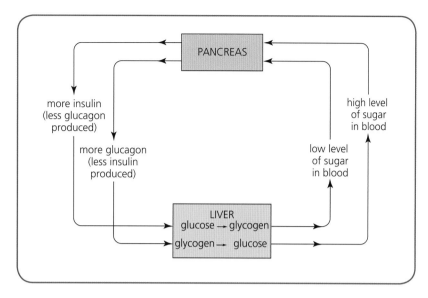

Figure 11.13 Regulation of blood glucose

Osmotic imbalance

Control of blood glucose level is important in relation to **osmosis** in cells. The presence of too much or too little glucose in cells could lead to **osmotic imbalances**. For example, it could result in the cells gaining too much water from, or losing too much water to, the surrounding intercellular fluid by osmosis.

Diabetes

People who suffer from **diabetes** are unable to control their blood glucose level. Diabetes is the result of a communication pathway that has broken down for one of the following reasons:

- the person's pancreatic cells are unable to make insulin (for example in people with type 1 diabetes)
- the target tissues in the person's body do not respond to insulin arriving in the bloodstream (for example in people with type 2 diabetes).

Consequences

If left untreated, diabetes results in a rapid **increase in blood glucose** concentration occurring after each meal. As the kidneys filter the blood, the filtrate formed is so rich in glucose that much of the glucose is excreted in **urine**. This increase in glucose concentration in urine is accompanied by the loss of additional water. The untreated diabetic produces excessive volumes of urine and is persistently thirsty. Over the long-term, people with **untreated** diabetes run a high risk of developing a variety of health problems including kidney disease and a form of eye condition that can result in blindness.

Treatment

Treatment for those people who fail to produce insulin takes the form of regular injections of insulin and a careful diet. Treatment for those people whose target tissues fail to respond to insulin takes the form of exercise, weight loss, diet control and additional insulin in some cases.

Causes

Type 1 diabetes is thought to be caused by a combination of some or all of the following:

- genetics
- environmental factors
- autoimmune factors.

Type 2 diabetes is thought to be caused by a combination of some or all of the following:

- unhealthy diet leading to obesity
- physical inactivity
- genetics.

To a certain extent, type 2 diabetes is a 'self-inflicted disorder'. Many cases could be prevented by people adopting a healthy lifestyle early in life and avoiding obesity throughout life.

Related Activity

Investigating trends in diabetic statistics

The number of people in Scotland with diabetes is increasing year on year, as shown in Figure 11.14.

The results of a recent Scottish diabetes survey are shown in Table 11.2. It shows that:

- many more cases of type 1 than type 2 diabetes are found amongst children, teenagers and young adults
- many more cases of type 2 than type 1 diabetes are found to occur amongst middle-aged and older people
- overall, people with type 2 diabetes greatly outnumber those with type 1 diabetes.

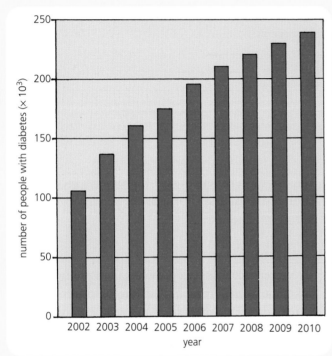

Figure 11.14 Incidence of diabetes

Age (years)	Number of people registered with diabetes	
	type 1	type 2
0–9	582	6
10–19	3084	70
20–29	4270	765
30–39	4700	4175
40–49	5858	17 740
50–59	4521	39 588
60–69	2788	59 297
70–79	1609	57 619
80 and over	493	29 009
totals	27 905	208 269

Table 11.2 Types of diabetes and age groups

Testing Your Knowledge 2

1. Rewrite the following sentences selecting only the correct answer from each underlined choice. (14)
   a) Environmental stimuli are detected by <u>receptors</u>/<u>effectors</u>.
   b) Responses to nerve impulses are brought about by <u>receptors</u>/<u>effectors</u>.
   c) The first nerve cell in a reflex arc is called a <u>motor</u>/<u>sensory</u> neuron.
   d) The final nerve cell in a reflex arc is called a <u>motor</u>/<u>sensory</u> neuron.
   e) An electrical impulse is transmitted towards the cell body of a neuron by <u>an axon</u>/<u>a sensory fibre</u>.
   f) An electrical impulse is carried away from the cell body of a neuron by <u>an axon</u>/<u>a sensory fibre</u>.
   g) The gap between two neurons is called <u>a synapse</u>/<u>an inter neuron</u>.
   h) A response made by a skeletal muscle is normally <u>faster</u>/<u>slower</u> than that made by a gland.
   i) A rapid, automatic, involuntary response to a stimulus is called a reflex <u>arc</u>/<u>action</u>.
   j) Chemical messengers secreted directly into the bloodstream are called <u>enzymes</u>/<u>hormones</u>.
   k) Cells on a target tissue bear specific <u>receptors</u>/<u>effectors</u> for a particular hormone.
   l) Insulin and glucagon are made in the <u>liver</u>/<u>pancreas</u>.
   m) The conversion of glucose to glycogen in the liver is promoted by <u>glucagon</u>/<u>insulin</u>.
   n) The conversion of glycogen to glucose in the liver is promoted by <u>glucagon</u>/<u>insulin</u>.

What You Should Know Chapters 9–11

action	electrical	organs
animal	endocrine	pancreatic
arc	glucagon	plant
brain	glucose	receptor
cerebellum	glycogen	sensory
cerebrum	hormones	slower
chemicals	insulin	specialised
CNS	medulla	stem
coordinated	meristematic	synapses
cord	motor	target
diabetes	nervous	tissues
division	neurons	unspecialised

1 In a multicellular organism, groups of _____ cells are organised as _____, which are grouped together to form _____.

2 Stem cells are _____ cells involved in the growth and repair of a multicellular _____. Division of _____ cells produces cells that have the potential to become different types of specialised cell.

3 Meristems are regions where cell _____ and growth take place in a multicellular plant. _____ cells are non-specialised and are capable of becoming any type of specialised _____ cell.

4 To survive, a multicellular animal needs the activities of all of its working parts to be _____. The _____ system provides the means by which the necessary internal communication is achieved.

5 In humans, the central nervous system (CNS) consists of the spinal _____ and the _____.

6 The brain is made up of the _____, which controls mental processes, the _____, which controls muscular coordination and the _____, which controls rate of breathing and heart beat.

7 The nervous system is composed of nerve cells called _____. A reflex _____ is an arrangement of a sensory neuron, an inter (relay) neuron and a _____ neuron along which an _____ impulse passes from a _____ to an effector. A reflex _____ is a rapid, automatic response to a stimulus.

8 _____ are gaps between neurons where _____ are released allowing the transfer of an impulse from neuron to neuron.

9 _____ neurons pass information to the _____ where it is processed. Motor neurons transmit impulses to effectors enabling a rapid response to be made by a muscle or a _____ response to be made by a gland.

10 Chemical messengers released directly into the bloodstream by _____ glands are called _____. A hormone recognises its _____ tissue by the presence of specific receptors present on its cells.

11 The concentration of glucose in the bloodstream is regulated by two _____ hormones. Insulin promotes the conversion of glucose to _____ in the liver; _____ promotes the conversion of glycogen to _____ as required.

12 _____ is a disorder caused by the person's lack of ability to make _____ or the failure of their body cells to respond to it.

12 Reproduction

In multicellular animals and plants, normal body cells are **diploid** and sex cells (gametes) are **haploid** (see page 20).

Sexual reproduction

Reproduction is the process by which the members of a species produce offspring. **Sexual** reproduction involves the fusion of two **gametes** during **fertilisation**.

Gamete production in mammals

The human reproductive organs are shown in Figures 12.1, 12.2, 12.3 and 12.4. The **testes** are the site of **sperm** production; the **ovaries** are the site of **egg** production. Such sites of gamete production are called gonads.

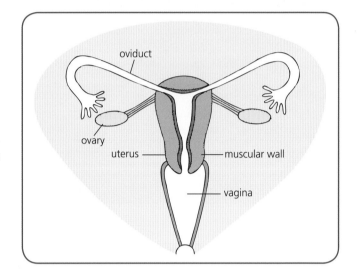

Figure 12.2 Human female reproductive organs

A male mammal produces a very large number of sperm and a female mammal produces a much smaller number of eggs. A sperm (see Figure 12.5) consists of

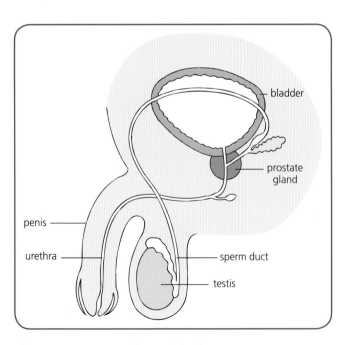

Figure 12.1 Human male reproductive organs

Figure 12.3 Sperm production in a human testis

Figure 12.4 Model showing human ovaries and oviducts

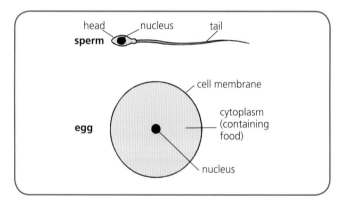

Figure 12.5 Sex cells (not drawn to scale)

a **head** region (mainly a nucleus containing genetic material) and a **tail** that enables it to move. An egg is larger than a sperm because in addition to its nucleus, it contains a **store of food** in its cytoplasm.

Events leading to fertilisation

The release of an egg from a mammalian ovary is called **ovulation**. Eggs are released at regular intervals into the oviducts (see Figure 12.6). The inner lining of an oviduct bears hair-like cilia that beat and gently move the egg along towards the uterus. The journey takes about three days in humans. Following copulation (sexual intercourse in humans) and ejaculation (release of sperm by the male), sperm swim up the uterus and into the oviducts. It is here in an **oviduct** that **fertilisation** normally occurs.

Fertilisation

This process involves a haploid sperm reaching a haploid egg and then the sperm's nucleus entering the egg and fusing with the egg's nucleus to form a single diploid cell called a **zygote**. The zygote formed contains genetic information from both parents and it is the first cell of a new individual. (Note: Although many sperm may meet an egg, only one sperm fertilises the egg.)

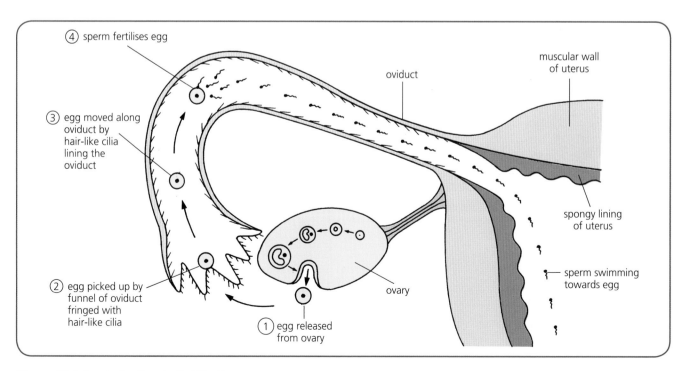

Figure 12.6 Events leading to fertilisation

Gamete formation in flowering plants

Flowers are the structures responsible for sexual reproduction in flowering plants. Although flowers often appear to be very different from one another (see Figures 12.7 and 12.8), they are built to the same basic plan. Usually the male and female reproductive organs are both present in the same flower (see Figure 12.9).

Figure 12.7 Insect-pollinated flower

Figure 12.8 Wind-pollinated flower

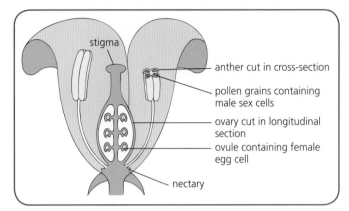

Figure 12.9 Half section of a flower

Pollen grains contain the plant's male sex cells and are produced in the **anthers**, the male sex organs of the flower. **Ovules** contain the plant's female sex cells (egg cells) and are produced in the **ovary**, the female sex organ of the flower.

Pollination

Pollination is the transfer of pollen grains from an anther to a stigma. It should not be confused with fertilisation, the process by which the nucleus of a male sex cell from a pollen grain fuses with the nucleus of an egg cell to form a zygote.

Growth of a pollen tube

Once a pollen grain has landed on a stigma, it responds to the presence of sugar on the stigma and uses the sugar as an energy source to form a **pollen tube** (see Figures 12.10 and 12.11). As the pollen tube grows down through the female tissues, the pollen grain's nucleus in

Figure 12.10 Pollen tubes

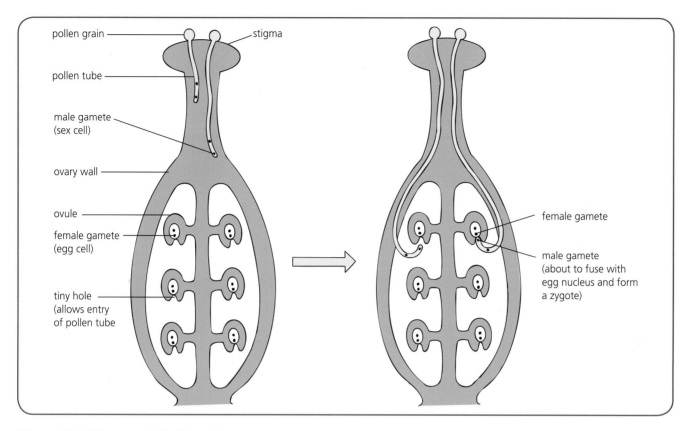

Figure 12.11 The growth of pollen tubes

the region behind the tip of the tube divides into two male gametes. When the tip of the tube reaches an ovule, it enters through a tiny hole and comes into contact with a tiny sac containing the female gamete.

Fertilisation

The tip of the pollen tube bursts and the two haploid male gametes enter the sac. One fuses with the

haploid egg cell to form a diploid **zygote**. (The other fuses with a second nucleus in the sac to form a type of cell that gives rise to the food store present in a seed.) Following mitosis and cell division, the zygote becomes an embryo, which grows into a plant when the seed containing it germinates.

Testing Your Knowledge

1 With reference to the relative numbers produced and their structure, draw up a table to show THREE differences between a mammalian sperm and an egg. (3)

2 a) Where are:
  i) sperm
  ii) eggs produced in the body of a mammal? (2)
 b) Identify the site of fertilisation in a mammal's body. (1)

3 Describe the process of fertilisation in a mammal using all of the following words in your answer: *diploid, egg, gamete, haploid, nucleus, sperm,*

zygote. (You may wish to use some words more than once.) (4)

4 a) Which structures in a flower contain pollen grains? (1)
 b) Of which sex are the gametes present in the pollen grains? (1)
 c) Which structure in a flower contains egg cells in ovules? (1)
 d) By what means does a male sex cell reach and fertilise a female sex cell in a flower? (1)

13 Variation and inheritance

Although the members of the same species are very similar to one another, they are not identical. This is because **variation** exists amongst the members of a species.

Types of variation

Discrete variation

A characteristic shows **discrete variation** if it can be used to divide up the members of a species into two or more distinct groups. For example, ivy plants can be divided into two separate groups according to leaf type (green or variegated, as shown in Figure 13.1). Similarly, humans can be split into two separate groups depending on their ability or inability to roll their tongue (see Figure 13.2) and into four groups based on blood group types A, B, AB and O.

Continuous variation

A characteristic shows **continuous variation** when it varies amongst the members of a species in a **smooth, continuous way** from one extreme to the other and does not fall into distinct groups. For example, seed length in broad beans varies continuously as shown in Figure 13.3. Similarly shell length in mussels (see Figure 13.4) and height in humans (see Figure 13.5) vary continuously.

Figure 13.2 Discrete variation in tongue-rolling ability

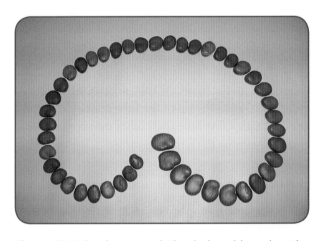

Figure 13.3 Continuous variation in broad bean length

Figure 13.1 Discrete variation in ivy leaf type

Figure 13.4 Continuous variation in mussel shell length

Figure 13.5 Continuous variation in human height

Related Activity

Investigating a variety of discrete and continuous characteristics

Table 13.1 shows some further examples of variation.

Discrete variation	Continuous variation
• ear lobe type in humans (attached or unattached – see Figure 13.6) • fingerprint type in humans (loop, whorl, arch or compound – see Figure 13.7) • hair type in humans (straight, curly or wavy) • eye colour in fruit flies (red or white) • wing length in fruit flies (long or short) • coat colour in guinea pigs (black or white) • flower colour in foxglove plants (purple or white • seed shape in garden pea plants (round or wrinkled) • height in garden pea plants (tall or dwarf) • colour of grain in maize plants (purple or yellow)	• body mass in humans • hand span in humans • foot length in humans • resting heart rate in humans • length of index finger in humans • height and diameter of shell in limpets (see Figure 13.8) • body length in trout • milk yield in cattle • mass of seeds in sunflower plants • mass of fruits on apple trees • length of petals in daisy flowers (see Figure 13.9) • breadth of tap root in dandelion plants

Table 13.1 Examples of discrete and continuous variation

earlobe unattached   earlobe attached

loop

whorl

arch

compound

Figure 13.6 Discrete variation in ear type

Figure 13.7 Discrete variation in fingerprint type

Figure 13.8 Continuous variation in height and diameter of limpet shells

Figure 13.9 Continuous variation in length of petals in daisies

Presentation of data

Discrete variation

The data obtained from a survey of a characteristic that shows discrete variation is normally presented as a **bar graph**. Figure 13.10 shows a bar graph of the blood groups of 100 people with each distinct group represented by a separate bar.

Continuous variation

Table 13.2 shows the heights of the members of a sample group of 50 people arranged in increasing order. They do not fall naturally into distinct groups. For convenience, the entire range of the characteristic is divided into small groups (subsets) of 5 cm. For example, eight people are found to fall into the subset 155–159 cm whereas only two people fall into the subset 180–184 cm.

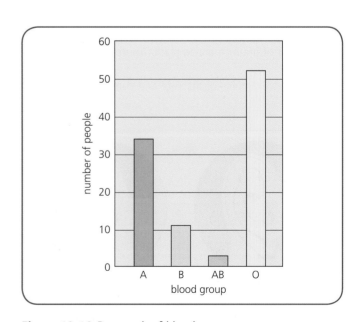

Figure 13.10 Bar graph of blood groups

Person	Height (cm)
1	144
2	145
3	148
4	151
5	152
6	152
7	153
8	154
9	155
10	155
11	156
12	156
13	157
14	158
15	158
16	159
17	160
18	160
19	161
20	161
21	162
22	162
23	162
24	163
25	163

Person	Height (cm)
26	164
27	164
28	164
29	165
30	165
31	165
32	166
33	166
34	167
35	167
36	168
37	168
38	169
39	170
40	171
41	172
42	172
43	174
44	174
45	176
46	178
47	179
48	181
49	183
50	186

Table 13.2 Continuous variation in human height

Grouping the data into subsets allows a **histogram** to be drawn, as shown in Figure 13.11. The majority of the people in the sample group have a height that is close to the centre of the range with fewer at the extremities. When a curve is drawn, a bell-shaped **normal distribution curve** is produced. In this example, the range in height extends from subset 140–144 cm to subset 185–189 cm and the most common height is the subset 160–164 cm.

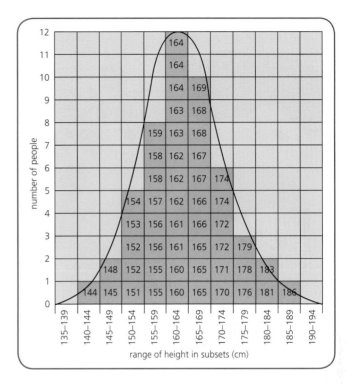

Figure 13.11 Histogram of human height

Variation and genetics

The genetic information responsible for the variation that exists amongst the members of a species is contained in genes on chromosomes (see chapter 4). The study of this genetic material and its transmission from generation to generation is called **genetics**.

Significance of sexual reproduction

Each new member of a species formed by **sexual reproduction** receives half of its genetic material from one parent and half from the other parent. It therefore resembles each parent in some ways but differs from each parent in other ways. By combining genes from separate parents, sexual reproduction produces individuals that are genetically distinct from other members of the species and therefore it **contributes to variation within a species**.

Inheritance

Phenotype

Coat colour in guinea pigs, leaf shape in tomato plants, wing type in fruit flies and grain colour in maize plants, as shown in Figure 13.12, are a few examples of the many physical characteristics possessed by living

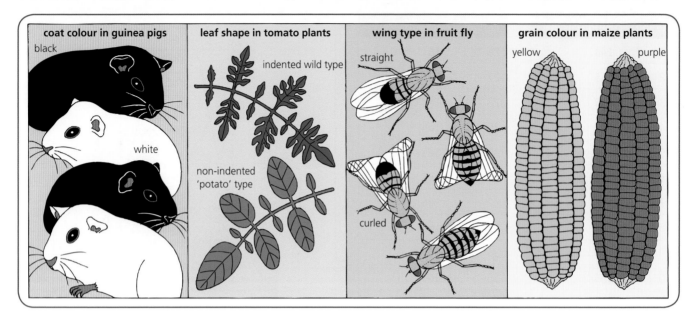

Figure 13.12 Phenotypes

organisms. These physical characteristics make up the organism's **phenotype**. Such characteristics are determined by genetic information.

True-breeding strains

Flower colour is a characteristic feature of pea plants that is controlled by genetic information. Purple and white are the two phenotypic expressions of flower colour in pea plants. Figure 13.13 shows three generations of a strain of pea plants with purple flowers; Figure 13.14 shows three generations of a strain of pea plants with white flowers. In each case the flower colour of the offspring is always identical to that of the parents and the members of the strain are described as being **true-breeding**.

Similarly, black guinea pigs that interbreed to form only black offspring and long-winged fruit flies that interbreed to produce only long-winged offspring are described as true-breeding strains.

Single gene inheritance

A characteristic such as coat colour in guinea pigs or grain colour in maize that shows discrete variation is controlled by different forms of a **single** gene. Geneticists often begin their investigation of inheritance in a species of plant or animal by studying a characteristic that shows discrete variation.

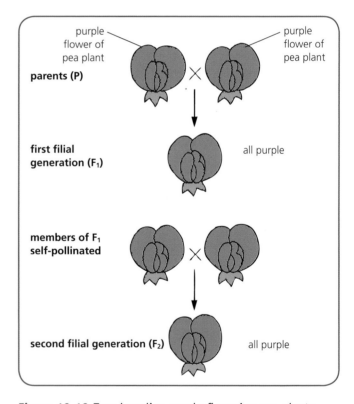

Figure 13.13 True-breeding purple-flowering pea plants

They set up a cross between two true-breeding strains of the organism that differ from one another in only one way. In guinea pigs, for example, a cross could be set up between two true-breeding strains differing only in coat colour. In fruit flies a cross could be set up between two true-breeding strains differing only in

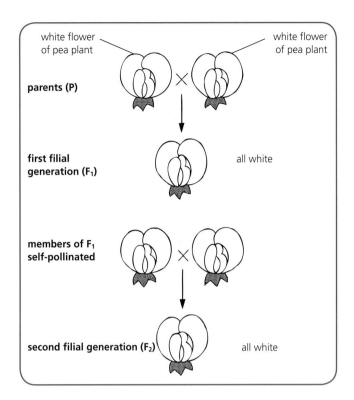

Figure 13.14 True-breeding white-flowering pea plants

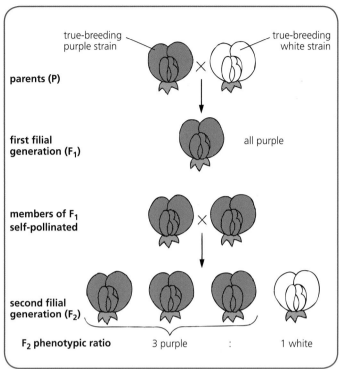

Figure 13.15 Single gene cross in pea plants

wing type. In pea plants, the example that follows – a cross between two true-breeding strains differing only in flower colour – is followed through two generations.

Inheritance of flower colour in pea plants

Figure 13.15 summarises a single gene cross for flower colour in pea plants. The phenotypes of the members of the F_1 generation are always found to be the same. In this case, they all bear purple flowers. The white

characteristic has disappeared in the F_1 because it has been masked by the purple characteristic. Purple flower colour is therefore said to be the **dominant** characteristic and white colour the **recessive** one.

The F_2 generation does not contain any new 'in-between' forms of flower colour. Both purple and white flower colour appear in the F_2 generation in their original form, unaffected by their union in the F_1 generation. All single gene crosses of this type produce a **3:1 phenotypic ratio** in the F_2 generation.

Testing Your Knowledge 1

1 a) Explain what is meant by the terms *discrete* and *continuous* variation. (2)
 b) Give TWO examples of each type of variation that exist amongst a large population of humans. (4)
2 The crosses shown in Figure 13.16 refer to a genetics experiment using pea plants.

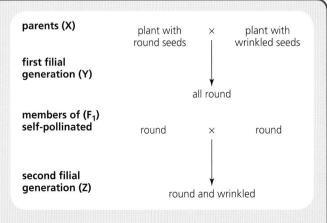

Figure 13.16

a) Before being used in the experiment, the parent plants were tested to ensure that they were true-breeding. How would this be done? (2)

b) Supply the symbols that would normally be used at positions X, Y and Z in Figure 13.16 to denote the different generations. (3)

c) i) Which seed shape characteristic is recessive and which is dominant?

ii) Explain how you arrived at your answer. (2)

d) What can always be said about the phenotypes of the members of the F_1 generation resulting from a cross between two true-breeding parents? (1)

e) Predict the ratio of the two phenotypes that would occur in the F_2 generation. (1)

Genes and genotype

Each **gene** is a unit of heredity that controls an inherited characteristic such as flower colour in pea plants (or contributes in part to a polygenic characteristic such as human height – see page 105). Each gene occupies a specific site on a chromosome (see Figure 13.17). The complete set of genes possessed by an organism is called its **genotype**.

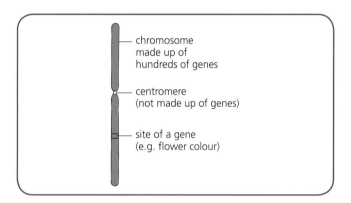

Figure 13.17 Site of a gene

Alleles

At least two forms of each gene normally exist among the members of a species. For example, the gene controlling flower colour in pea plants may be the dominant form that produces purple flowers or the recessive form that produces white flowers. These different forms of a gene are called **alleles**.

Every normal body cell in an organism carries two matching sets of chromosomes, one originating from each parent. Thus every body cell has two alleles of each gene, one from each parent. These two alleles may be the same or different depending on which alleles an organism inherits from its parents. Each gamete, on the other hand, has only one set of chromosomes and therefore carries only one allele of each gene.

Symbols

For convenience, the dominant and recessive alleles of a gene are often represented by **symbols**. In pea plants, for example, the two alleles of the gene for flower colour can be represented by the letters P for the dominant allele (purple) and p for the recessive allele (white). Since every **body cell** has two alleles of each gene, one from each parent, an organism's genotype is always represented by **two letters** per gene. A **gamete** only carries one allele of each gene and is always represented by **one letter** per gene. The cross in Figure 13.15 can be represented as shown in Figure 13.18, which includes a Punnett square.

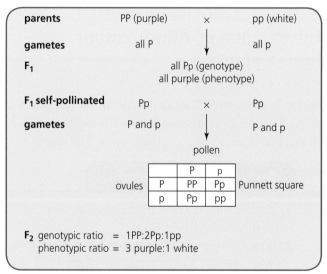

Figure 13.18 Use of symbols

Homozygous and heterozygous

When an organism possesses two identical alleles of a gene (such as P and P or p and p) its genotype is said to be **homozygous** and it is true-breeding. When an organism has two different alleles of a gene (such as P and p) its genotype is said to be **heterozygous** and it is not true-breeding.

Same phenotype, different genotype

In the above example, if a pea plant's phenotype is white flowers then its genotype must be pp. However, if a pea plant's phenotype is purple flowers, its genotype may be PP or Pp. In other words, the two **different genotypes** PP and Pp have the **same phenotype** (purple).

Polygenic inheritance

A characteristic showing continuous variation is controlled by the alleles of more than one gene and is said to show **polygenic inheritance**. The more genes that are involved, the greater the number of intermediate phenotypes that can be produced.

Additive effect

The genes involved in polygenic inheritance are transmitted from generation to generation by sexual reproduction in the normal way. What makes them different from other genes is that their effects are **additive**. This means that each dominant allele of each gene **adds a contribution** towards the characteristic controlled by the genes.

Polygenic inheritance in humans

Many human characteristics such as height, weight, skin colour, hand span and foot size show a pattern of polygenic inheritance. Since there are many different expressions of height, weight, etc., each of these characteristics must be controlled by two or more genes. Detailed studies suggest that **three or more genes** are probably involved in each case, with every dominant allele making an individual contribution to the characteristic.

Research Topic	**Mendel's work using pea plants**

Gregor Mendel (1822–84) carried out single gene crosses using true-breeding varieties of pea plant that possessed characteristics showing discrete variation (Figure 13.19). He carefully isolated plants and transferred pollen from one plant to another manually when cross-fertilisation was required. He collected and sowed the seeds formed by each generation of plants. He is regarded as being ahead of his time because he appreciated the importance of:

- working with **large numbers** of plants
- studying **one characteristic** at a time
- **counting the number** of different types of offspring produced and calculating a ratio.

By doing so, he was the first to put genetics on a firm scientific basis and his work is looked upon as the birth of genetics.

Figure 13.20 shows a summary of his single gene inheritance experiments. From the results of these experiments, Mendel drew the following conclusions (expressed in modern terms):

- The inheritance of characteristics is determined by factors (genes).
- In an individual organism, the alleles of a gene exist in pairs.
- At gamete formation, each gamete only receives one of a pair of alleles.
- Alleles retain their identity from generation to generation.

Figure 13.19 Seed shape (smooth or wrinkled) is one characteristic Mendel studied

Characteristic	Dominant trait	Recessive trait	F$_2$ products	Ratio
flower colour	purple	white	705 purple, 224 white	3.15:1
seed colour	yellow	green	6022 yellow, 2001 green	3.01:1
seed shape	smooth	wrinkled	5474 smooth, 1850 wrinkled	2.96:1
pod colour	green	yellow	428 green, 152 yellow	2.82:1
pod shape	inflated	constricted	882 inflated, 299 constricted	2.95:1
flower position	axial	terminal	651 axial, 207 terminal	3.14:1
plant height	tall	dwarf	787 tall, 277 dwarf	2.84:1

Figure 13.20 Mendel's single gene crosses

Research Topic — Polygenic inheritance in grain colour

Grain colour in a certain type of cereal can be explained on the basis that it is determined by two genes, each with two alleles, as shown in Table 13.3. Each dominant allele codes for a quantity of red colour equal to 25% of the maximum amount that can occur in this type of cereal. Thus a strain with the genotype $R^1R^1R^2R^2$ would possess the maximum amount of pigment and be 100% red, strain $R^1R^1R^2r^2$ would be 75% red, and so on to strain $r^1r^1r^2r^2$, which would be white.

Figure 13.21 shows how a cross between a 100% red strain and a white strain gives a 50% red strain in the F_1 generation. Self-pollination of the F_1 generation produces an F_2 whose members display a range of colour types.

Gene	Dominant allele	Recessive allele
1	R^1 (codes for red colour)	r^1 (does not code for red colour)
2	R^2 (codes for red colour)	r^2 (does not code for red colour)

Table 13.3 Genes for cereal grain colour

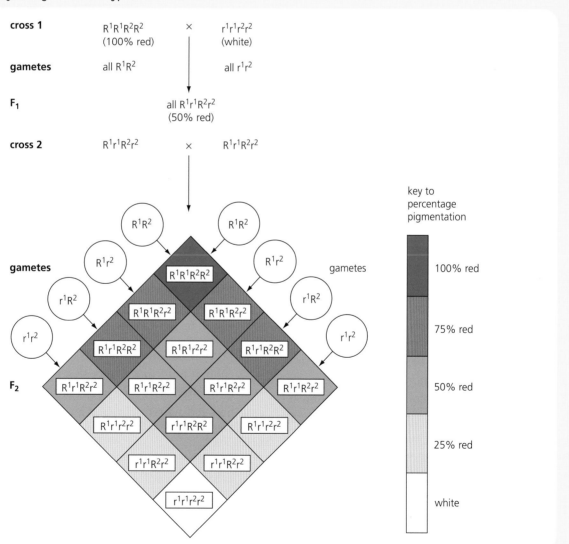

Figure 13.21 Genetic control of cereal grain colour

Related Topic

Observed versus predicted figures for number of offspring

Single gene crosses of the type shown in Figure 13.18 always produce a 3:1 phenotypic ratio in the F₂ generation. However, there is often a difference between the **observed** and the **predicted** numbers of the different types of offspring, as shown in Figure 13.20. In each of these single gene crosses, the F₂ offspring do not show the predicted ratio of 3:1 exactly, although each ratio is very close to it.

Continuing with flower colour in Figure 13.18 as our example, an exact 3:1 ratio would have occurred in the F₂ generation if during the **Pp × Pp** cross exactly half of the **P** ovules had been fertilised by **P** pollen grains and the other half of the **P** ovules by **p** pollen, while at the same time exactly half of the **p** ovules had been fertilised by **P** pollen and the other half by **p** pollen. However, this rarely happens in nature because fertilisation is a **random** process involving the element of **chance**.

Environment

Whereas characteristics that show discrete variation (such as tongue rolling and ABO blood group) are unaffected by environmental factors, many characteristics that show continuous variation (such as height and foot size) are influenced by the **environment**. They are dependent on favourable environmental conditions for their full phenotypic expression. For example, regardless of how many dominant alleles for height a person inherits, they will not reach their full potential height without consuming an adequate diet during childhood and adolescence.

Thus a combination of polygenic inheritance and environmental factors produces phenotypic characteristics that show a wide range of continuous variation.

Family trees

Unlike pea plants, human beings do not breed to suit the geneticist. In addition, they produce too few offspring to allow reliable conclusions to be drawn about the phenotypic ratios produced. Nevertheless the laws of genetics still apply to humans and particular traits can be traced through several generations of a family by constructing a **family tree** (pedigree chart).

Hair colour

In humans, the allele for red hair colour (h) is recessive to the dominant allele for non-red hair (H). If a person such as Sandy in Figure 13.22 has red hair yet neither of his parents has red hair, then it can be concluded that Sandy must have the **homozygous** genotype (hh) and that both of his parents must have the **heterozygous** genotype (Hh).

Since Sandy's aunt and maternal grandmother are red-haired they must be hh and his maternal grandfather must be Hh and so on. Piecing together such information for several generations of a family enables a geneticist to construct a family tree, as shown in Figure 13.22.

Element of chance

Each time Sandy's maternal grandparents produced a child, it was a 1 in 2 chance that the child would be non-red-haired (Hh) and a 1 in 2 chance that the child would be red-haired (hh).

Every time Sandy's parents (Hh and Hh) produce a child, it is a 1 in 4 chance that the child will be non-red-haired (HH), a 1 in 2 chance that the child will be non-red-haired (Hh) and a 1 in 4 chance that the child will be red-haired (hh).

Use of family trees

A family tree may be constructed and used by a **genetic counsellor** when advice is needed by a couple concerned about passing on a genetic disorder (known to exist in their families) to their children.

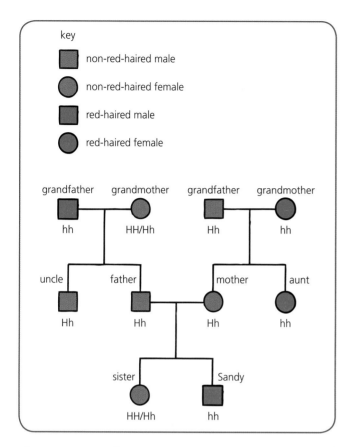

Figure 13.22 Family tree for hair colour

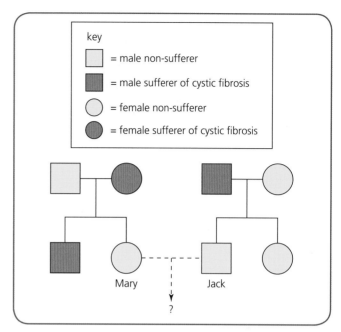

Figure 13.23 Family tree with phenotypes

Cystic fibrosis

Cystic fibrosis is a genetic disorder caused by a change (mutation) to one gene. It results in the sufferer producing mucus that is thicker and stickier than normal. This causes congestion of the lungs and other organs.

Let us consider the case of a couple (Mary and Jack) who want advice about the risk of their children inheriting the allele of the gene for cystic fibrosis. A genetic counsellor would interview the couple and construct their family trees as shown in Figure 13.23. She would then be able to deduce the genotypes and add them to the tree as shown in Figure 13.24 (where M = normal allele and m = allele for cystic fibrosis).

She would conclude that both Mary and Jack are heterozygous for this gene and are therefore **carriers** of

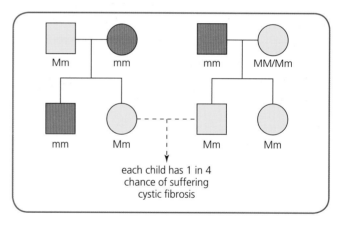

Figure 13.24 Family tree with deduced genotypes

the recessive cystic fibrosis allele. The counsellor would then advise the couple that each child they produce would run a 1 in 4 chance of suffering cystic fibrosis and a 1 in 2 change of being a carrier of the allele for the disorder.

Testing Your Knowledge 2

1 a) What name is given to the basic unit of inheritance that controls a characteristic that is passed on from generation to generation? (1)
   b) Of what structures found in a cell's nucleus do such units form a part? (1)
2 State the meaning of the terms *genotype* and *phenotype*. (2)
3 a) What term is used to refer to the different forms of a gene? (1)
   b) How many forms of a gene does a zygote receive from each parent? (1)

4 Explain the difference between the terms *homozygous genotype* and *heterozygous genotype* with reference to a named example. (2)
5 a) i) Which type of variation, discrete or continuous, is controlled by alleles of more than one gene?
       ii) What term is used to refer to this type of inheritance? (2)
   b) Apart from genetic factors, what other type of factors influences the wide range of phenotypic expression shown by some characteristics such as human body mass? (1)
6 Under what circumstances would a couple seek advice (based on family trees) from a genetic counsellor? (1)

What You Should Know Chapters 12–13

alleles	genes	pollen
anthers	genotype	polygenic
chromosome	haploid	recessive
continuous	heterozygous	risk
counsellor	homozygous	smaller
diploid	more	sperm
discrete	numerous	testes
dominant	ovaries	tree
egg	ovules	uninterrupted
fertilisation	phenotype	zygote

1 In a multicellular organism, the body cells are _____ and the sex cells (gametes) are _____.

2 In male animals, the _____ are the site of _____ production; in females, the _____ are the site of egg production.

3 Sperm are _____ in size and more _____ than eggs.

4 In flowering plants, the male gametes are contained in _____ produced in _____. The female sex cells (_____ cells) are contained in _____ produced in the ovary.

5 _____ is the process by which a haploid male gamete fuses with a haploid female gamete to produce a diploid _____.

6 Variation exists amongst the members of a species. When a characteristic can be used to divide the species into distinct groups, it is said to show _____ variation. When the characteristic varies in an _____ way from one extreme to the other, it is said to show _____ variation.

7 An organism's physical characteristics are known collectively as its _____.

8 Each inherited characteristic is controlled by one or more units of heredity called _____. Each gene is part of a _____.

9 Each gene normally has two or more different forms called _____. An allele that always shows its effect and masks the presence of the other form is said to be _____. An allele that is masked by the dominant form is said to be _____.

10 The complete set of genes possessed by an organism is called its _____. The genotype of an organism with identical alleles of a gene is described as _____; the genotype of an organism with two different alleles of a gene is described as _____.

11 A characteristic that shows continuous variation is controlled by alleles of _____ than one gene and is said to show _____ inheritance.

12 A pattern of inheritance amongst the members of a family can be established by constructing a family _____. Analysis of a family tree relating to a genetic disorder enables a genetic _____ to help people to make decisions about parenthood based on assessment of _____.

14 Transport systems in plants

Surface area to volume ratios

A small organism (such as a unicellular plant or animal) has a **large surface area** in relation to its volume; a large organism (such as a multicellular plant or animal) has a **smaller surface area** in relation to its volume.

Need for a transport system

Once essential substances have entered a living organism, they must be spread through its body since all of its living parts need a supply. In a tiny **unicellular organism**, only very short distances are present between the body's relatively large surface area and the parts needing essential substances. Therefore the passive process of **diffusion** is adequate to transport materials to all parts of the cell.

In a large **multicellular organism**, the body's surface area is small in relation to its volume and its absorbing organs are often located at a considerable distance from most of the cells in need of essential substances. Diffusion alone is too slow. A specialised **transport system** is needed to deliver essentials to living cells at a rate that is rapid enough to keep pace with their continuous demands.

Plant transport systems

Green plants need water for transporting materials and for photosynthesis. A land plant's roots are buried in the ground where they absorb water. The green leaves are above ground where they make sugar by photosynthesis. Therefore the plant needs **two transport systems** (see Figure 14.2) to enable water to travel up to the leaf cells and sugar to pass down to the root cells.

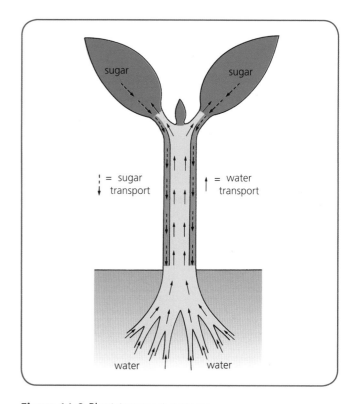

Figure 14.2 Plant transport systems

Related Activity

Calculating surface area to volume ratios

Table 14.1 shows how a '1 centimetre cube' has a surface-area-to-volume ratio of 6:1 and a '6 centimetre cube' has a surface-area-to-volume ratio of 1:1. In effect this means that a small organism has nearly all of its body tissue close to the outside surface (see Figure 14.1). A large organism, on the other hand, has much less of its inner tissue close to the outside surface with most of it buried in the body core.

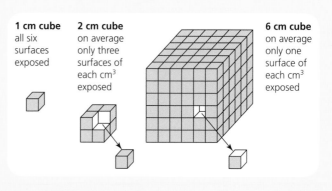

1 cm cube all six surfaces exposed

2 cm cube on average only three surfaces of each cm³ exposed

6 cm cube on average only one surface of each cm³ exposed

Figure 14.1 Relative surface areas

Length of one side of cube (cm)	Surface area of one side (cm²)	Total surface area (cm²) (SA)	Volume (cm³) (VOL)	SA/VOL	Ratio (SA:VOL)
1	1	6	1	6	6:1
2	4	24	8	3	3:1
3	9	54	27	2	2:1
6	36	216	216	1	1:1

Table 14.1 Size and relative surface area

Related Activity

Investigating the site of water transport in a plant

Stem structure
Figure 14.3 shows where the **xylem** and **phloem** tissue are found in the stem of a plant such as *Impatiens* (Busy Lizzy) that is a few months old and in the woody stem of a plant such as privet that is 1 year old.

Red dye experiment
The cut end of a leafy shoot from each type of plant is placed in **red dye** for at least 30 minutes. A portion of stem is then cut out and examined as shown in Figure 14.4. Red dye is found to be present only in the xylem cells (vessels) showing that **xylem** is the site of **water transport** in a plant. (A set of different experiments, not shown here, can be used to demonstrate that phloem is the site of sugar transport in a plant.)

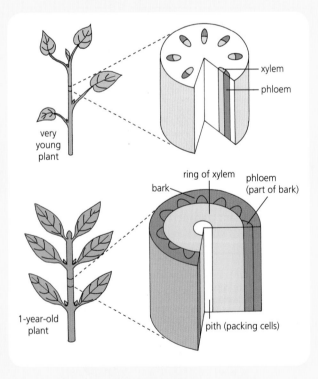

Figure 14.3 Sites of xylem and phloem in stems

Figure 14.4 Red dye experiment

Water transport in a plant

Figure 14.5 shows the route taken by water as it passes up through a plant from root to leaf. Figure 14.6 shows **root** **hairs** on the young roots of germinating seeds. A root hair is an extension of an epidermal cell and it presents a **large absorbing surface** to the surrounding soil solution.

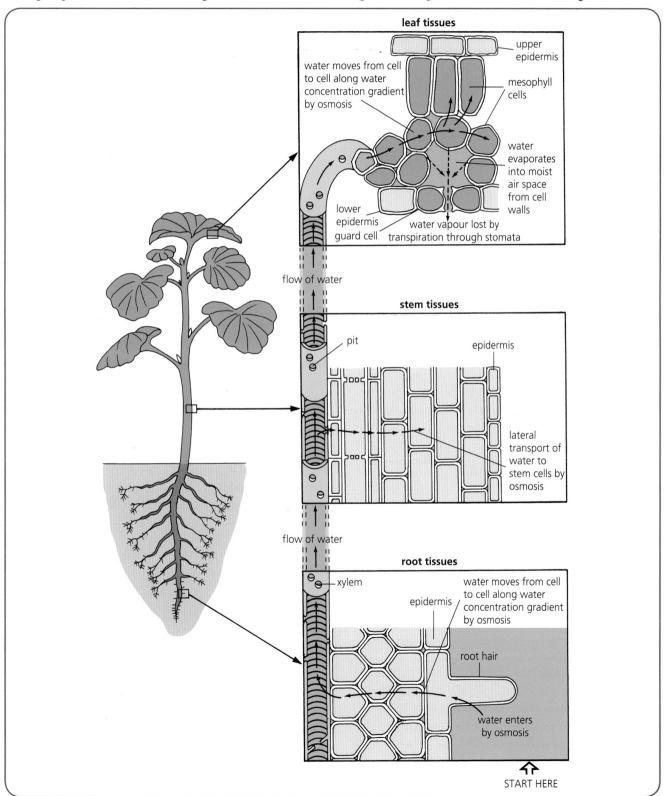

leaf tissues

upper epidermis

water moves from cell to cell along water concentration gradient by osmosis

mesophyll cells

water evaporates into moist air space from cell walls

lower epidermis guard cell

water vapour lost by transpiration through stomata

flow of water

stem tissues

pit

epidermis

lateral transport of water to stem cells by osmosis

flow of water

root tissues

xylem

epidermis

water moves from cell to cell along water concentration gradient by osmosis

root hair

water enters by osmosis

START HERE

Figure 14.5 Water transport system

Figure 14.6 Root hairs

Since a root hair is a region of low water concentration compared with the soil solution (a region of higher water concentration), water enters a root hair by **osmosis**. Water then passes from the root hair (which now has a higher water concentration) into a neighbouring cell (which by comparison has a lower water concentration) and so on across the root to the **xylem** vessels. The xylem vessels transport **water** and **mineral salts** up through the stem to all parts of the plant. **Mesophyll** cells in the leaf need water for photosynthesis.

Exit of water

Transpiration is the process by which water is lost by evaporation from the aerial parts of a plant. Most transpiration occurs through tiny pores in the leaves called **stomata**.

Related Activity

Investigating transpiration

Site of transpiration

When the experiment shown in Figure 14.7 is examined after several days, much condensation is found to be present on the inner surface of bell jar A, very little on the inside of B and none in C. It is therefore concluded that most water is lost by a plant's **leaves** during transpiration.

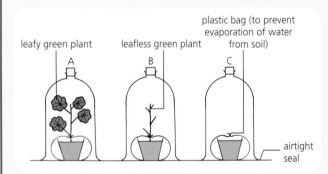

Figure 14.7 Investigating the site of transpiration

Rate of transpiration

A **bubble potometer** (see Figure 14.8) is an instrument used to measure **rate of water uptake** by a leafy shoot. This water uptake is only approximately equal to the transpiration rate because some water is normally retained by the leafy shoot for other processes such as photosynthesis.

An **air bubble** is allowed to enter the system and its rate of movement along the horizontal tube is measured (for example in mm/min). The syringe is used to inject water

and return the bubble to the start of the scale, allowing the experiment to be repeated. Table 14.2 gives the reasons for adopting certain techniques and precautions during the investigation. Table 14.3 gives a specimen set of results for three different environmental conditions.

From the results it is concluded that **wind** increases the rate of transpiration. This occurs because the air outside the stomata is continuously being replaced with drier air that accepts more water vapour from the plant. Increased **humidity** of the air surrounding the plant results in decreased transpiration rate. This occurs because the difference in concentration of water vapour between the inside and the outside of the leaf is reduced and therefore rate of diffusion of water molecules from the plant slows down.

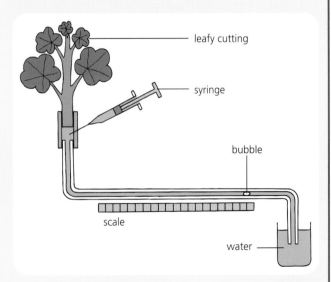

Figure 14.8 Bubble potometer

Design feature or precaution	Reason
stem cut under water and end of stem, rubber tubing and capillary tubing all connected under water	to prevent air entering xylem and forming air locks
tightly fitting rubber tubing used	to prevent leakage of water and ensure that system is airtight
time allowed for plant to equilibrate between different environmental conditions	to ensure that rate of movement of bubble is governed by factor being investigated and not the previous one
repeat measurements of rate of movement of bubble taken for each condition and average calculated	to obtain a more reliable result for each condition
all factors kept equal except for one change in environmental conditions	to ensure that the experiment is valid by only altering one variable factor at a time

Table 14.2 Experimental design features and precautions

Environmental condition	Additional apparatus needed to create condition	Average rate of movement of bubble (mm/min)
normal day	none	5
windy day	electric fan	20
humid day	transparent plastic bag	1

Table 14.3 Bubble potometer results

Related Activity

Investigating stomata

Location of stomata
When a leaf from a non-grass-like plant such as geranium is immersed in very hot water, many tiny bubbles appear on the leaf's lower surface and a very few on its upper surface. Each bubble indicates the **position of a stoma** through which hot expanded air has escaped from a **moist air space** (see Figures 14.5 and 14.13). It is concluded that in this type of plant, most stomata are located on the **underside** of the leaf.

When the procedure is repeated using a leaf from a grass, approximately equal numbers of tiny bubbles appear on both surfaces. It is therefore concluded that the stomata are **equally distributed** on the two surfaces of a grass leaf.

Structure of a stoma
A **stoma** is a slit-like pore enclosed by two **guard cells** (see Figure 14.9). Stomata and their guard cells can be seen under a microscope by preparing and viewing a **leaf peel** (see Figure 14.10). Figure 14.11 shows a microscopic view of a leaf surface using a thin layer of nail varnish.

Model of a stoma
When a sausage-shaped balloon that has had a strip of adhesive tape stuck to one of its sides is inflated, it bends over towards the reinforced side. Two balloons treated in this way and tied together at their ends act as a model of an open stoma.

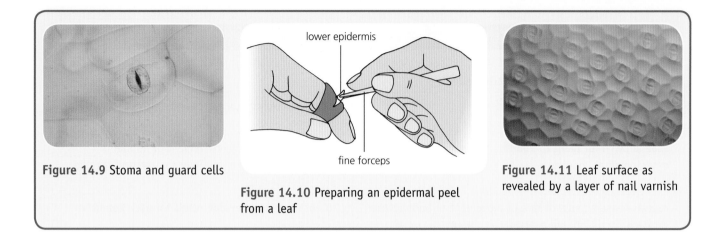

Figure 14.9 Stoma and guard cells

Figure 14.10 Preparing an epidermal peel from a leaf

Figure 14.11 Leaf surface as revealed by a layer of nail varnish

Stomatal mechanism

Guard cells (see Figure 14.12) differ from other epidermal cells in three ways. Guard cells are **sausage-shaped** and possess **chloroplasts**. In addition, the inner regions of their cell walls (those facing the stomatal pore) are **thicker** and **less elastic** than the outer regions of their cell walls.

Opening and closing of stomata occur as a result of **changes in turgor** of guard cells. When water enters a pair of flaccid guard cells, turgor increases. Due to their larger surface area and greater elasticity, the thin outer parts of the two guard cells' walls become stretched more than the thick inner parts. As the two guard cells bulge out, the thick inner walls become pulled apart, **opening** the stoma. This occurs in **light**.

When water leaves a pair of guard cells, they lose turgor and return to a flaccid condition. This results in the **closing** of the stoma. It occurs in **darkness**.

Leaf structure

Figure 14.13 gives a summary of the **internal structure** of a leaf and the functions of its various parts.

Sugar transport

Sugar is transported through a plant in **phloem** cells. This occurs in both an **upward** and a **downward** direction depending on circumstances. For example, sugar made in leaves by photosynthesis may be transported up to the plant's growing points and

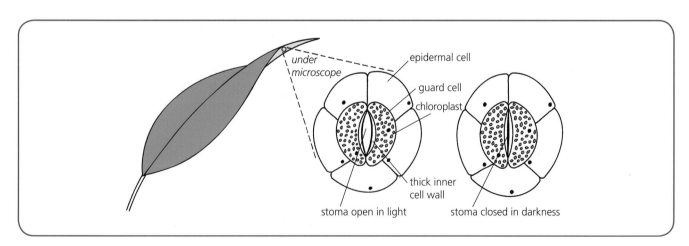

Figure 14.12 Stomata in light and dark

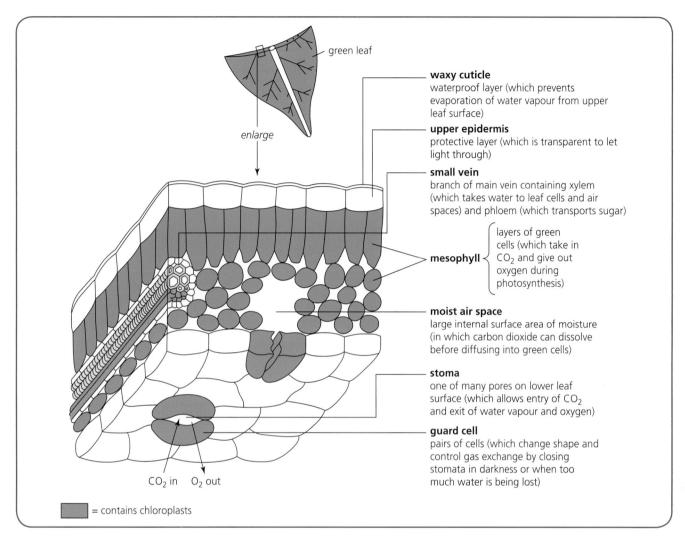

Figure 14.13 Structure of a leaf

flowers or down to its stem and roots. Furthermore, starch in a storage organ such as a bulb may be converted to sugar and transported up to growing leaves and flowers.

Comparison of xylem and phloem

Figure 14.14 shows both types of transport tissue in longitudinal section. **Xylem** is composed of non-living, hollow tubes (vessels) that are described as being **lignified** because they bear rings or spiral bands of strong **lignin** (see Figure 14.15). These structures provide **support** and enable the xylem vessels to

withstand pressure changes that occur when water is drawn up through them to replace water lost by transpiration.

Phloem is living tissue composed of **sieve tubes** and **companion cells**. The cytoplasm in sieve tubes is continuous from cell to cell through holes in sieve plates (the name given to the perforated walls at the ends of the sieve tubes). The continuity of cytoplasm allows sugar to be transported to all parts of the plant. Sieve tubes lack nuclei and their activities are controlled by neighbouring companion cells.

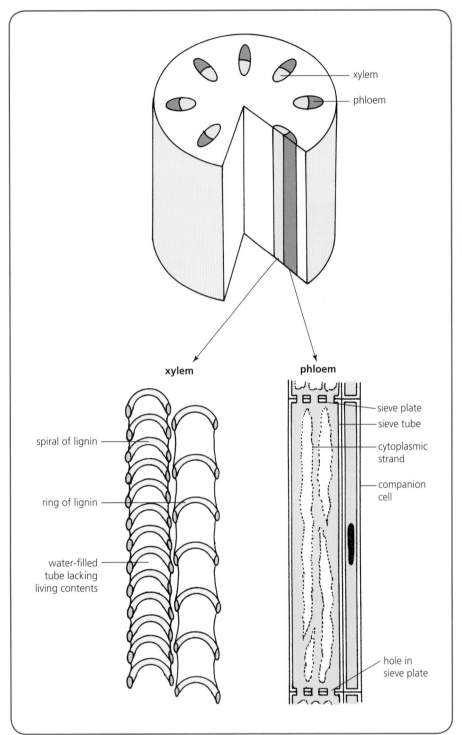

Figure 14.14 Comparison of xylem and phloem

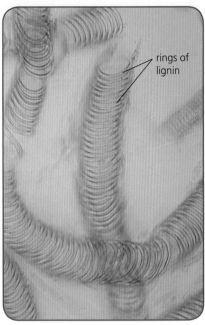

Figure 14.15 Xylem

Testing Your Knowledge

1 Explain why a plant needs two different transport systems. (2)

2 Copy and complete Table 14.4. (6)

Type of cell or tissue	Description
	absorbs water from soil solution
	lignified to withstand pressure changes during transport of water
	main site of photosynthesis in a leaf
	controlled by a companion cell
	protective layer on outside of plant organs
	controls opening and closing of stomata

Table 14.4

3 Which ONE of the following is correct? (1)
Transpiration is the:

A transport of water up the xylem vessels

B movement of sugars up to new growing points

C transport of glucose down sieve tubes

D evaporation of water from leaf surfaces.

4 a) Construct a table to compare the transport of substances in phloem and xylem with respect to:

　i) type of substance transported

　ii) direction taken by substance

　iii) state of tissue (dead or alive). (6)

b) Name ONE other function of xylem in addition to transport. (1)

15 Animal transport and exchange systems

A large multicellular animal has a **small surface area** relative to its volume (see page 111). Therefore it needs **additional absorbing areas** to take in oxygen and food. In human beings, for example, alveoli in the lungs (see page 125) and villi in the small intestine (see page 127) greatly increase the surface area for the absorption of oxygen and digested food respectively.

Once these essential substances have entered the animal's body, they must be carried to all of its living cells at a rate faster than is possible by diffusion. In mammals, this rapid transport of essential materials is achieved by the animal's **circulatory system**.

Mammalian circulatory system

The circulatory system consists of the **heart** (a muscular pump) and the **blood vessels** (a system of tubes), which carry **blood** to all parts of the body. Nutrients, oxygen, carbon dioxide and hormones are transported in the blood.

Heart

The **heart** is divided into two separate sides, as shown in Figure 15.1. Each side has two hollow chambers: an **atrium** and a **ventricle**. The diagram shows the four heart chambers viewed from the front of the person. The right-hand side of the heart is therefore on the left side of the diagram and vice versa. The wall of the heart is made of cardiac muscle.

Blood flow

The path taken by blood as it flows through the heart and its associated blood vessels is shown in Figure 15.2. Blood from the body enters the right atrium by the main vein called the **vena cava**. The right atrium contracts, pumping blood into the right ventricle. Contraction of the muscular ventricle wall forces blood into the **pulmonary artery**. This vessel carries blood from the heart to the lungs where it takes up oxygen.

The **pulmonary vein** returns oxygenated blood from the lungs to the heart's left atrium. The blood is then pumped into the left ventricle where strong contraction of the muscular wall forces blood into the main artery called the **aorta**. The aorta takes blood to all parts of the body. These tissues and organs remove the oxygen as the blood passes through, making it become deoxygenated.

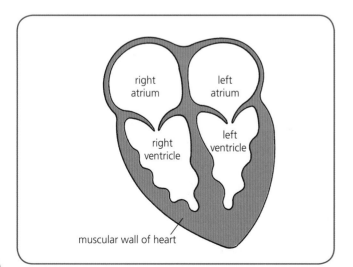

Figure 15.1 Chambers of the heart

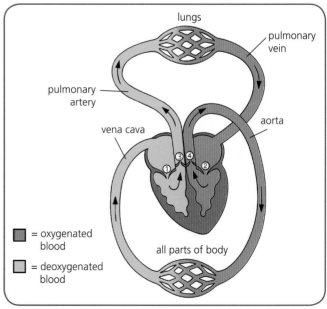

Figure 15.2 Heart and associated blood vessels

Investigating heart structure

With the hands protected by disposable gloves, a **sheep's heart** is held with both hands to examine it closely, feel its muscular wall and observe its associated blood vessels. The heart is then returned to the teacher for dissection.

Figure 15.3 shows a sheep's heart before dissection and after the front half has been cut away. The heart's four chambers are numbered 1–4 in the diagram.

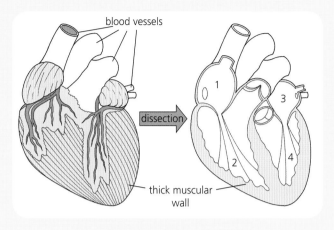

Figure 15.3 Structure of a sheep's heart

Deoxygenated blood returns by the vena cava to the heart's right atrium to repeat the cycle.

Thickness of ventricle walls

The wall of the left ventricle is particularly thick and muscular since it is required to pump blood all round the body. The wall of the right ventricle is less thick since it only pumps blood to the lungs.

Valves

Figure 15.2 shows the positions of the four heart **valves**. Valves 1 and 2 are situated between the atria and the ventricles. When they are open, blood passes from the atria into the ventricles. When the ventricles contract, the blood, under pressure, closes valves 1 and 2. This prevents blood from flowing back into the atria.

Valves 3 and 4 are situated between the ventricles and the two arteries that leave the heart. Once blood has been pumped through valves 3 and 4 they close, **preventing backflow** of blood from the arteries into the ventricles. Blood is therefore only able to travel in **one direction** through the heart. Figure 15.4 shows an artificial heart valve.

Figure 15.4 Artificial heart valve

is able to withstand the **high pressure** of oxygenated blood coming from the heart. (The pulmonary artery is exceptional in carrying deoxygenated blood.) Each time the heart beats, blood is forced along the arteries at high pressure and this pressure wave can be felt as a **pulse** beat.

A **vein** is a vessel that carries blood **back** to the heart. Although muscular, its wall is thinner than that of an artery (see Figure 15.5) since deoxygenated blood

Blood vessels

Arteries and veins

An **artery** is a vessel that carries blood **away** from the heart. It has a **thick muscular wall** (see Figure 15.5) that

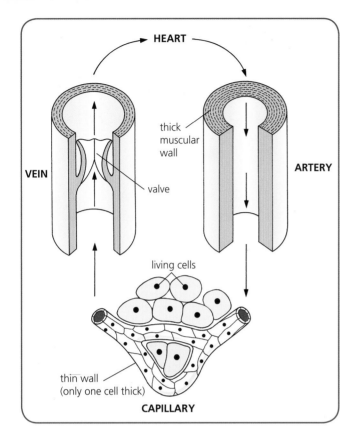

Figure 15.5 Types of blood vessel

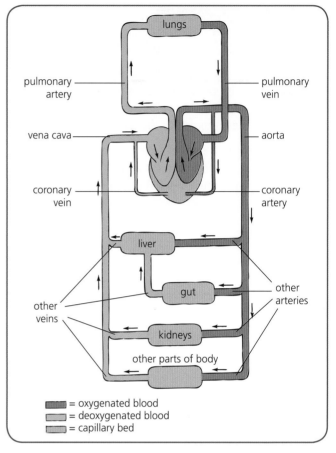

Figure 15.6 Human circulatory system

flows along a vein at **low pressure**. (The pulmonary vein is exceptional in carrying oxygenated blood.) Compared with an artery, the central cavity of a vein is wider. This helps to reduce resistance to the flow of blood along a vein. **Valves** are present in veins to prevent backflow.

Capillaries

An artery divides into smaller vessels and finally into a dense network of tiny, thin-walled **capillaries** (see Figure 15.5). Capillaries are the most numerous type of blood vessel in the body. They present a **large surface area** and are in close contact with the living cells in tissues and organs.

Capillaries are often referred to as **exchange vessels** since all exchanges of materials between blood and living tissues take place through their **thin walls** (only one cell thick). Capillaries unite to form larger vessels that converge to form veins. A simplified version of the human circulatory system is shown in Figure 15.6.

Coronary artery

The first branch of the main artery (aorta) leaving the heart is called the **coronary artery** (see Figures 15.6, 15.7 and 15.8). This artery supplies the muscular wall of the heart itself with oxygenated blood. If this vessel becomes blocked, blood flow to the heart wall is prevented and the person suffers a **heart attack**.

Figure 15.7 Coronary artery

Figure 15.8 Details of the coronary artery

Figure 15.9 Red blood cells in a capillary

Red blood cells

Red blood cells (see Figure 15.9) are very small and extremely numerous (approximately 5 million per mm^3). Their biconcave disc shape (see Figure 15.10) presents a **large surface area** for the uptake of oxygen. The red pigment present in red blood cells is called **haemoglobin**. As blood passes through lung capillaries, haemoglobin (dark red in colour) combines with oxygen to form oxyhaemoglobin (bright red in colour). When blood reaches the capillaries beside respiring cells, oxyhaemoglobin quickly releases the oxygen, which then diffuses into the cells (see Figure 15.11).

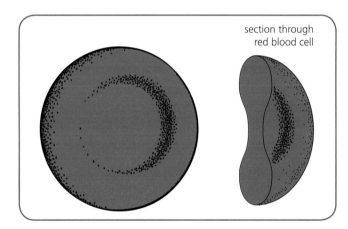

Figure 15.10 Shape of a red blood cell

Figure 15.11 Role of haemoglobin

Testing Your Knowledge 1

1 a) Name the FOUR chambers of the human heart. (2)
   b) Which of the simplified diagrams of a mammalian heart in Figure 15.12 shows the blood flowing in the correct direction? (1)

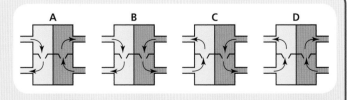

Figure 15.12

c) i) Identify blood vessels 1, 2 and 3 in Figure 15.13.
  ii) From where has the blood in vessel 1 come?
  iii) Why is a blood clot at position A or B of particular danger to the affected person? (5)

2 Draw a table to show THREE structural differences between an artery and a vein. (3)

3 a) Name the type of blood vessel shown in Figure 15.14. (1)

  b) i) Identify the type of blood cell present in the vessel.
    ii) What is the red pigment that this type of cell contains?
    iii) Briefly describe the function of the red pigment. (4)

Figure 15.13

Figure 15.14

Organs of gaseous exchange

The **lungs** (see Figure 15.15) are a mammal's organs of gaseous exchange. Air enters the nose or mouth and passes down through a system of tubes of decreasing diameter – the trachea, bronchi (singular bronchus) and bronchioles. The larger airways are supported and held open by rings of **cartilage**.

Cilia and mucus

The trachea and bronchi are lined with tiny hair-like **cilia** (see Figure 15.16) and cells that secrete sticky **mucus**. Rhythmic beating of the cilia sweeps mucus containing trapped dirt and micro-organisms upwards and away from the lungs.

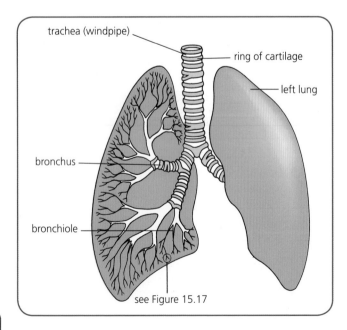

Figure 15.15 Organs of gas exchange

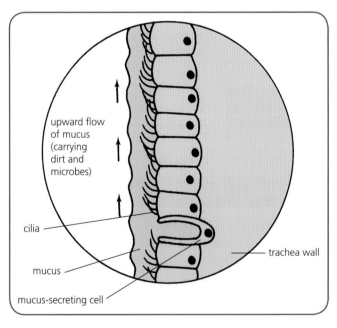

Figure 15.16 Cilia and mucus

Internal structure of the lung

Air passing along the narrow bronchioles ends up in tiny air sacs deep in the lungs (see Figure 15.17). These air sacs are called **alveoli** (singular alveolus). The alveoli are so numerous that they provide a very **large surface area** for gas exchange. The total internal surface area of the two lungs is approximately $90\,m^2$ (roughly the area of one side of a tennis court).

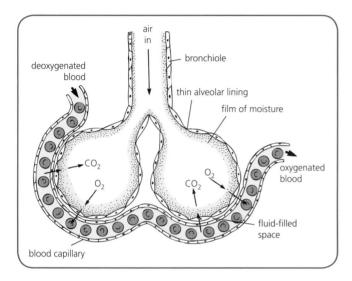

Figure 15.17 Gas exchange in alveoli

Capillary network

Each alveolus is surrounded by a **dense network** of blood capillaries. The lining of an alveolus is very **thin** and in **close proximity** to the walls of the blood capillaries, which are themselves only one cell thick. This combination of:

- large surface area
- short distance
- thin walls
- good blood supply

presents ideal conditions for **gas exchange** to occur between alveolar air and blood.

Gas exchange

Blood arriving in a lung is described as **deoxygenated** because it contains a low concentration of oxygen.

Since air breathed into an alveolus contains a higher concentration of oxygen, diffusion occurs. Oxygen first dissolves in the moisture on the inner surface of the thin lining of an alveolus (see Figure 15.17) and then diffuses into the blood in the surrounding capillaries. The blood therefore becomes **oxygenated** (rich in oxygen) before leaving the lungs and passing to all parts of the body.

Deoxygenated blood contains a higher concentration of carbon dioxide than the air entering the alveoli. Therefore carbon dioxide diffuses from the blood into the alveoli from where it is exhaled.

Food transport system

The alimentary canal (see Figure 15.18) is the body's **digestive system**. As insoluble molecules of food pass along this muscular tube they are broken down to a soluble state by digestive enzymes. The salivary glands, liver and pancreas, which are connected by ducts to the alimentary canal (gut), are described as associated organs.

Peristalsis

The oesophagus is a muscular tube that connects the back of the mouth with the stomach. Once food has been swallowed, it is moved down the oesophagus by a form of muscular activity called **peristalsis**.

Mechanism of peristalsis

Part of the gut wall is composed of **circular muscle**. When this **contracts** behind a portion of food, the central hole of the tube becomes narrower (see Figures 15.19 and 15.20) and the food is pushed along. At the same time the circular muscle in front of the food becomes **relaxed** allowing the central hole to enlarge and let the food slip along easily.

Functions of peristalsis

Peristalsis also squeezes semi-solid food through the stomach and along the intestines. This movement helps to mix the food with digestive juices. Following absorption of the end products of digestion in the small intestine, peristalsis keeps unwanted wastes on the move through the large intestine on their way to the rectum to be eliminated.

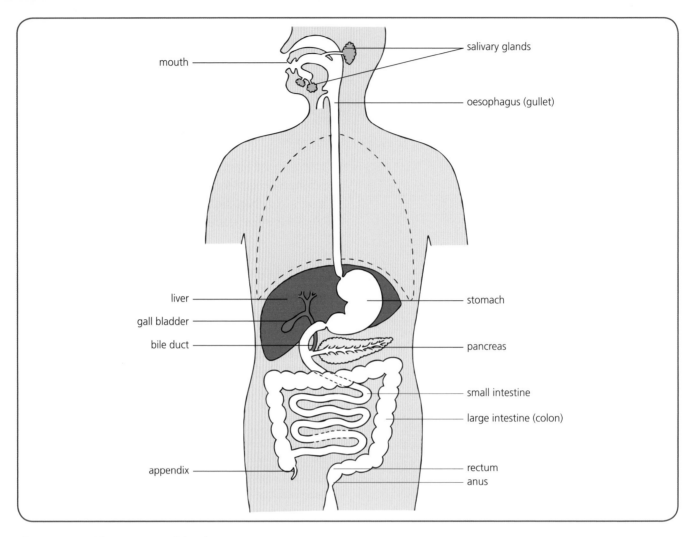

mouth

salivary glands

oesophagus (gullet)

liver

stomach

gall bladder

bile duct

pancreas

small intestine

large intestine (colon)

appendix

rectum

anus

Figure 15.18 Alimentary canal (gut)

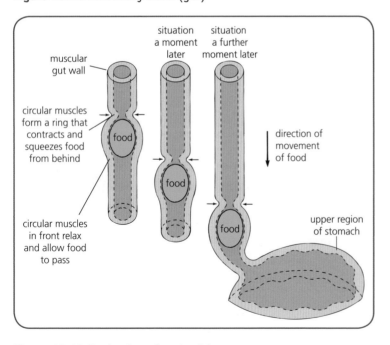

muscular
gut wall

situation
a moment
later

situation
a further
moment later

circular muscles
form a ring that
contracts and
squeezes food
from behind

food

direction of
movement
of food

food

circular muscles
in front relax
and allow food
to pass

food

upper region
of stomach

Figure 15.19 Mechanism of peristalsis

Figure 15.20 Model of peristalsis

End products of digestion

Imagine the small intestine of a person who has eaten an egg sandwich. As a result of complete digestion, the starch in the bread has been broken down to **glucose**, the protein in the egg to **amino acids** and the fat in the butter or margarine to the **products of fat digestion**. All of these different substances must now be absorbed and transported round the body.

Absorption in the small intestine

The main function of the small intestine is to absorb the end products of digestion through its wall and then pass them into the circulatory system. The small intestine is very efficient at this job because of its structure (see Figure 15.21). It is very **long** and its internal surface is **folded** and bears thousands of tiny, finger-like projections called **villi** (singular villus). As a result, the small intestine presents a **large absorbing surface area** to the digested food.

Role of villi

The internal structure of a **villus** is shown in Figures 15.22 and 15.23. In addition to presenting a large surface area, villi are ideally suited to the jobs of absorption and transport of digested food because each villus:

- is covered by a cellular lining that is only **one cell thick**. The soluble end products of digestion are therefore able to pass through rapidly.

- contains a dense network of **blood capillaries** into which glucose and amino acids pass. These end products of digestion are then carried by the blood transport system to the liver.
- contains a tiny lymphatic vessel called a **lacteal** that collects the products of fat digestion and passes them into the lymphatic system.

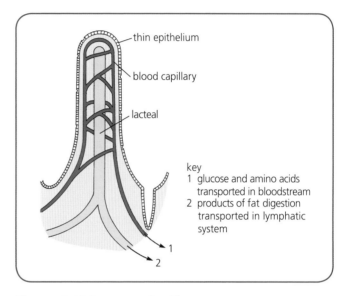

Figure 15.22 Structure of a villus

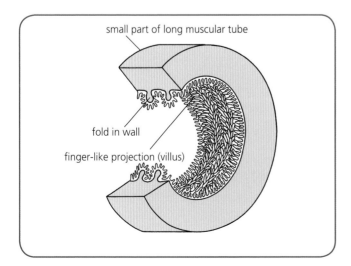

Figure 15.21 Structure of the small intestine

Figure 15.23 Microscopic view of villi

127

Testing Your Knowledge 2

1 a) Why does the trachea not close during movements of the head and neck? (1)
   b) What is the purpose of:
      i) the mucus secreted by cells lining the airways?
      ii) the cilia that line the surfaces of the airways? (2)
2 a) What is an *alveolus*? (1)
   b) Copy and complete Table 15.1 (which refers to features of alveoli) using the following answers: *alveolar wall is thin; to pick up and transport oxygen; inner alveolar surface is moist*. (2)

3 Describe the mechanism of peristalsis with reference to a mouthful of food that has just been swallowed. (2)
4 a) State THREE ways in which the structure of the small intestine creates a large surface area suited to the efficient absorption of digested food. (3)
   b) What feature of the lining epithelium of the small intestine enables digested food to pass through easily? (1)
   c) Explain how the internal structure of a villus is suited to the transport of digested food. (2)

Feature	Function
alveoli present a large surface area	to absorb much oxygen
	to allow oxygen to dissolve
	to allow oxygen to diffuse through into blood easily
network of tiny blood vessels surrounds alveoli	

Table 15.1

16 Effects of lifestyle choices

Inherited and environmental factors both play their part in contributing to the healthy or unhealthy state of a person's body. The human body normally has a natural tendency to **healthiness** if given the appropriate conditions. Nevertheless, it is also subjected to a variety of environmental factors that have the potential to cause a **disorder** or **disease**. Some of these factors are controlled to some extent by the society in which the person lives, employing techniques such as immunisation programmes against disease-causing micro-organisms. However, the control of many other potentially damaging factors depends on the behaviour of the individual, who has **free will** and is at liberty to create their own environment.

The government produces materials aimed at persuading people to adopt practices that will improve their physical and mental health while rejecting those that will have an adverse effect on them. However, the ultimate state of a person's health is directly and indirectly affected by the **lifestyle choices** that they make.

Poor lifestyle choices

High-fat diet

Some people consume a **high-fat diet**. This may take the form of 'comfort-eating' in response to some underlying condition such as anxiety, depression or low self-esteem. It often leads to **obesity**, which is accompanied by several health risks, as shown in Figure 16.1.

High-salt diet

Some people consume a diet containing a **high concentration of salt**. This may occur unwittingly, to some extent, because the person is unaware of the salt content of many of the processed foods that they are eating (see Table 16.1). Excess salt in the diet increases the risk of **high blood pressure**, which in turn increases the chance of the person suffering heart disease or a stroke.

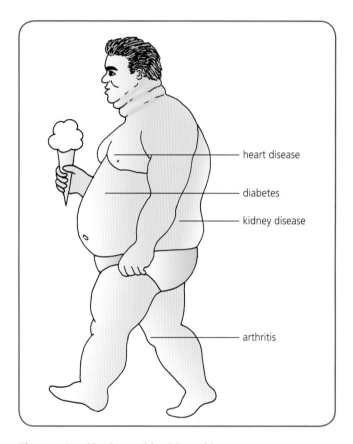

heart disease

diabetes

kidney disease

arthritis

Figure 16.1 Obesity and health problems

Lack of exercise

Medical experts recommend that for a healthy life, people should take **regular exercise**, with the amount varying from one age group to another. For example, to maintain a basic level of health, people aged 5–18 years should do at least 1 hour of physical activity *every day*. This should be a mix of **moderate-intensity activity** (such as fast walking or riding a bike) and **vigorous-intensity activity** (such as playing football or dancing energetically).

However, many people do not take enough regular exercise and their sedentary lifestyle increases the risk of obesity.

Food	Sodium content (g/100 g)	Salt content (g/100 g)	High (H), medium (M) or low (L) salt content
banana	trace	trace	L
beef (minced)	0.32	0.80	M
biscuits (ginger nuts)	0.32	0.80	M
butter (unsalted)	trace	trace	L
cabbage	0.01	0.03	L
cake (sponge)	0.35	0.88	M
cheese (cheddar)	0.61	1.53	H
hamburger	0.66	1.65	H
noodles	0.41	1.03	M
omelette	1.03	2.58	H
pizza	0.34	0.85	M
potato (boiled)	0.02	0.05	L
quiche	0.61	1.53	H
soup (vegetable)	0.50	1.25	M
spaghetti	trace	trace	L
tuna (canned in oil)	0.42	1.05	M

Table 16.1 Salt content of foods

Related Information

Sodium and salt content

Salt is a chemical called sodium chloride. Sometimes information about salt is presented as '**sodium** content'. This only represents 40% of the overall salt content.

Table 16.1 shows the salt content of some common foods. More than 1.5 g per 100 g is regarded as a high salt content, whereas 0.3 g or less per 100 g is a low salt content. The daily recommended maximum amount of salt that should be eaten depends on age, as shown in Table 16.2.

Age (years)	Daily recommended maximum amount of salt (g)
1–3	2
4–6	3
7–10	5
11 and over	6

Table 16.2 Recommended maximum salt intake

Use of tobacco

Nicotine is the addictive substance in tobacco. It stimulates the central nervous system and increases pulse rate and blood pressure. Tobacco smoke also contains many other harmful substances including **carbon monoxide** (see page 133). In the UK, treating diseases caused directly by smoking costs more than £5 billion each year and around 100 000 people die annually as a result of smoking.

A direct relationship exists between number of cigarettes smoked daily and death rate from **lung cancer** (see Figure 16.3). Several other diseases such

Investigating the effect of exercise on pulse rate

The volunteer sits quietly for 3 minutes to allow their **pulse rate** to settle at a steady pace. A stopwatch is then used to measure the person's pulse rate for 30 seconds while they continue to sit quietly. Their pulse rate is measured a second time and an average resting pulse rate in beats per 30 seconds is calculated.

The person exercises vigorously by running on the spot for 2 minutes and then, on stopping, immediately has their pulse rate taken as before. Their pulse is measured every minute for up to 7 minutes from the end of exercise. Figure 16.2 shows a graph of a typical set of results using pulse values converted to beats per minute. The person's recovery time can be calculated from the data. **Recovery time** is the time taken for pulse rate to return to its normal resting value after exercise. The shorter the recovery time, the fitter the person.

Figure 16.2 Effect of exercise on pulse rate

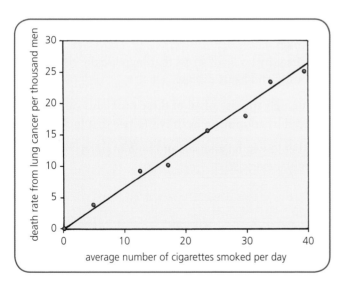

Figure 16.3 Death rate from lung cancer

as emphysema, bronchitis, coronary heart disease and throat cancer are caused or aggravated by smoking. It also has an adverse effect on the fetus during pregnancy.

In the UK, about a third of adults choose to lead this risky lifestyle, though the number of smokers is gradually decreasing year by year. (An exception to this trend is found amongst teenage girls where an increase is reported.) Most smokers admit that they would like to give up but find it extremely difficult to stop. Some smokers do not want to stop, are happy to adopt this high-risk activity and often become annoyed at 'infringements of their personal liberty' as smoking becomes banned in public places.

Use of alcohol

In the UK, **alcohol** is the most commonly used 'recreational drug of choice'. Once consumed, alcohol is absorbed from the stomach (and other parts of the gut) and carried in the bloodstream. When it reaches the brain, it affects the brain's activity and often makes the person feel relaxed and uninhibited. The alcohol is slowly broken down into harmless substances by the liver and its effect wears off. Alcoholic drinks have a high energy content and therefore can contribute to **weight gain**.

One **unit** of alcohol is the quantity that can be broken down by a healthy adult's liver in about 1 hour. Figure 16.4 shows three different drinks (a small glass of wine, a half pint of beer and a small measure of whisky) where each contains about one unit of alcohol. Currently the recommended upper limit per week for women is 14 units and for men is 21 units.

Figure 16.4 Examples of one unit of alcohol

Harmful effects

If a large quantity of alcohol is consumed, the liver does not have time to break it down before the alcohol has caused the following harmful effects.

In the **short term**, excess alcohol in the bloodstream leads to:

- longer (slower) reaction time
- poorer control and coordination of muscles
- poorer judgement when faced with a decision to make
- in extreme cases, loss of consciousness and blackout for several hours.

All of these effects increase the risk of an **accident** taking place. Women who take alcohol during pregnancy can damage the health of the unborn baby.

In the **long term**, drinking alcohol to excess on a regular basis frequently leads to **cirrhosis** of the liver and brain damage. It also increases the risk of cancer. In the UK, alcohol is responsible for 33 000 deaths each year.

Stress

Most people find that they have to cope with **stress** in their life from time to time and it is generally accepted that a certain amount of low-level stress is good for the

body because it keeps the person alert. However, the choice of a lifestyle that contains **continuous high levels of stress** or a job that involves **high-stress experiences** (such as having no control over events and being constantly hounded to complete excessive workloads against tight deadlines) may lead to ill health. This is often indicated by one or more of the following:

- headaches
- anxiety
- irritability
- loss of sleep
- inability to concentrate
- depression.

Adverse effects of poor lifestyle choices

The six examples discussed on pages 129–132 contribute directly or indirectly to an increased chance of the person suffering:

- fatty deposits in blood vessels (see Figure 16.5)
- blood clots (see Figure 16.6)
- diabetes
- heart attacks
- strokes
- unhealthy levels of stress that increase the risk of obesity and heart disease.

Fortunately the risk of all of these problems can be reduced by adopting a healthy lifestyle that includes:

- a diet low in fat and salt and high in fibre
- regular exercise

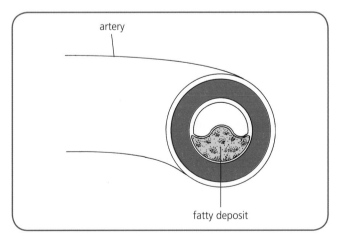

Figure 16.5 Fatty deposit in wall of blood vessel

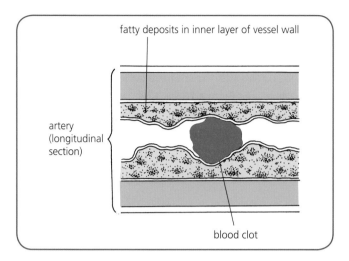

Figure 16.6 Blood clot in artery

- complete abstinence from smoking
- reduction of alcohol consumption to recommended levels or less
- reduction of stress by seeking professional help to address the underlying causes.

Iron

Iron is an essential constituent of **haemoglobin**, the respiratory pigment in red blood cells. A small quantity of iron is lost every day by the human body in dead skin cells, bile and urine, and needs to be replaced. Growth and menstruation make further demands (see Table 16.3).

It is therefore essential that growing children and pregnant women consume a diet rich in iron. Many foodstuffs such as meat, eggs, fish, green vegetables and cereals are rich in iron. If the diet lacks iron,

haemoglobin cannot be produced and the person may suffer **anaemia** (a deficiency in red blood cell number resulting in shortness of breath and lack of energy).

Environmental factors with adverse effects

Toxic heavy metals

Some **heavy metals** such as lead, cadmium, mercury and chromium cannot be broken down by the human body and are toxic if they accumulate in the tissues over time. **Lead**, for example, harms the body by inhibiting enzymes that control essential processes such as respiration and growth. Lead poisoning may occur in young children if they ingest flakes of peeling paint containing lead. Lead is also found in old pipes and in some pesticides. **Cadmium** is used in pesticides and in some batteries. It is present in cigarettes, enabling it to gain access to the body via the respiratory system.

The best method of dealing with heavy metal pollution is **prevention**. In the UK, leaded petrol is being rapidly phased out and lead is no longer used for pipes in new homes. At a level of individual lifestyle choice, people can avoid the use of paints and pesticides containing lead and replace lead pipes in older properties. Similarly, unnecessary exposure to cadmium can be reduced by avoiding the use of pesticides containing cadmium, recycling batteries and refraining from smoking.

Carbon monoxide pollution

Carbon monoxide (CO) is a colourless, odourless gas. If it is breathed in, it reduces the concentration of oxygen that the blood can carry. In high concentrations, CO leads to drowsiness and even death. CO pollution is caused primarily by **exhaust emissions** released by vehicles burning fossil fuels. However, faulty gas appliances burning natural gas in an enclosed environment containing a very low level of oxygen also produce CO.

Individuals can make lifestyle choices that reduce CO pollution and the risk of CO poisoning by:

- ensuring that efficient catalytic converters are fitted to vehicles
- purchasing small rather than large vehicles, thereby reducing the quantity of exhaust fumes emitted

Factors creating demand for iron	Average mass of iron required to satisfy demand (mg/day)
basic loss in skin cells, bile and urine	0.5–1.0
growth, aged 0–12 months	0.7–0.8
growth, aged 1–11 years	0.3
growth during adolescence	0.5
normal menstruation	0.5–1.6
pregnancy	6.0

Table 16.3 Iron demands

changing to a hybrid vehicle (see Figure 16.7) that would release even less CO in its emissions

making use of public transport instead of a private vehicle when possible

ensuring regular maintenance of gas-burning appliances and installing CO alarms.

Figure 16.7 Hybrid vehicle

Radiation

Deficiency of vitamin D in young children leads to the formation of soft, abnormal bones. The long bones of the legs tend to bend under the weight of the body, making the child bow-legged. This condition is known as rickets. Vitamin D is formed in the human skin when it is exposed to the **ultraviolet rays** present in sunshine. Therefore a low level of exposure of the skin to the sun's rays (such as 15 minutes per day) is a good lifestyle choice because it boosts the body's supply of vitamin D and helps to prevent rickets in growing children.

However, excessive, unprotected exposure to solar radiation is a poor lifestyle choice since it greatly increases the risk of **skin cancer** (see Figure 16.8). The incidence of this life-threatening condition is increasing year on year (see Figure 16.9). The use of an appropriate high-factor barrier cream when sunbathing for more than a few minutes is therefore a further example of a good lifestyle choice.

Figure 16.8 Skin cancer

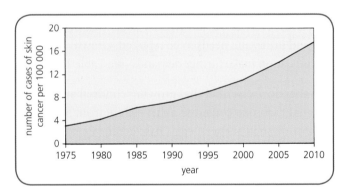

Figure 16.9 Incidence of skin cancer

Testing Your Knowledge

1 a) Give FOUR examples of poor lifestyle choices and for each briefly describe how it could undermine the person's health. (4)

b) Poor lifestyle choices increase directly and indirectly the chance of suffering which of the following: *strokes, diabetes, blood clots, heart attacks, fatty deposits in blood vessels*? (1)

2 a) What is *haemoglobin*? (1)

b) Which metallic element is required in the diet for the formation of haemoglobin? (1)

c) What disorder of the blood may arise if the body fails to make enough haemoglobin? (1)

3 a) Why has the use of leaded petrol as a fuel for vehicles been almost completely phased out in the UK? (1)

b) Give ONE example of a way in which an individual can make a lifestyle choice that would help to reduce the pollution of the atmosphere by carbon monoxide. (1)

c) Why is it important to wear a barrier cream with a high protection factor when sunbathing? (1)

Related Activity

National Health Service debate

At present the **National Health Service (NHS)** provides the residents of the UK with a comprehensive range of health services. Almost all of these are free at the point of use and patients are not involved personally in the financial consequences resulting from the treatment. This situation begs the question: *'Should all illnesses be treated for free under the NHS or should some (or even all) be paid for?'*

Those people in favour of **all illnesses being treated for free** argue that the present system is, in fact, not free. It is financed by national insurance contributions and taxation. They argue that as medicine advances and new drugs and services come on stream, they must be made available to everyone and not just to a wealthy minority. When challenged about the amount of money that this would cost, they insist that it would be a valid use of a large proportion of the nation's gross national product. They are quick to remind people of the vast sums of money the Government is able to find to finance nuclear weapons and to fight wars in distant foreign countries.

Some people support an NHS where the **vast majority of services and treatments are free**, but accept that the amount of money available to finance them is finite. Therefore they would argue that some restrictions need to be imposed. For example, they would probably not be in favour of free prescriptions for a prohibitively expensive drug that would extend a terminally ill patient's life by only a few months. In their opinion the money would be better spent elsewhere in the system.

Some people argue that **partial privatisation** of the NHS is the answer. In their opinion, patients who are ill through no fault of their own would receive free treatment. However, those who were suffering any illness or condition that had been 'self-inflicted' as a result of poor lifestyle choices would have to pay for their treatment. For example, the following people would have to pay:

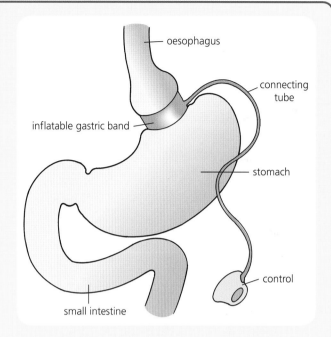

Figure 16.10 Gastric band

- smokers suffering chronic bronchitis, emphysema or lung cancer
- alcoholics in need of a liver transplant
- heroin addicts requiring methadone
- those suffering sexually transmitted diseases following casual sex encounters
- obese people wanting gastric band surgery (see Figure 16.10) or in need of surgery for knee or hip problems
- sufferers of type 2 diabetes brought on by obesity.

However, many of the people who hold this view, when pressed, have to agree that illness is not a black-and-white issue. Conditions can rarely be categorised one way or the other since they are the result of both genetic and environmental factors.

Some people take an even more extreme view and would like to see the NHS **completely privatised**. They claim that this would produce a transformation and modernisation of a public service. In their opinion, it would result in greater competition and a subsequent improvement in quality of care. They envisage everyone being obliged to take out private health insurance cover in order to be able to pay for treatment, as required, during their lifetime.

What You Should Know Chapters 14-16

alveoli	exchange	red
amino acids	guard	salt
aorta	haemoglobin	sieve
area	hairs	stomata
capillaries	heart	stress
carbon	lacteal	sugar
cartilage	lifestyle	surface
cava	lignin	thick
cilia	low	transpiration
companion	mesophyll	transport
coronary	mucus	veins
dead	oxygen	ventricles
diabetes	peristalsis	villi
dioxide	phloem	water
epidermis	pressure	wider
excess	pulmonary	xylem

1 The body of a large multicellular organism has a small _____ area relative to its size and needs one or more _____ systems to move essential substances to all parts of its body efficiently.

2 Plants need a transport system to carry _____ to the leaves for photosynthesis and a second transport system to carry _____ from the leaves to all other parts of the plant.

3 Water and mineral salts enter a plant by its root _____. These materials are transported up through the plant in _____ cells (vessels), which are supported by _____ and are _____.

4 Some water arriving in the leaves is used by _____ cells for photosynthesis.

5 Much of the water is lost as water vapour through tiny holes in the leaf _____ called _____. The opening and closing of each stoma is controlled by two _____ cells. The loss of water by evaporation from leaves is called _____.

6 The site of sugar transport in a plant is the _____ tissue. It is alive and composed of _____ tubes and _____ cells.

7 In mammals, the blood circulatory system transports nutrients, _____ and carbon _____ round the body.

8 The _____ is a muscular pump made up of four chambers, the right and left atria and right and left _____.

9 The vena _____ carries blood from the body's tissues and organs to the heart. Blood is transported to the lungs in the _____ arteries and back from the lungs in the pulmonary _____.

10 The _____ carries blood from the heart to the body's tissues and organs. The first branch of the aorta is the _____ artery, which supplies the heart wall itself with oxygenated blood.

11 Arteries carry blood at high _____. They have _____ muscular walls and a narrow central channel. Veins carry blood at _____ pressure and have thinner walls and a _____ central channel.

12 _____ are tiny, thin-walled vessels that present a large surface _____ in tissues and organs, allowing materials to be exchanged.

13 _____ blood cells are specialised to carry oxygen. They contain the red pigment _____.

14 The body's main airways are supported and kept open by rings of _____. Their lining secretes _____ to trap dirt and this is swept up and away from the lungs by _____.

15 The lungs contain many tiny air sacs called _____. These are thin-walled and present a large surface area in contact with blood capillaries allowing _____ of oxygen and _____ dioxide to occur.

16 Food is moved through the digestive system by muscular activity called _____.

17 The wall of the small intestine bears tiny projections called _____, which are thin-walled and present a large surface area for the absorption of digested food. Each villus contains a blood capillary that absorbs glucose and _____ and a _____ that absorbs the end products of fat digestion.

18 Human transport and exchange systems are affected by _____ choices. Undesirable choices include the regular consumption of a diet high in _____ and/or rich in fat, use of tobacco, consumption of alcohol to _____ and high levels of _____. These increase the risk of _____, strokes and heart attacks.

Applying Your Knowledge and Skills Chapters 9–16

1 'A red blood cell is an example of a cell whose structure can easily be related to its function.' Justify this statement. (2)

2 Copy and complete Table KS2.1, which refers to structures present in the human body. (9)

System	Organ(s)	Function
digestive	stomach, intestines	
excretory		elimination of wastes
	lungs, trachea	
	ovaries, testes	production of sex cells
nervous	brain	

Table KS2.1

3 The eight statements shown in Figure KS2.1 were made by people being interviewed about the use of human embryos for stem cell research.

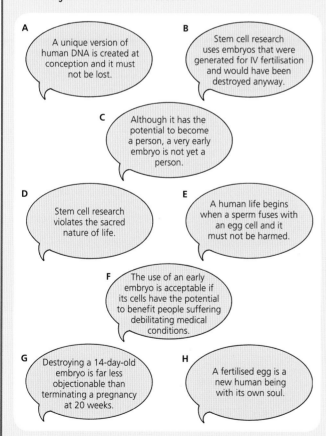

A A unique version of human DNA is created at conception and it must not be lost.

B Stem cell research uses embryos that were generated for IV fertilisation and would have been destroyed anyway.

C Although it has the potential to become a person, a very early embryo is not yet a person.

D Stem cell research violates the sacred nature of life.

E A human life begins when a sperm fuses with an egg cell and it must not be harmed.

F The use of an early embryo is acceptable if its cells have the potential to benefit people suffering debilitating medical conditions.

G Destroying a 14-day-old embryo is far less objectionable than terminating a pregnancy at 20 weeks.

H A fertilised egg is a new human being with its own soul.

Figure KS2.1

Classify the statements into two groups:
a) those in favour of this type of research (1)
b) those opposed to this type of research. (1)

4 Figure KS2.2 shows the reflex action that happens when the foot comes into contact with a sharp tack.

foot about to stand on tack

reflex action

Figure KS2.2

a) Match numbers 1 to 6 with the following statements:
   A Leg muscles contract, removing foot from danger.
   B Impulse enters spinal cord.
   C Impulse travels through motor neuron.
   D Pain receptors in sole of foot are stimulated.
   E Impulse passes through spinal cord.
   F Nerve impulse travels up sensory neuron. (1)
b) Explain why this response is protective. (1)
c) When a piece of dirt lands in the eye, it makes the eye water. Describe this reflex action by identifying the *stimulus, receptor, effector, response* and *protective value*. (5)

5 An experiment was set up to investigate the effect of a pituitary hormone called somatotrophin. The pituitary gland was surgically removed from each of 30 rats of equal mass and age. The rats were divided into two groups, P and Q. Those in P were given daily injections of somatotrophin; those in Q were used as the control. The results are shown in Table KS2.2.

Time (days)	Mean mass (g)	
	group P	group Q
0 (first injection)	220	220
40	240	230
80	250	220
120	280	220
160	320	230
200	390	220
240	410	220
280	410	210
320	430	220
360	440	210
400	440	220

Table KS2.2

a) Present the data as a line graph. (4)

b) Make a generalisation about the mean body mass of the control group of rats during this investigation. (1)

c) What conclusion can be drawn about the normal role of the hormone somatotrophin? (1)

d) i) Why were rats of equal mass and age used?

   ii) Identify TWO other factors that would need to be kept constant in this investigation. (3)

e) Suggest TWO ways in which the reliability of the results could be increased. (2)

6 Figure KS2.3 shows half of a flower.

Figure KS2.3

a) Which letter indicates the location of an egg cell? (1)

b) Which letter shows the site of pollen grain production? (1)

c) Which letter indicates the point where a zygote could be formed? (1)

7 Figure KS2.4 represents the life cycle of human beings.

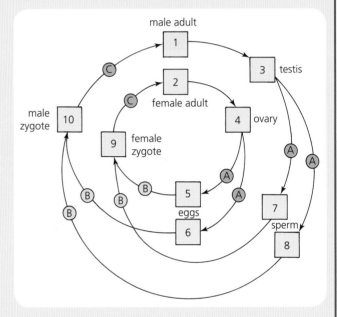

Figure KS2.4

a) Match boxes 1, 2, 3, 4, 5 and 7 with the descriptions haploid or diploid. (2)

b) Identify the process that occurs at all the arrows marked A. (1)

c) What process takes place when two arrows marked B meet? (1)

d) Name the process that occurs at each arrow marked C. (1)

8 a) Which ONE of the following is an example of discrete variation amongst humans? (1)

   A   waist circumference

   B   male or female gender

   C   length of hand span

   D   breadth of foot

   b) Which ONE of the following is an example of continuous variation amongst humans? (1)

   A   intelligence

   B   ear lobe type

   C   wavy or straight hair

   D   blood group

   c) Table KS2.3 gives the results from a survey of forefinger print types found amongst the students in a college.

Type of forefinger print	Number of forefinger prints	Percentage number of forefinger prints
arch	90	
compound	45	
loop	630	
whorl	135	

Table KS2.3

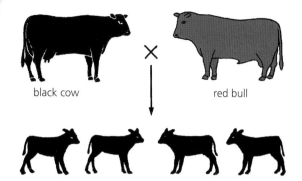

black cow ✕ red bull

Figure KS2.5

i) Calculate the percentage number of each type of forefinger print.
ii) Present these percentages as a bar chart. (4)

d) Under the headings *discrete variation* and *continuous variation*, list TWO ways in which identical twins reared in different environments:
   i) would definitely be exactly alike
   ii) could differ from one another. (4)

9 The cross shown in Figure KS2.5 involves the gene for coat colour in cattle.
   a) State the two phenotypes of coat colour in this cross. (2)
   b) Which form of the gene for coat colour is dominant? (1)
   c) Using symbols of your own choice draw a keyed diagram to represent the cross. (2)
   d) i) When the calves reach sexual maturity, will they be true-breeding?
      ii) Explain your answer. (2)

10 The data in Table KS2.4 refer to a series of experiments in which a large, leafy shoot attached to a bubble potometer (see Figure 14.8 on page 114) was subjected to various conditions of several environmental factors.

a) Consider each of the following pairs of experiments in turn and for each pair draw a conclusion about the effect of a named factor on the time taken by the bubble to travel 100 mm:
   i) 1 and 2
   ii) 3 and 7
   iii) 6 and 10. (3)

b) Why is it impossible to draw a valid conclusion about the effect of an environmental factor on the time taken by the bubble to travel 100 mm from a comparison of experiments 3 and 8? (1)

c) Which experiment in Table KS2.4 should be compared with experiment 5 to find out about the effect of darkness on time taken by the bubble to travel 100 mm? (1)

d) Which TWO experiments should be compared in order to find out about the effect of wind speed on time taken by the bubble to travel 100 mm when the plant is in light at 25 °C and in air at 95% humidity? (1)

		Experiment number									
		1	2	3	4	5	6	7	8	9	10
Environmental factor	wind speed (m/s)	0	0	0	0	15	15	15	15	15	15
	temperature (°C)	5	25	5	25	5	25	5	25	5	25
	air humidity (%)	75	75	95	95	75	75	95	95	75	75
	light (L)/ dark (D)	L	L	L	L	L	L	L	L	D	D
Time taken by bubble to travel 100 mm		3 min 3 s	1 min 35 s	4 min 28 s	3 min 2 s	1 min 56 s	0 min 30 s	3 min 22 s	1 min 57 s	24 min 10 s	22 min 4 s

Table KS2.4

e) Which TWO experiments should be compared in order to find out about the effect of temperature on transpiration rate by the plant when exposed to wind speed of 15 m/s, in light and in air of 75% humidity? (1)

11 Ringing is the process by which a band of outer tissues containing the phloem is peeled away from the stem of a plant. Before being ringed, the plant in Figure KS2.6 was left in bright light for 2 days and then leaves A and B were tested for the presence of starch. Next the plant was ringed and kept in darkness for 24 hours. Then leaves A and B were tested again for starch. The results are shown in Table KS2.5.

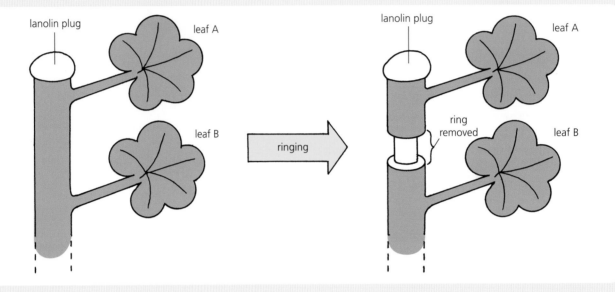

Figure KS2.6

	Leaf A	**Leaf B**
result of starch test after 2 days in light	+	+
result of starch test after 2 days in dark	+	−

Table KS2.5

a) Account for the presence of starch in leaves A and B after 2 days of bright sunlight. (1)
b) Starch, on being converted to soluble sugar, can be transported from a leaf to other parts of the plant. In which tissue does this transport of sugar occur? (1)
c) Explain why starch is absent from leaf B after 24 hours of darkness. (1)
d) Account for the presence of starch in leaf A after 24 hours of darkness. (2)

12 The relative concentrations (in units) of carbon dioxide in the air in an alveolus and in the blood in a pulmonary capillary are shown in Figure KS2.7.

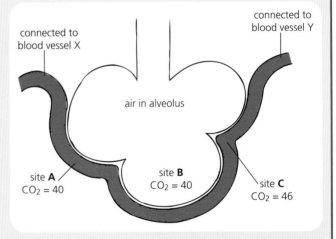

Figure KS2.7

a) At which site is the blood:
  i)   deoxygenated?
  ii) oxygenated?
  iii) Explain your choice. (3)
b) Match the following relative concentrations (in units) of oxygen with sites A, B and C:
  i)   40
  ii) 95
  iii) 100. (2)
c) Match X and Y with the two main vessels that connect the lungs with the heart. (2)
d) The following list gives the substances and layers through which a molecule of oxygen passes on its way from being part of alveolar air to entering a red blood cell. Put them into the correct order. (1)
  1) blood plasma
  2) capillary wall
  3) film of moisture
  4) fluid-filled space
  5) thin alveolar lining

13 The risk of suffering from heart disease depends on several factors and can be calculated by referring to Figure KS2.8, where each * counts as one risk point.
a) Calculate the level of risk of heart disease for each of the following:
  i) A woman aged 45 with an upper blood pressure of 120 who eats a diet containing 20% animal fat. Her weight is ideal for her height but she smokes 20 cigarettes a day and takes very little exercise.
  ii) A 16-year-old with an upper blood pressure of 120 who eats a diet containing 30% animal fat. He is a non-smoker but is 4 kg above his correct weight. He takes a moderate amount of exercise.

age (years)	10–20	21–30	31–40	41–50	51–60	61 and over
	*	**	***	****	*****	******

+

upper blood pressure (mm Hg)	100	120	140	160	180	200 or more
	*	**	***	****	******	********

+

animal fat in diet (%)	0	10	20	30	40	50
	*	**	***	****	*****	*******

+

variation from ideal weight	0	up to 2 kg above	3–9 kg above	10–16 kg above	17–23 kg above	24 kg or more above
		*	**	***	*****	******

+

daily smoking habit	none	cigar/pipe	10 cigarettes	20 cigarettes	30 cigarettes	40 or more cigs.
		*	**	****	******	**********

+

exercise taken	major amounts with workouts	major amount	moderate amount	minor amount	very little	none
	*	**	***	*****	******	********

Key to total * score
4–11 = below average risk
12–17 = average risk
18–24 = above average risk
above 24 = high risk

Figure KS2.8

iii) A 61-year-old man who takes very little exercise. He does not smoke but he eats a diet containing 30% animal fat and he is 28 kg above his correct weight. His upper blood pressure is 140. (3)

b) A 45-year-old man was found to have a score of 19 risk points. He normally took a moderate amount of exercise, was 4 kg overweight, had an upper blood pressure of 120 and ate a diet containing 30% animal fat. How many cigarettes did he smoke daily? (1)

c) Name THREE changes to lifestyle that people can make in order to reduce their risk of heart disease. (3)

14 Figure KS2.9 shows eight conversation bubbles from a debate about whether or not treatment for obesity should be funded by the NHS.

a) Classify them into two distinct categories – for or against. (2)

b) What is your opinion on this matter?

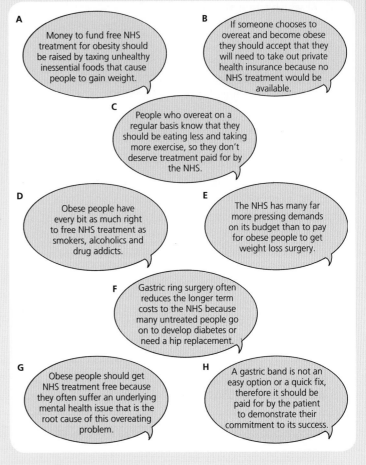

Figure KS2.9

Unit 3

Life on Earth

17 Biodiversity and the distribution of life

Biodiversity means the **total variation** that exists amongst all living things on Earth. So far, scientists have studied about 1.75 million different species and many more await discovery and investigation. Scotland alone is thought to possess about 50 000 different land and freshwater species and about 39 000 species in the surrounding seas (see Figure 17.1).

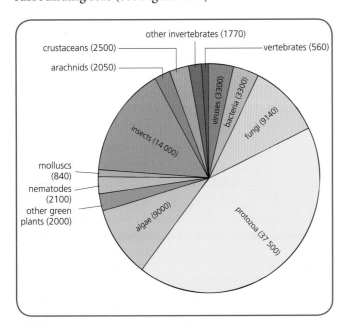

other invertebrates (1770)
crustaceans (2500)
vertebrates (560)
arachnids (2050)
viruses (3300)
bacteria (3300)
insects (14 000)
fungi (9140)
molluscs (840)
nematodes (2100)
other green plants (2000)
algae (9000)
protozoa (37 500)

Figure 17.1 Scottish biodiversity

Biotic and abiotic factors

Factors affecting a species that are directly related to, or are the result of, activities of **living** things are called **biotic** factors. These include, for example, amount of available food, number of predators, incidence of disease and level of competition with other species for the necessities of life.

Non-living factors such as temperature, rainfall, light intensity, concentration of oxygen and pH are called **abiotic** factors.

Ecosystem and habitat

An **ecosystem** is a natural biological unit of the environment (such as a forest) and is made of living and non-living parts (also see page 152). An ecosystem contains one or more **habitats**. These are the places such as burrows and tree branches where organisms live.

Biodiversity in an ecosystem is affected by biotic and abiotic factors and by many human influences such as over-hunting and habitat destruction. Some factors increase the biodiversity in an ecosystem but many bring about its decline.

Related Activity

Investigating human influences on environments

Today there are so many human beings in the world that we no longer form a small, natural part of a balanced, stable ecosystem. As we strive to support the ever-increasing world population and its energy demands, we pursue activities that cause pollution, deforestation and desertification. These processes destroy natural habitats and reduce biodiversity.

Air pollution

When fossil fuels (such as coal and oil) are burned in power stations to generate electricity, sulphur dioxide (SO_2) gas is released into the air (see Figure 17.2 and page 148). Vehicle exhaust fumes also contain SO_2. Even in low concentrations this harmful gas aggravates human respiratory ailments and causes damage to many types of plant.

Figure 17.2 Air pollution

Deforestation

Tropical rainforests cover only about 6% of the Earth's land surface, yet they are estimated to contain half or more of all the existing species of plants, animals and micro-organisms. When this type of forest is cleared (see Figure 17.3) not only is a **natural resource** destroyed but the ecosystem and its wide variety of independent species are lost forever. For every plant species that becomes extinct through human activities, several animal species that were dependent on the plant for food and shelter are threatened and may also become extinct.

Desertification

In some dry parts of the world, the area of land covered by desert is increasing. When this process is largely the result of human activities it is called **desertification**.

The top part of Figure 17.4 shows a typical scene at the edge of a desert as it was in 1960. The rainfall is erratic but adequate to sustain the plants and maintain the water table. Marginal land (territory on the edge of a cultivated zone) and forests hold soil and form a windbreak. Some land is used for grazing. Traditional agricultural practices are employed on cropland. For example, crops are rotated, allowing each piece of land in turn to lie fallow for a spell and recover its fertility.

The bottom part of Figure 17.4 shows the situation today. The land has been lost to the desert and there is little chance of such land being returned to cultivation.

all lost forever?

Figure 17.3 Clearing the rainforest

The people can no longer feed themselves and their supply of drinking water has dried up. Out of desperation they may try to cultivate other areas of marginal land, which in turn accelerates the process of desertification.

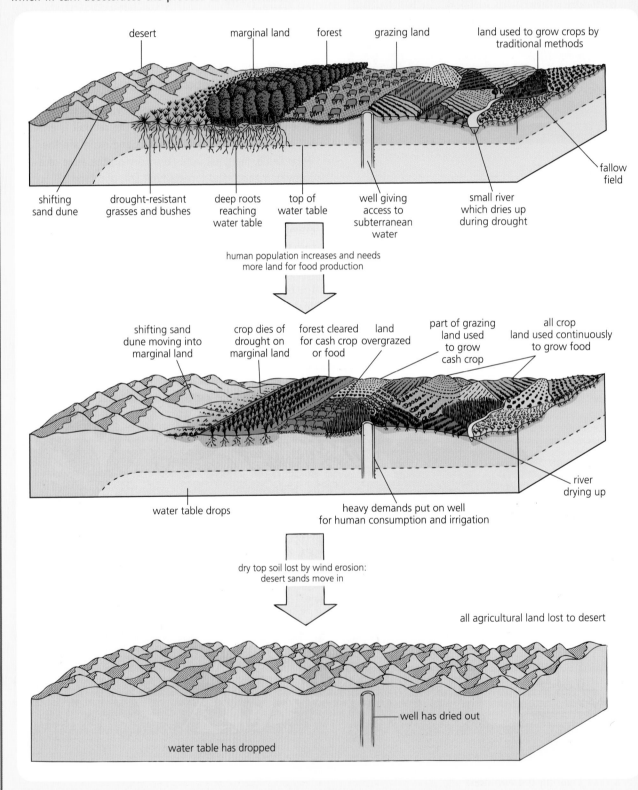

Figure 17.4 Desertification

Grazing

Grazing is a biotic factor that can affect species diversity in a grassland.

Rabbits

Natural grassland normally contains a rich variety of plant species. Some types of grass are especially sturdy and show vigorous growth; others are more delicate.

Rabbits are relatively unselective grazers. Their effect on a grassland's plant community depends on the level of grazing pressure applied. At low levels of grazing pressure, the aggressive dominant grasses are not held in check and tend to drive out the less vigorous plants. Species diversity amongst the plant community under these circumstances is low.

As grazing pressure increases (see Figure 17.5) more and more of the competitive dominant grasses are eaten and kept in check. This tends to free resources and space for the smaller, more delicate plant varieties and promotes an **increase in biodiversity** of species. However, at high intensities of grazing pressure, species **biodiversity decreases** again as the dense population of rabbits struggle to find food and drive some of the more delicate species within the plant community to extinction.

Sheep

When grazing pressure is intense on Scottish grassland that was once forest, such as Scots pine or birch,

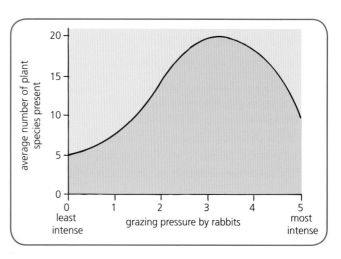

Figure 17.5 Effect of grazing on species diversity

sheep eat any tree saplings that appear among the grass. Regeneration of a forest community is therefore prevented and **biodiversity** of plant species is **decreased**. However, when grazing pressure is kept low on the same type of land, Scots pine and birch woodland communities are able to develop giving an **increase in species biodiversity**.

Predation

Predation is a biotic factor that affects the numbers of both the population of a prey animal and the population of its predator because a delicate balance exists between the two.

Interpreting predator–prey interaction graphs

The graph in Figure 17.6 shows that an increase in number of prey (perhaps due to climatic conditions favouring growth of their plant food) leads to an increase in predation. As the size of the prey population decreases, competition between predators for the remaining prey becomes more and more intense until eventually the number of predators drops. This in turn allows the prey population to build up again, which leads to a corresponding increase in the predator population and so on. In this series of events, the predator curve takes the same shape as that of the prey but lags behind it since time is required for each change to take effect.

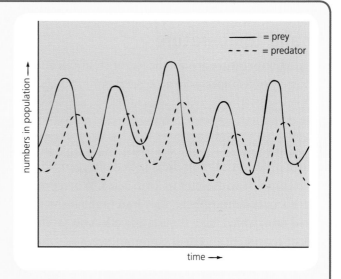

Figure 17.6 Predator–prey interactions

Related Activity

Analysing barn owl pellets

Barn owls are unable to digest the fur and bones of their prey. Once swallowed, these materials are bound into dark-coloured **pellets** in the bird's gut. The owl then gets rid of the pellet by regurgitation ('throwing it up'). An analysis of the pellets littering the ground near a barn owl's roost allows scientists to identify the bird's prey.

A pellet (see Figure 17.7) is dissected using forceps and a magnifying lens while wearing disposable gloves. When the bones present in the pellet are identified (by using, for example, information available on the Barn Owl Trust's website) they are found to have belonged to

small mammals such as shrews, voles and mice, which an owl usually swallows whole. Less commonly a pellet may contain the remains of a rat, a frog or another bird. The bar graph in Figure 17.8 shows the percentage of different prey types present in an analysis of a large number of pellets.

Figure 17.7 Dissection of an owl pellet

Figure 17.8 Analysis of barn owl pellets

pH and temperature

pH and **temperature** are abiotic factors that can affect the variety of fish species in an ecosystem.

pH and acid rain

The combustion of coal by electricity-generating power stations produces sulphur dioxide and nitrogen oxides, which combine with water to form acids. When present in excess in the atmosphere, they lead to the formation of **acid rain**, which has a devastating effect on several types of ecosystem and their communities.

Figure 17.9 shows the effect of the decrease in pH of loch water on the variety of fish species found in this aquatic ecosystem. The length of each bar represents the lower range of pH that can be tolerated by the species of fish.

Temperature and thermal pollution

Some types of electricity-generating power station use local river water as a coolant. When the water is returned to the river, it is considerably warmer and causes **thermal pollution**. The increase in temperature of river water is accompanied by a decrease in

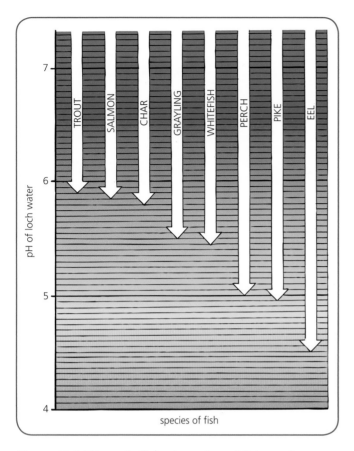

Figure 17.9 Effect of pH on the variety of fish species

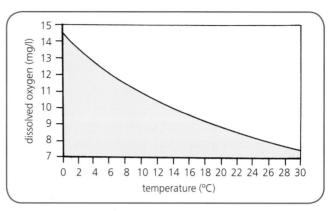

Figure 17.10 Effect of temperature on dissolved oxygen content of water

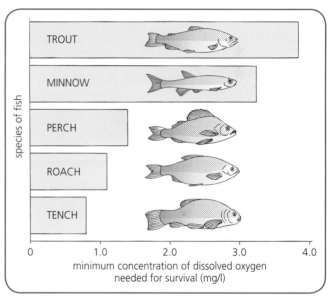

Figure 17.11 Effect of oxygen concentration on the variety of fish species

its dissolved oxygen content (see Figure 17.10) and a decrease in the variety of fish species in the river (see Figure 17.11). Whereas all of the species shown in the diagram could be present in water containing 4 mg/l of oxygen, only tench would be found at 1 mg/l of oxygen.

Biome

A **biome** is a large region of the Earth that can be distinguished from other biomes by:

- the characteristic abiotic factors that affect it
- the particular animal community (fauna) and plant community (flora) that it possesses.

Freshwater and marine biomes are examples of **aquatic** biomes. Desert, forest, grassland and tundra are examples of biomes that are **terrestrial**. A biome can also be described as a major ecosystem.

Global distribution of biomes can be influenced by abiotic factors such as rainfall and temperature. Tropical forests are only found in those parts of the world that receive high levels of rainfall and high temperatures. Desert biomes occur in those regions of the world that receive little (or no) rain and are affected by extremes of temperature.

Related Topic

Climograph

Figure 17.12 shows a 'climograph' that maps the ranges of temperature and precipitation (rain, hail or snow) occurring in six types of biome. Biomes are not sharply defined in reality. For example, the landscape changes gradually from forest to grassland and from grassland to desert.

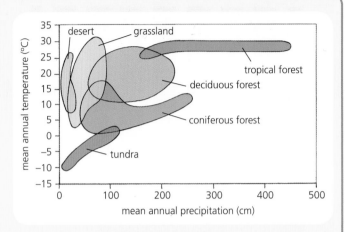

Figure 17.12 Climograph for six biomes

Research Topic   Range of biomes

Figure 17.13 shows the distribution of the world's terrestrial biomes. Table 17.1 gives further details about four of these biomes.

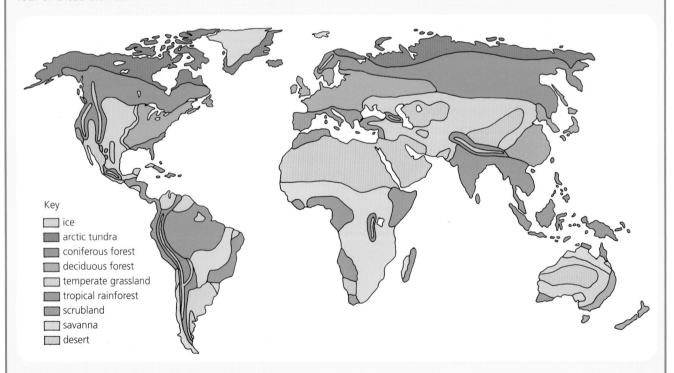

Key
- ice
- arctic tundra
- coniferous forest
- deciduous forest
- temperate grassland
- tropical rainforest
- scrubland
- savanna
- desert

Figure 17.13 Global distribution of terrestrial biomes

Biome	Characteristic abiotic factors	Examples of flora and fauna
tropical rainforest (see Figure 17.14)	high temperature, high rainfall	tall trees, woody vines and bromeliads; many species of tree-living frogs, snakes, lizards, birds and mammals such as monkeys
temperate grassland (see Figure 17.15)	moderate temperature, low to moderate rainfall	many species of grass and other small flowering plants; large grazing mammals, wolves and coyotes
arctic tundra (see Figure 17.16)	low temperature, lack of available water since precipitation is mostly snow	lichens, mosses and grasses; snowshoe hares, ptarmigan and arctic foxes
desert (see Figure 17.17)	high temperature during daylight, low temperature at night; very low rainfall	cacti, deeply-rooted shrubs and thorny bushes; desert rats, scorpions and snakes

Table 17.1 Characteristics of four biomes

Figure 17.16 Arctic tundra biome

Figure 17.14 Tropical rainforest biome

Figure 17.15 Temperate grassland biome

Figure 17.17 Desert biome

Ecosystem

An **ecosystem** comprises two closely interrelated parts:

- the entire **community** of living organisms (plants, animals and micro-organisms) that inhabit a particular area.
- the **abiotic factors** present in that area with which the living things interact and by which they are affected.

Put more simply, an ecosystem consists of a **living community** and its **physical environment**.

Ecosystems range in size from the very small (such as a freshwater pond – see Figure 17.18) to the medium-sized (such as Caledonian forest – see Case Study below) and finally to the very large (such as the arctic tundra biome).

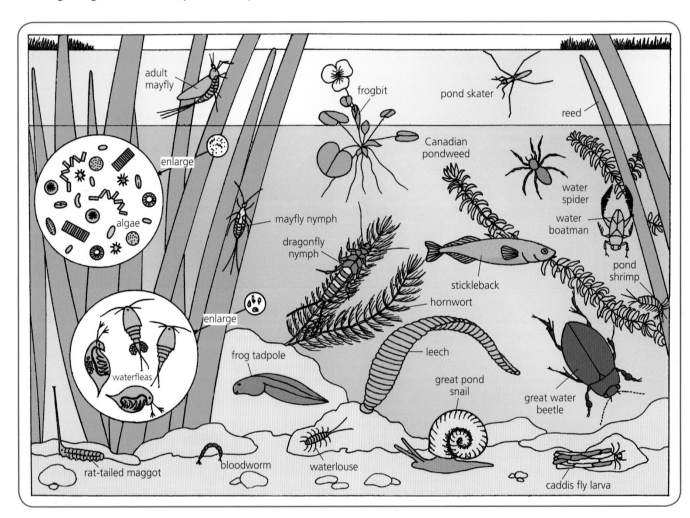

Figure 17.18 Freshwater ecosystem

Case Study | **Caledonian forest ecosystem**

Caledonian forest is a type of ecosystem that once covered large parts of Scotland at the time when trees recolonised the UK after the last ice age. This type of forest is dominated by Scots pine trees but also contains other species of tree such as birch, oak and rowan and smaller plants such as ferns, mosses and lichens.

The 1% of the original native pinewood that survives to the modern day is one of the UK's last remaining wildernesses and it is home to some of the country's rarest wildlife. Some species of bird such as the capercaillie (see Figure 17.19) and Scottish crossbill (see page 154) depend on the Caledonian forest ecosystem as a breeding site and normally fail to breed successfully elsewhere in the UK.

Some birds such as the black grouse and the long-eared owl are rarely found living in ecosystems other than the Caledonian forest. This **unique ecosystem** is also the home of many types of mammal including pine marten, red deer, wildcat, red squirrel and European beaver (recently reintroduced to Scotland). Much of the Caledonian forest ecosystem that remains is protected by law. Furthermore, several projects are under way to regenerate and restore more of the forest in the future.

Figure 17.19 Capercaillie in Caledonian forest

Case Study | Heather moorland

About 12% of Scotland is covered by moorland, much of it dominated by heather plants. A **heather moorland** ecosystem (see Figure 17.20) is characterised by low-growing vegetation that thrives on uncultivated acidic soil in conditions of high rainfall, low temperatures and exposure. In addition to heather, the moor contains a variety of other plants such as grasses, cotton-grass and mosses. It also supports a varied animal community such as red deer, red grouse, lapwing, golden plover, hen harrier (predator of red grouse), adder and many insects.

Management
Traditionally heather moorland has been managed for grouse-shooting and much of the land would

Figure 17.20 Heather moorland ecosystem

eventually revert to woodland if it were not **burned** and **grazed**. The moor is burned in patches every 7–15 years so that it is made up of:

- some areas where tall, unburnt heather plants provide **cover** for red grouse
- some areas where recently burnt heather plants produce **new shoots** as food for adult grouse.

Both fire and limited grazing by sheep maintain the moorland's open character. In addition, sheep droppings act as an energy source for insects that are, in turn, eaten by red grouse chicks.

Decline
In recent years, grouse numbers have decreased and many moorland estates have run at a loss. Instead of being carefully managed for shooting and limited grazing, some moorlands have become coniferous forest plantations or have been over-grazed by sheep and red deer. When moorland is overgrazed, many heather plants are replaced by coarse unpalatable grasses and bracken (see page 155). This leads to **reduced biodiversity** amongst the animal community. Therefore the future of some regions of heather moorland is threatened and they will only survive if the land is carefully managed for grouse-shooting and low-level grazing by sheep.

Niche

An organism's **niche** (more correctly, ecological niche) is the role that it plays within a community. This refers to its **whole way of life** and includes the use that it makes of the resources in its ecosystem and its interactions with other members of the community. A red fox, for example, is a nocturnal predator. Its food includes small mammals, amphibians, insects and fruit, which it finds in the forests, meadows and river banks that make up its natural habitat. The uneaten remains of the fox's prey provide food for members of the community that act as scavengers and decomposers. The fox's live body, in turn, provides a habitat and food supply (blood) for various parasitic insects.

In recent years, the 'urban' red fox has become very successful by adapting to life in many cities and towns. Its niche is different from that of its 'country cousin' in that its food consists largely of materials discarded by humans and its habitat has become city gardens – a constant source of annoyance to many city dwellers who have no prior experience of interacting with the red fox and who regard their gardens as their own private territory.

Related Activity

Investigating examples of niches

Niche of wild cat
The **wild cat** (see Figure 17.21) is a rare Scottish mammal. Normally its habitat is an inaccessible mountainside or a secluded wooded place amongst rocks. It is a **nocturnal predator** most active at dawn and dusk because its sight and hearing are its primary senses when hunting. (It has a poor sense of smell.) Its main food is mountain hare, grouse and rabbit and it will sit and wait patiently above a rabbit's warren for its prey to emerge. When food is scarce it will eat any small mammal or bird that it can catch in addition to fish and insects.

The wild cat has few natural enemies, though pine martens may take its kittens. Its main adversaries are human beings, who have wiped it out almost to extinction because of its tendency to create havoc amongst lambs and poultry. The wild cat's niche also includes playing host to various parasitic worms, ticks and fleas.

Niche of Scottish crossbill
Crossbills are parrot-like finches with a beak in which the upper and lower halves cross over one another. The **Scottish crossbill** (see Figure 17.22) is a rare species of crossbill. Experts estimate that there are only about 2000

Figure 17.21 Wild cat

Figure 17.22 Scottish crossbill

in the population. They are found in the Caledonian forest and nowhere else. They live and breed in this coniferous forest where their niche includes competing with other species of crossbill for resources. The females make use of thin twigs, needles and moss to build untidy nests amongst the evergreen foliage of Scots pine trees where they lay batches of 2–5 eggs.

The Scottish crossbill is a **specialist feeder** and depends on pine, larch and spruce cones for their seeds. It only eats other seeds when cones are scarce. The bird's unusual beak shape is an adaptation that helps it to extract seeds from cones while the cones are still attached to the tree. The crossed bill is used to wrench off the cone's scales. The bird then extracts the seed using its tongue.

The Scottish crossbill may help to disperse some of the conifer seeds around the forest, especially when parent birds are collecting many seeds to feed their young. The bird's natural enemies include the pine marten, which raids nests and eats eggs and nestlings.

Niche of bracken

Bracken (see Figure 17.23) is the most common fern in the UK. It plays host to a varied community of animals. For example, it provides **food** for the larvae of many butterflies and moths and a **habitat** for the sheep tick, which carries the micro-organism responsible for Lyme disease. Several types of bird including the skylark are found to nest in bracken and use it for **cover**. Adders may even be found basking on bracken on a sunny day. In the absence of woodland, bracken often provides a **canopy** for shade plants such as bluebell and wood anemone and several types of woodland fungi.

Figure 17.23 Bracken

However, bracken produces and releases **poisonous chemicals**. This characteristic enables it to dominate an ecosystem (especially during regrowth after a fire), prevent tree seedlings from growing and choke out rival plants. Normally bracken is not trampled down by cattle or horses because it is poisonous to these animals and farmers try to prevent them from coming into contact with it.

Bracken is a **versatile plant** that can tolerate a range of soil pH from 2.8 to 8.6 (though it does not thrive on marshy soil). It survives adverse conditions by means of **underground stems**, some of which act as storage organs and others as collections of frond (leaf)-forming buds. It is such a successful plant that in many areas it has managed to spread from its traditional hillside habitat to heather moorland, grassland and wooded areas. Livestock farmers regard its continued invasion of pastureland as a major problem.

Related Activity

Analysing data related to distribution of ptarmigan

The **ptarmigan** (see Figure 17.24) is a plump game bird that lives and breeds in remote mountainous areas. Figure 17.25 shows the results from a recent survey. The managers of many estates in mountainous regions were asked to report whether or not the abundance and distribution of ptarmigan in their area had changed in the previous 25 years.

In regions 2 and 4, only 50% or less of estates reported an increase in ptarmigan abundance and distribution and no estates in regions 1, 3 or 5 reported an increase. In

Figure 17.24 Ptarmigan

Figure 17.25 Analysis of ptarmigan survey

regions 1 and 3, 60% or more of the estates reported the situation to be unchanged but in regions 2, 4 and 5, 30% or less of estates reported no change. In region 5, 75% of estates reported a decrease in ptarmigans and in all other regions a smaller percentage of estates also reported a decrease.

Testing Your Knowledge

1 a) In general, what is the difference between a *biotic* and an *abiotic* factor that can affect biodiversity? (2)

   b) Organise the following factors into two groups – biotic and abiotic: pH, competition, food supply, light intensity, predation, temperature, disease, grazing, rainfall. (2)

2 a) Distinguish between the terms *biodiversity* and *biome*. (2)

   b) Give THREE examples of terrestrial biomes. (3)

   c) Identify TWO abiotic factors that can influence the global distribution of biomes. (2)

3 a) Of what TWO interrelated parts does an ecosystem consist? (2)

   b) What is the difference between an organism's *community* and its *niche*? (2)

Energy flow in a food chain

A **food chain** is a relationship where one organism feeds on the previous one in the series and in turn provides food for the next one. A food chain begins with a **producer** (a green plant able to produce food by photosynthesis). Each arrow in a food chain indicates the direction of **energy flow**. When the plant is eaten by an animal (the **primary consumer**), energy is transferred from the plant to the animal. When this first animal is eaten by a second animal (the **secondary consumer**) energy is again transferred and so on through a series of organisms, as shown in Figure 18.1.

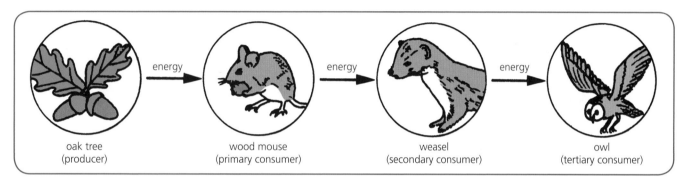

oak tree
(producer)

wood mouse
(primary consumer)

weasel
(secondary consumer)

owl
(tertiary consumer)

Figure 18.1 Food chain

Energy loss

As energy flows through a food chain or web, a progressive **loss** of about 90% occurs at each level for two reasons.

Firstly, an organism uses energy to build its body. However, this may include parts such as cellulose cell walls or bone or skin or horns that, when eaten by the next consumer, may turn out to have little or no nutritional value. These parts tend therefore to be left uneaten by the next consumer or to be expelled undigested as faeces. As a result, energy is lost from the food chain. Some of this energy is, however, gained by the ecosystem's decomposers (see page 158).

Secondly, most of the energy gained by a consumer in its food is used for **moving** about and, in warm-blooded animals, for keeping warm. Much energy is therefore **lost** as heat and only about 10% on average of the energy taken in by an organism is incorporated into its body tissues. Figure 18.2 shows the fate of energy as it is transferred along a marine food chain. Figure 18.3 shows an alternative way of presenting this information involving the flow and loss of energy in an ecosystem

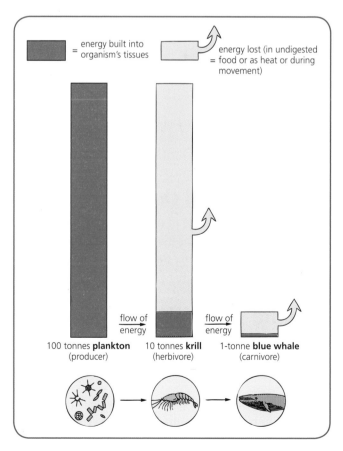

= energy built into organism's tissues

= energy lost (in undigested food or as heat or during movement)

flow of energy

flow of energy

100 tonnes **plankton**
(producer)

10 tonnes **krill**
(herbivore)

1-tonne **blue whale**
(carnivore)

Figure 18.2 Energy loss in a food chain

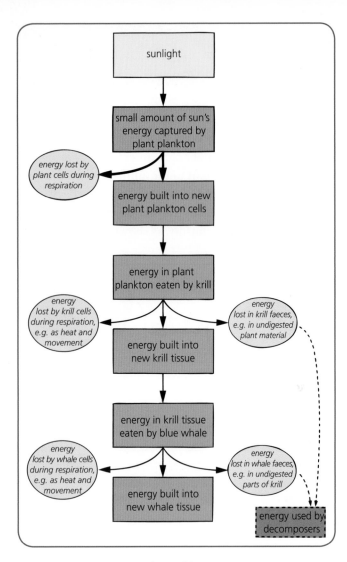

Figure 18.3 Energy transfer and loss

This numerical relationship is called a **pyramid of numbers** and is often illustrated in the form shown in Figure 18.4.

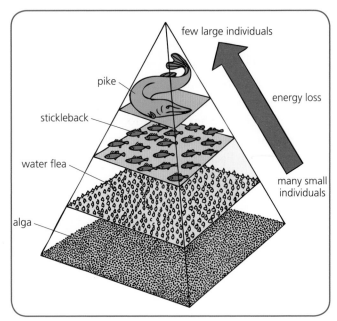

Figure 18.4 Pyramid of numbers

The relationship takes the form of a pyramid because:

- the **energy loss** at each link in the food chain limits the quantity of living matter that can be supported at the next level
- the final consumer tends to be **larger** in body size than the one below it, and so on.

A simpler way of representing a pyramid of numbers is shown in Figure 18.5.

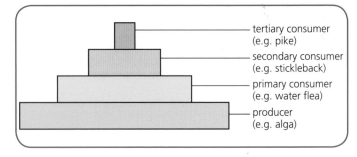

Figure 18.5 Pyramid of numbers (alternative style)

Length of a food chain

More efficient use is made of food plants by humans consuming them **directly** rather than first converting them into animal products, since this cuts out at least one of the energy-losing stages in the food chain.

Pyramid of numbers

Consider the following food chain:

alga → water flea → stickleback → pike

In terms of numbers, the producers (the algae) are found to be the most numerous followed by the primary consumers and so on along the chain, with the final consumer being the least numerous.

Pyramid of biomass

The **biomass** of a population is its total mass of living matter. In a food chain the biomass of the producer is greater than that of the primary consumer, which in turn is greater than that of the secondary consumer and so on along the chain. Since biomass decreases at each level, it can also be represented as a pyramid.

Figure 18.6 shows a **pyramid of biomass** for a rocky shore ecosystem where the average mass of dry material per square metre (g/m²) has been calculated.

Pyramid of energy

A more reliable comparison between the organisms found at the different levels in a food chain can be made based on **productivity**. This is measured as grams of dry mass per square metre per year and then converted into its energy equivalent in kilojoules per square metre per year. The results are used to construct a **pyramid of energy**, which illustrates the energy content at each level and the transfer of energy from one level to another. Figure 18.7 shows a pyramid of energy for a river ecosystem.

True pyramid

A pyramid of numbers may take an irregular shape because it is based on different body sizes (see the Related Activity below). However, when any pyramid

Figure 18.6 Pyramid of biomass

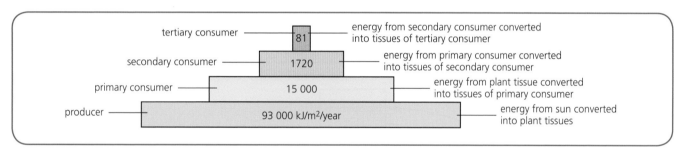

Figure 18.7 Pyramid of energy

Related Activity

Investigating irregular pyramids of numbers

Tree as producer

In some food chains the producer is a **single large plant** and the 'pyramid' therefore takes a different form. Figure 18.8, for example, shows the irregular pyramid of numbers for the food chain:

oak tree → caterpillar → shrew → owl

Figure 18.8 Pyramid with large single producer

Parasite as final consumer

In some food chains, the final consumer consists of a **large population of tiny parasites** and the 'pyramid' takes a different form. Figure 18.9 shows the irregular pyramid of numbers for the food chain:

grass → gazelle → lion → flea

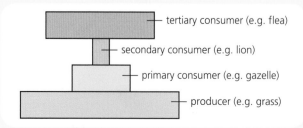

Figure 18.9 Pyramid with a large population of parasites

Testing Your Knowledge 1

1 Describe TWO ways in which energy may be lost from a food chain. (2)
2 a) Copy the pyramid of numbers shown in Figure 18.10 and complete it using the following organisms: *water flea, pike, alga, stickleback*. (2)
  b) Which of these organisms is the secondary consumer? (1)
  c) Which population of organisms in this pyramid contains most energy? (1)
  d) Give ONE reason why the numbers decrease towards the top of a normal, regular pyramid of numbers. (1)
3 Give the meanings of the terms *pyramid of biomass* and *pyramid of energy*. (2)

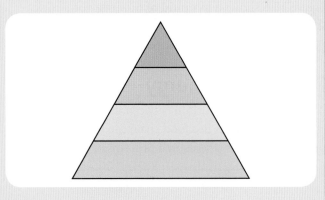

Figure 18.10

of numbers, regular or irregular, is represented as a pyramid of energy, it takes the form of a **true pyramid** because only a proportion of energy (about 10%) is successfully transferred from one level to the next.

Nitrogen cycle

About 80% of air consists of nitrogen gas. All living things need nitrogen to make protein. However, plants and animals cannot make use of nitrogen gas directly. Plants absorb nitrogen from the soil in the form of

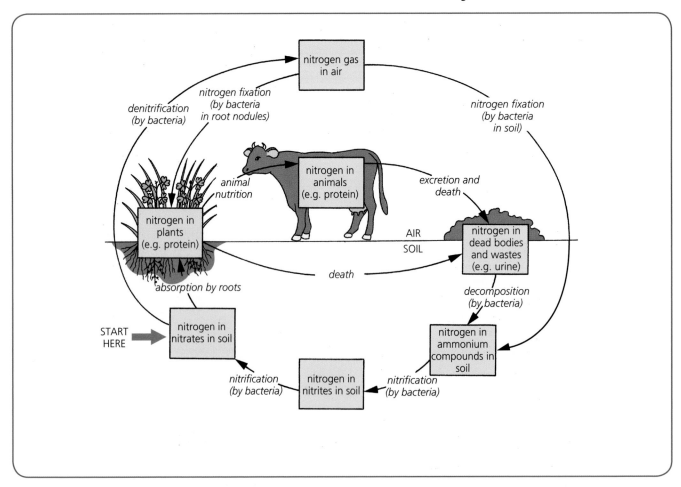

Figure 18.11 Nitrogen cycle

nitrate. Animals must eat plant or animal **protein** to obtain their supply of nitrogen. Nitrogen is a chemical element that is **cycled** around an ecosystem. Figure 18.11 shows the sequence of the main processes that occur during the **nitrogen cycle**.

Action of bacteria

The nitrogen cycle is dependent on the activities of several different types of **bacteria**, each playing a key role as indicated by the numbered arrows in Figure 18.12.

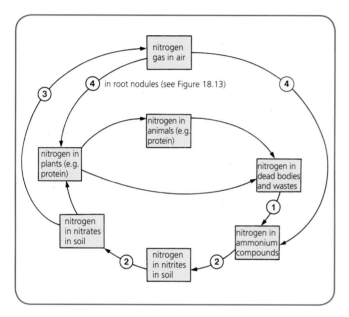

Figure 18.12 Role of bacteria in nitrogen cycle

- At arrow 1, decomposer bacteria bring about the decomposition of dead bodies and **nitrogenous waste**, releasing **ammonium compounds** into the soil.
- The arrows marked 2 represent the process of **nitrification**. This is brought about by nitrifying bacteria converting ammonium compounds to **nitrites** and then further nitrifying bacteria converting the nitrites to **nitrates** that can be used by plants.
- Arrow 3 represents the process of **denitrification**. Denitrifying bacteria deprive the soil of nitrogenous compounds by breaking down nitrates and releasing **nitrogen gas** into the air.
- This loss is compensated for by the activities of bacteria at the two arrows marked 4, which bring about **nitrogen fixation**. Free-living soil bacteria absorb **atmospheric nitrogen** and 'fix' it into **ammonium compounds**. Other bacteria live inside swellings called **nodules** on the roots of

leguminous plants such as pea, bean and clover (see Figure 18.13). These bacteria also absorb nitrogen gas from the air and 'fix' it into a form that the plant can use to build protein. It is for this reason that leguminous plants are able to thrive in soil deficient in nitrogenous compounds.

Without the activities of all these different types of bacteria, the nitrogen cycle would not turn and life on Earth would come to a halt.

Fertilisers

Many types of **fertiliser** contain **nitrate** to enrich the soil and bring about an increased yield of crops.

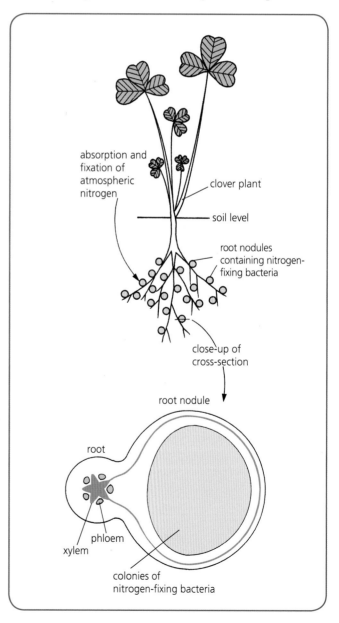

Figure 18.13 Root nodules

Competition in ecosystems

Competition occurs in an ecosystem whenever two or more members of the community need a particular **resource** that is in **short supply**. For example, green plants may compete for light, water and soil nutrients; animals may compete for water, food and nesting sites.

Interspecific and intraspecific competition

Interspecific competition occurs when members of **different** species compete for the same resource(s) in an ecosystem. **Intraspecific** competition occurs when the members of the **same** species compete for exactly the same resources in an ecosystem. Intraspecific competition is often even more intense than interspecific competition because the competing individuals have identical needs.

Evolutionary effect of intraspecific competition

Intraspecific competition regulates the size of the population of the species affected. The weaker members are weeded out by **natural selection** (see page 181).

Feeding in grasshoppers

Unlike territorial birds that interact with one another when competing for a scarce resource such as territory (see page 164), grasshoppers do not interact directly. When they do have to compete intraspecifically for a scarce resource such as a limited supply of grass, their effect on one another is indirect by adversely affecting one another's growth and reproduction.

Related Activity

Investigating interspecific competition

When two different species occupy the same ecological niche, competition may become so fierce that one species tends to force the other out.

Squirrels

The introduction of the North American **grey squirrel** (see Figure 18.14) to Britain has resulted in the widespread decline (almost to extinction) of the **red squirrel**. Both types of squirrel occupy a similar ecological niche in the woodland ecosystem. The grey squirrel is thought to have become so widely distributed and successful because it competes aggressively for food and is able to make use

of a wide variety of foodstuffs including acorns (despite their high tannin content). The grey squirrel is therefore continuing to populate areas at the expense of the more timid red squirrel whose digestive system cannot cope with large quantities of acorns and other seeds rich in tannins.

Trout

A similar situation is developing in some river ecosystems. **Rainbow trout** (see Figure 18.15) that have been introduced from North America are invading the river habitat of the native **brown trout**. The American fish are more aggressive and greedy for food. The fierce competition that has resulted is forcing the brown trout into decline.

Figure 18.14 Red squirrel and grey squirrel

Figure 18.15 Rainbow trout

Related Activity

Investigating intraspecific competition in plants

Plants of the same species have exactly the same growth requirements. When grown together, they will be in direct competition with one another if any resource is limiting and this competition will be intense.

Oak trees

The oak trees shown in Figure 18.16 are in direct competition for water, soil nutrients and light. The young plant in the centre of the picture is being shaded out by its elders and is unlikely to survive in this example of intraspecific competition.

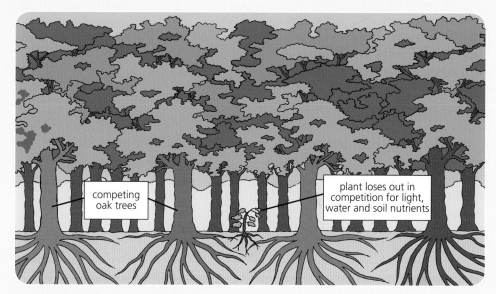

competing oak trees

plant loses out in competition for light, water and soil nutrients

Figure 18.16 Intraspecific competition in oak trees

Cress seedlings

The experiment shown in Figure 18.17 is set up to investigate the effect of density on germinating cress seeds. Carton A, with only 100 seeds, represents low density of planting; carton B, with 500 seeds, represents high density. After 5 days, almost all the seeds in A are found to have successfully germinated and grown into healthy seedlings. Although most of the seeds in B also germinate, many fail to grow into healthy plants and remain yellow and sickly. Of the seedlings that do grow successfully, most are found to be smaller than their counterparts in A.

From this experiment it is concluded that the spaced out plants in carton A grow well because each plant receives an adequate supply of each growth requirement. In carton B where the seedlings are densely packed, much of the light that might have reached each plant is intercepted by the leaves of other plants so that on average each plant receives less light for photosynthesis. In addition their rooting systems become interwoven and may be competing for water.

If a plant is short of water, its stomata stay closed for a longer time and carbon dioxide uptake needed for

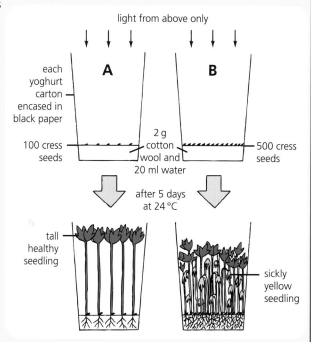

light from above only

each yoghurt carton encased in black paper

A   **B**

100 cress seeds

2 g cotton wool and 20 ml water

500 cress seeds

after 5 days at 24 °C

tall healthy seedling

sickly yellow seedling

Figure 18.17 Investigating intraspecific competition

photosynthesis is reduced. Thus intraspecific competition between densely populated plants results in many individuals growing more slowly.

Investigating intraspecific competition in animals

Territorial behaviour

Intraspecific competition in animals often takes the form of **territoriality**. This is the name given to behaviour that involves competition between members of the same species (especially birds) for territories. An animal's total **range** is the area that it covers during its lifetime. Within this range a male animal often establishes and inhabits a smaller area called its **territory**, which contains enough food for himself and eventually a mate and their young.

Robin

Robins defend their territory fiercely using **social signals** (sign stimuli) as shown in Figures 18.18 and 18.19. They are most aggressive at the centre of their territory. The further they move away from the centre, the less likely they are to attack intruders.

Red grouse

The red grouse (see Figure 18.20) lives on moorland and feeds on the shoot tips and flowers of heather plants. Young heather plants are more nutritious than older ones. Rather than compete directly for food, the male red grouse claims a territory large enough to provide food for his dependants during the breeding season.

Territorial size varies depending on the availability of food. Each enclosed space in Figure 18.21 represents

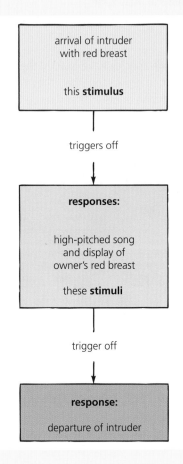

arrival of intruder with red breast

this **stimulus**

triggers off

responses:

high-pitched song and display of owner's red breast

these **stimuli**

trigger off

response:

departure of intruder

Figure 18.19 Flow chart of territorial behaviour

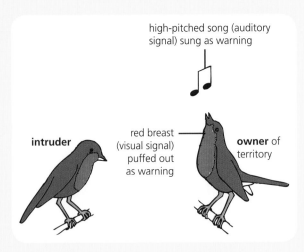

high-pitched song (auditory signal) sung as warning

intruder

red breast (visual signal) puffed out as warning

owner of territory

Figure 18.18 Territorial behaviour in robins

Figure 18.20 Red grouse

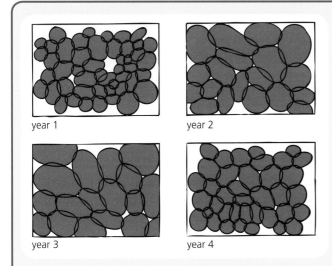

year 1   year 2

year 3   year 4

Figure 18.21 Sizes of red grouse territories

a red grouse's territory on the same piece of moorland over a period of 4 years. During years 1 and 4, food was plentiful and the birds only needed to defend small territories. During years 2 and 3, the heather was poor and a larger territory was required to supply a bird's needs. When times were lean, intraspecific competition was more intense and weaker birds that failed to establish a territory did not breed.

Advantages of territorial behaviour

Once territories have been established, aggression between neighbours is reduced to a minimum and **energy** is saved. Territorial behaviour **spaces out** the population in relation to the available food supply. This ensures that there will be enough food for the number of young produced.

Testing Your Knowledge 2

1 a) Which type of nitrogenous substance is absorbed by plants and used to make protein? (1)
   b) Explain the difference between the processes of *nitrification* and *denitrification* in the nitrogen cycle. (3)
   c) By what means do the colonies of bacteria in root nodules benefit leguminous plants? (2)

2 a) Under what conditions does competition between organisms occur? (1)
   b) Name TWO resources for which:
      i) plants and
      ii) animals could be competing. (4)

3 a) Explain the difference between *intraspecific* and *interspecific* competition. (1)
   b) Explain why competition between members of the same species is likely to be more intense than that between members of two different species. (1)

19 Sampling techniques and measurements

Practical investigation of an ecosystem

The study of an ecosystem involves:

- finding out which plants and animals live there
- finding out how abundant (rare, common, etc.) these organisms are
- investigating the reasons why the organisms live there.

Sampling the organisms in an ecosystem

It is rarely possible to count all of the plants and animals in an ecosystem because this would take too long and would probably cause permanent damage to the ecosystem. Instead, small **samples** that represent the whole ecosystem are taken. To make the procedure **valid**, each sampling unit must be **equal in size** and be chosen at random (so that the results are not biased). From the samples an estimate of an organism's **abundance** for the whole ecosystem can be calculated.

Quantitative techniques for measuring biotic factors

The use of **pitfall traps** and **quadrats** are two of the many different quantitative techniques for sampling and counting the organisms in a particular ecosystem.

Pitfall trap

Table 19.1 summarises the use of a **pitfall trap** for trapping and counting the numbers and types of animal present in a soil ecosystem such as the one shown in Figure 19.3.

Figure 19.1 Pitfall trap

Figure 19.2 Improved pitfall trap

Ecosystem	Sampling technique	Possible sources of error	Ways in which errors may be minimised
soil	trapping using a **pitfall trap** (see Figure 19.1) (this operates on the basis that animals that are active on the soil surface will fall into the trap and be unable to climb out again)	the numbers and types of animals may not be representative of the ecosystem as a whole (this source of error is true of all sampling techniques)	set up several traps (replication makes the results more reliable)
		birds may eat trapped animals	disguise the opening with a lid such as a leaf supported on sticks (see Figure 19.2)
		some animals may eat the others	check traps regularly or put preservative liquid such as 50% ethanol in the bottom of the traps

Table 19.1 Pitfall trapping technique

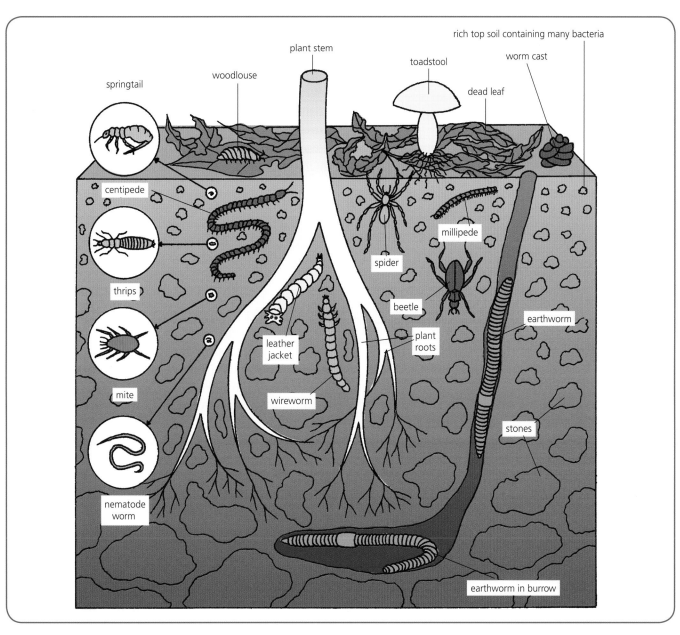

Figure 19.3 Soil ecosystem

Quadrats

A further method of sampling uses quadrats. A **quadrat** is a rectangular-shaped sampling unit of known area. Its frame is normally made of wood, metal or string. This form of sampling is often used to estimate the numbers of plants in an ecosystem (or slow-moving animals such as shellfish on a rocky shore).

Estimating the total number of thistles in a field

Figure 19.4 shows a quadrat that encloses an area of 1 square metre. The sites for several quadrats (say ten)

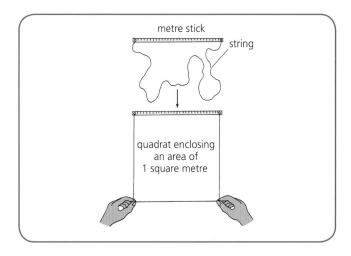

Figure 19.4 Quadrat

are chosen at random (see Figure 19.5) and the number of thistles present in each quadrat is counted. From this information the average number of thistles per square metre is calculated. The length and breadth of the field is measured and its area calculated. An estimate of the total number of thistles in the field is then worked out.

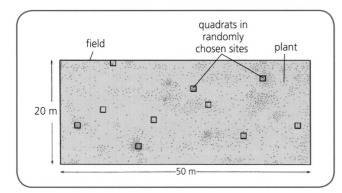

Figure 19.5 Sampling a field

Example of calculation

Table 19.2 shows a typical set of results.

Quadrat	Number of thistles
1	11
2	0
3	5
4	15
5	1
6	7
7	3
8	7
9	9
10	4

Table 19.2 Quadrat results

Total number of thistles in ten quadrats = 62

Average number of thistles per quadrat
(i.e. per m²) = 62/10 = 6.2

Total area of field
(length × breadth) = 50 m × 20 m = 1000 m²

Estimate of total number of thistles in
field = 6.2 × 1000 = 6200 thistles

Possible sources of error

Number of quadrats

Ten quadrats may be too small a number of samples to give a fair representation of the number of plants present in the ecosystem. This is especially likely if the plant being investigated tends to grow in clusters. Most or all of the quadrats might just happen to land in positions where none of the plants under investigation grow (see Figure 19.6).

In or out?

Some of the type of plant being considered might be located partly inside and partly outside a quadrat. Should they be included in the count or not?

Ways in which errors may be minimised

A much larger number of quadrats could be studied by the class working as, say, ten groups with each group doing ten quadrats and the whole class pooling their results. This would improve the **reliability** of the results and therefore give a more accurate representation of the number of plants present.

A basic rule could be established and followed by everyone involved (see Figure 19.7). Any plant partly in and partly out falling on the bottom or left-hand side of the quadrat counts as in, whereas any plant on the top or right-hand side counts as out.

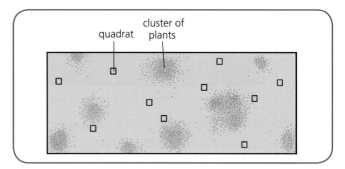

Figure 19.6 Too few quadrats

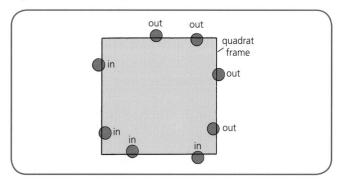

Figure 19.7 In or out?

Measuring abundance of plant types

The **abundance** of a plant type is a measure of the extent to which it occurs in an environment. For example, one type of plant might be found to occur frequently and another only rarely in an ecosystem. Abundance can be measured using the type of quadrat shown in Figure 19.8.

Figure 19.8 Frame quadrat

The quadrat is placed at randomly chosen sites in the ecosystem being studied. The number of squares that contain the type of plant being investigated is counted

(up to a maximum of 25). This method does not involve counting the number of plants. Figure 19.9 shows an example. The abundance of plantains = 3 (out of 25), dandelions = 5, buttercups = 8 and grass = 24.

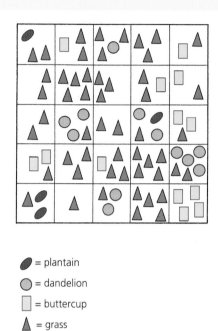

= plantain
= dandelion
= buttercup
= grass

Figure 19.9 Measuring abundance

Further techniques for biotic factors

Use of a Tullgren funnel

A **Tullgren funnel** (see Figure 19.10) is used to extract tiny animals that live in the soil's air spaces. The animals in the soil sample move down and away from the hot, dry, bright conditions created by the light bulb and fall through the sieve into the water below.

Pond netting

The **net** (see Figure 19.11) is moved rapidly through the water, catching animals that are quickly transferred to screw-top jars containing pond water. When investigating the bottom of the pond, the handle of the net is rotated as shown in Figure 19.12. This keeps the net closed on

the way down and on the way back up again. It prevents entry of surface animals and escape of animals collected at the bottom.

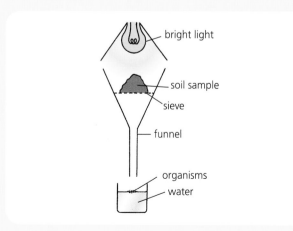

bright light

soil sample

sieve

funnel

organisms
water

Figure 19.10 Tullgren funnel

Figure 19.11 Net

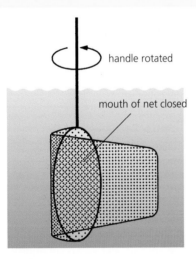

Figure 19.12 Careful use of net

Tree beating

A branch of a tree is held over a tray and given a few sharp taps with a **walking stick,** as shown in Figure 19.13. Small organisms that fall onto the tray are transferred to a large plastic bag. Back in the laboratory, a **pooter** (see Figure 19.14) is used to trap animals for close inspection.

Figure 19.13 Tree beating

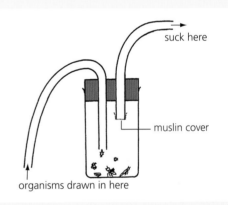

Figure 19.14 Pooter

Identifying the organisms collected

Each organism can be identified by comparing it to pictures in a suitable book. However, this method can take a very long time. A much better method is to use a **key**. A key may be branched or in the form of paired statements. Figures 19.15 and 19.16 give keys to animals commonly found in soil and pond ecosystems. (After identification organisms should be returned to their natural habitats so that as little disturbance as possible is caused to the ecosystem.)

1	body has no legs	go to 2
	body has legs	go to 6
2	body not divided into sections (segments)	go to 3
	body divided into segments	go to 5
3	body worm-like	**nematode worm** (a)
	body not worm-like	go to 4
4	shell present	**snail** (b)
	no shell present	**slug** (c)
5	no more than 13 segments present	**fly maggot** (d)
	more than 13 segments present	**earthworm** (e)
6	6 jointed legs present	go to 7
	more than 6 jointed legs present	go to 11
7	grub-like insect	go to 8
	adult insect	go to 9
8	non-jointed legs present on abdomen	**caterpillar** (f)
	non-jointed legs absent from abdomen	**beetle larva** (g)
9	thin waist between thorax and abdomen	**ant** (h)
	no thin waist between thorax and abdomen	go to 10
10	spring attached to abdomen	**springtail** (i)
	no spring attached to abdomen	**beetle** (j)
11	8 legs present	go to 12
	more than 8 legs present	go to 13
12	body divided into 2 parts	**spider** (k)
	body not divided into 2 parts	**mite** (l)
13	14 legs present	**woodlouse** (m)
	more than 14 legs present	go to 14
14	each body segment has 1 pair of legs	**centipede** (n)
	each body segment has 2 pairs of legs	**millipede** (o)

(not drawn to scale)

Figure 19.15 Key to soil animals

| 1 | shell present | go to 2 |
| | shell absent | go to 3 |

(a)

| 2 | shell made of 2 halves | **freshwater mussel** (a) |
| | shell made of 1 part | **pond snail** (b) |

(b)

| 3 | body not divided into segments | go to 4 |
| | body divided into segments | go to 5 |

(c)

| 4 | body threadlike | **nematode worm** (c) |
| | body flat | **flatworm** (d) |

(d)

| 5 | no obvious jointed legs present | go to 6 |
| | jointed legs present | go to 8 |

(e)

| 6 | feelers and tail hooks present | **midge larva ('bloodworm')** (e) |
| | no feelers or tail hooks present | go to 7 |

(f)

| 7 | suckers present at both ends | **leech** (f) |
| | no suckers present | **freshwater worm ('redworm')** (g) |

(g)

| 8 | 6 legs present | go to 9 |
| | more than 6 legs present | go to 13 |

(h)

| 9 | lives in protective tube | **caddis fly larva** (h) |
| | free living | go to 10 |

(i)

| 10 | 2 pairs of wings present | go to 11 |
| | no wings present | go to 12 |

(j)

| 11 | large dark body, threadlike feelers present | **water beetle** (i) |
| | small light body, no threadlike feelers present | **water boatman** (j) |

(k)

| 12 | 2 tail appendages ('prongs') present | **stonefly** (k) |
| | 3 tail appendages ('prongs') present | **mayfly nymph** (l) |

(l)

| 13 | 8 legs present | go to 14 |
| | more than 8 legs present | go to 15 |

(m)

(n)

| 14 | small body in 1 part | **water mite** (m) |
| | large body in 2 parts | **water spider** (n) |

(o)

| 15 | body flattened downwards like a woodlouse | **waterlouse** (o) |
| | body flattened sideways, gills on front legs | **freshwater shrimp** (p) |

(p)

(not drawn to scale)

Figure 19.16 Key to pond animals

Abiotic factors

Abiotic factors are non-living factors present in an ecosystem such as light intensity, temperature, soil moisture and pH (see Appendix 2). A living organism is only able to survive in a certain habitat and play its part in an ecosystem if a combination of abiotic factors suited to its needs is present there.

Measuring abiotic factors

Light intensity

Light intensity can be measured using the **light meter** part of a light/moisture meter (see Figure 19.17). The switch on the meter is set at the light meter position. The meter is held so that the **light sensitive panel** is directed towards the light source to be measured. The reading is taken from the light intensity scale once the pointer has stopped moving. All measurements are taken as near the same time as possible during a period of constant light intensity so that a comparison between readings at different locations is valid.

Figure 19.17 Light/moisture meter

Soil moisture content

Soil moisture content can be measured using the **moisture meter** part of a light/moisture meter. The switch on the meter is set at the moisture meter position. The **moisture probe** is pushed into the soil to a depth of 40 mm. The reading is taken from the moisture meter scale once the pointer has stopped moving. The probe is wiped with a tissue between samples to prevent moisture from one reading affecting the next one.

Temperature

A **thermometer** or a **temperature probe** can be used to measure the temperature of soil or of pond water, for example. The probe may be linked to appropriate data-logging software on a computer.

pH

A **pH meter** can be used to measure the pH (acidity or alkalinity) of soil (or pond water). The meter's probe is inserted into the soil and it is connected to data-logging software on a computer. Alternatively the pH of soil can be tested using the apparatus shown in Figure 19.18. The tube is shaken vigorously and then allowed to settle. A clear zone of liquid appears and its colour is compared with a chart of pH colours to identify the soil's pH.

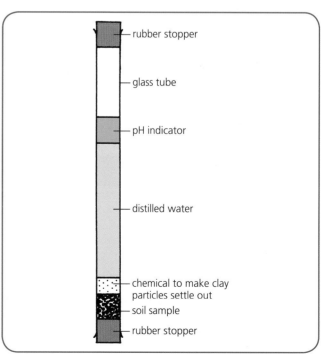

Figure 19.18 Measuring pH of soil

Related Activity

Investigating the effect of light intensity on distribution of daisies

In this investigation the area being studied contains a grassy field and part of an oak wood. On a sunny day the abiotic factor (light intensity) shows a wide range of variation from high in the middle of the field to low in the wood. To investigate if light intensity affects the distribution of daisy plants, a **line (belt) transect** is set up, as shown in Figure 19.19. A length of string is pegged from point X in the field to point Y in the wood. The string has been marked in advance at 1 metre intervals, giving ten sample sites.

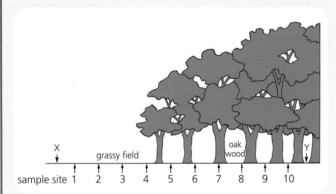

Figure 19.19 Line transect

A quadrat of the type used to measure abundance (see Figures 19.8 and 19.9 on page 169) is placed at each sample site and the number of squares containing daisies is counted. The light meter part of the meter shown in Figure 19.17 is used to measure the light intensity at each sample site. Table 19.3 gives a typical set of results. The results show that the daisies are most abundant in light of high intensity and become less frequent as light intensity decreases.

Possible mechanism determining distribution of daisies

Daisies are green plants that make their food by photosynthesis using light energy. In conditions of low light intensity, it is possible that they are unable to obtain sufficient light energy to produce food. They are therefore unable to survive in the dimly lit conditions in the oak wood. This investigation suggests that the abiotic factor, **light intensity**, determines the distribution of daisies. However, it is possible that other abiotic factors such as soil moisture content or soil pH could also be playing a part in their distribution.

Sample site	1	2	3	4	5	6	7	8	9	10
Abundance of daisies (score out of 25)	19	20	18	21	12	8	4	1	0	0
Light intensity (A = low, H = high)	H	H	H	H	G	F	E	D	C	C

Table 19.3 Abundance of daisies

Testing Your Knowledge

1 a) Name a technique that could be used to sample the invertebrate animals living in a garden's soil. (1)
  b) Name the apparatus that you would use and describe how you would use it. (2)
  c) i) Identify a possible source of error when using this technique.
    ii) State how this error could be minimised. (2)

2 a) Name a technique that could be used to estimate the total number of dandelion plants in a large patch of grass. (1)
  b) Describe how you would use the apparatus. (2)

  c) i) Identify a possible source of error when using this technique.
    ii) State how this error could be minimised. (2)

3 a) Describe how a light/moisture meter could be used to measure:
    i) light intensity
    ii) soil moisture content. (4)
  b) Identify a precaution that should be adopted in each case so that a comparison between readings at different locations is valid. (2)

What You Should Know Chapters 17 -19

abiotic	decreases	nitrogen
ammonium	ecosystem	numbers
animals	energy	pH
bacteria	heat	pitfall
base	human	predation
biomass	interspecific	protein
biomes	intraspecific	pyramid
biotic	level	quadrats
chain	light	rainfall
climate	many	sampling
community	meters	temperature
consumer	niche	transfer
decomposers	nitrification	valid

1 Biodiversity in an ecosystem can be affected by _____ and abiotic factors and _____ influences that can increase or decrease it.

2 Biotic factors such as grazing and _____ are caused by living things; abiotic factors such as pH and _____ are non-living.

3 Various large regions of the Earth, distinguished by their _____ and native plants and _____, are called _____. Their global distribution can be affected by _____ and temperature.

4 An _____ is made up of a community of living organisms and the non-living factors with which they interact. A _____ is the role that an organism plays within a _____.

5 About 90% of _____ is lost at each level in a food _____ as undigested material or as _____ or during movement. Some of the energy in waste material is gained by the ecosystem's _____.

6 A pyramid of _____ illustrates the numerical relationship between the organisms in a food chain, with the producer (the most numerous) at the _____ and the final _____ (the least numerous) at the top.

7 A pyramid of _____ shows that the producer at the base has the greatest biomass and that this _____, level by level, to the final consumer, which has the smallest biomass.

8 A _____ of energy illustrates the energy content at each _____ in a food chain and the _____ of energy from one level to another.

9 _____ is cycled round ecosystems. Nitrate absorbed by plants is made into plant _____, which becomes converted to animal protein on being consumed.

10 Several different types of _____ play essential roles in the nitrogen cycle by bringing about the processes of _____, nitrogen-fixation and the decomposition of wastes to _____ compounds.

11 When competition for the same resource(s) occurs between individuals of different species in an ecosystem, it is called _____ competition and when it occurs between individuals of the same species it is called _____ competition.

12 Biologists investigate an ecosystem's community by _____ its plants and animals. To do this, they often use quantitative techniques such as _____ traps and _____.

13 For sampling to give a _____ representation of the community, _____ samples must be taken and mean results calculated.

14 An ecosystem is affected by many _____ factors including _____ intensity, temperature, moisture content and _____. These can be measured using appropriate _____ and probes linked to computer software.

20 Adaptation, natural selection and evolution

Mutation

A **mutation** is a change in the structure or composition of an organism's genetic material. If such a change in genotype produces a change in phenotype, the affected individual (such as the albino ivy plant shown in Figure 20.1) is called a **mutant**. In the absence of outside influences, mutations arise spontaneously and at random but only rarely.

Mutagenic agents

The mutation rate of a gene is expressed as the number of mutations that occur at that gene site per million gametes. The normal spontaneous rate of mutation can be increased by exposing cells to **mutagenic agents**. These are environmental factors such as some types of radiation and certain chemicals.

Figure 20.1 Albino ivy plant

Research Topic | Mutagenic agents

Mutagenic agents can be used by geneticists to try to create **new mutant varieties** of organism that are useful to humans. For example, the exposure of an enormous number of plants to X-rays occasionally produces an improved variety such as:

- a mutant strain of barley with an upright growth form that is resistant to heavy rain
- a mutant type of rice plant that shows improved hardiness to cold.

However, for the most part, mutagenic agents are **environmental hazards** that damage the genetic material of living things. In the experiment shown in Figure 20.2 an increased level of radiation brings about an increased rate of mutation but no new improved varieties are formed.

Mutagenic agents fall into three categories as follows.

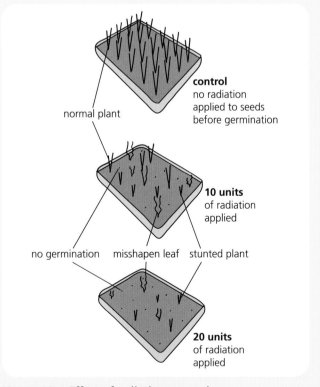

Figure 20.2 Effect of radiation on seeds

Ionising radiation

This group includes **X-rays** and radiation such as alpha, beta and gamma rays from **radioactive sources**. These rays damage genetic material directly by breaking it up. Occasional exposure of an individual's cells to X-rays for medical purposes is not harmful. However, the radiographer operating the equipment is at risk of frequent exposure and must be protected (for example, by a lead screen).

High levels of radiation from the fallout of a **nuclear bomb** or following an accident at a **nuclear power station** are seriously harmful or even lethal. The incidence of many forms of cancer (caused by mutations affecting stem cells) rose dramatically amongst the population living close to the Chernobyl nuclear power station in Ukraine following the disastrous accident that occurred there in 1986. Figure 20.3 shows one of the victims after thyroid cancer surgery.

Figure 20.3 Victim of Chernobyl disaster

Ultraviolet radiation

This form of radiation is also known as **UV light**. It is absorbed by some of the bases in DNA, which then become altered and linked together. Potentially this has a disruptive effect on the functioning of the DNA. However, in the absence of UV light, the linked bases are returned to normal by the action of **repair enzymes**.

Some people do not possess the correct allele of the gene that codes for one of the repair enzymes and may therefore develop **skin cancer** if exposed to high levels of ultraviolet radiation for prolonged periods. It is for this reason that people are advised to use a barrier cream with a high protection factor when sunbathing.

Chemical mutagens

Mustard gas is an example of a chemical mutagen. It acts by affecting one of the bases in DNA and making the molecule become unstable and ineffective. Mustard gas was first used as a chemical weapon in the First World War. It continues to be produced by several countries around the world and to be stock-piled as a means of defence in the event of war. When the gas comes into contact with humans, it acts as a powerful irritant that causes blistering of the skin, eyes and respiratory tract prior to damaging the cells' DNA.

Research Topic | Different types of mutation

The sequence of bases along a DNA strand contains genetic information that determines the sequence of amino acids in a protein (see Figure 4.4 on page 32). Mutations bring about changes to the genetic information held in the 'codewords' in the DNA.

Neutral mutation

A mutation may alter one base in the DNA strand and form a new codeword. The presence of this codeword introduces a chemically **similar amino acid** into the protein. The protein (and the mutant organism possessing it) remains unaffected. Such a mutation is described as **neutral**.

Disadvantageous mutation

If a DNA codeword is altered by mutation, this may lead to the **wrong amino acid** being introduced into the protein molecule at some point along its chain of amino acids or **no amino acid** being introduced at that point. This results in an inferior or non-functional version of the protein molecule being produced. For example, in humans a certain mutation on chromosome 7 leads to the formation of a protein that lacks one copy of an essential amino acid and is therefore non-functional. In the absence of the normal protein, the person secretes mucus that becomes thicker and stickier than normal. It causes congestion of organs such as the lungs and pancreas. This condition is called **cystic fibrosis** and a sufferer needs regular pounding on the chest to clear the thick mucus (see Figure 20.4).

Advantageous mutation

On rare occasions there occurs a mutant organism that is **better** than the original. For example, unusual varieties of plants possessing several extra complete sets of chromosomes occur as a result of a type of chromosome mutation. These mutant plants are called polyploids and normally they are larger than their diploid relatives. This increase in size often includes seed and fruit size, which make the plants of **economic importance**. Many commercially developed crop plants such as wheat, tomatoes and strawberries (see Figure 20.5) are polyploid mutants and give bigger yields than their non-polyploid relatives.

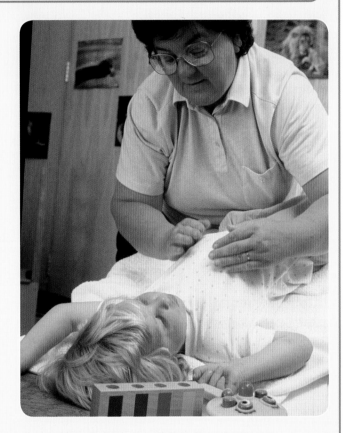

Figure 20.4 Treating a sufferer of cystic fibrosis

original strawberry plant

polyploid strawberry plant

Figure 20.5 Mutant strawberry plant

Mutation as a source of variation

Mutation is the only source of **new variation** amongst living things. It is the process by which new alleles of genes are produced. Without mutation, all organisms would be homozygous for all genes and no variation would exist.

Result of mutation

Most mutations are harmful (or even lethal) and therefore confer a **disadvantage** on the mutant organism's phenotype. On rare occasions there occurs by mutation a mutant allele that confers an **advantage** on the organism that receives it. Such mutant alleles provide the alternative choices upon which **natural selection** can act (see page 181) and bring about evolutionary change.

Adaptation

An **adaptation** is an inherited characteristic that makes an organism well suited to its environment. The members of a species possess certain **evolutionary adaptations**. These are the phenotypic expressions of changes that have occurred in the species' genotype as a result of mutations over a very long period of time. Possession of these adaptations gives the species some advantage and increases its chance of survival in its environment.

Related Activity

Investigating examples of adaptation

Desert mammal
Since the desert is a region of very low rainfall where drought conditions persist for most of the year (accompanied by high daytime and low night-time temperatures), the kangaroo rat, a desert mammal, has only a limited supply of available water. It is able to gain all of its water from its food ('dry' seeds) and remain in water balance (see Figure 20.6) without drinking water at all. This is made possible by the possession of the following **adaptations**:

- Its mouth and nasal passages are **dry**, thereby reducing water loss during breathing.
- Its bloodstream contains a high concentration of **antidiuretic hormone** (see page 89).

- Its kidney tubules are **very long** and promote water reabsorption so effectively that it can produce urine 17 times as concentrated as its blood.
- Its large intestine is efficient at **reabsorbing water** from waste material and producing faeces with a low water content.
- It does **not sweat**.

Behavioural adaptations
The kangaroo rat is **active at night** and goes out searching for food when the conditions are cool. Therefore it has no need to produce sweat to give a cooling effect and water is conserved. The animal remains in its **underground burrow** in a fairly **inactive state** during the extreme heat of the day. Unlike the hot, dry air above ground, the air inside the burrow is cooler and

water gain		water loss
6 g in food		44 g in expired air from lungs
		13.5 g in urine from kidneys
54 g in metabolic water produced during tissue respiration		2.5 g in faeces from large intestine
		0 g in sweat
60 g = total gain		60 g = total loss

Figure 20.6 Water balance in kangaroo rat (fed 100 g seeds over 1 month)

more humid. Therefore the air being inhaled by the rat is almost as damp as the air being exhaled and minimum net loss of water occurs.

Desert plant

A normal land plant (such as an oak tree) would be unable to survive in the desert. Its leaves would present an enormous surface area of thin tissue from which water would be rapidly lost as water vapour by transpiration. At the same time, its roots would be unable to find water in the ground to replace this loss.

A desert plant such as a cactus is able to survive in such an extreme habitat because it possesses certain **adaptations**. Figure 20.7 shows the prickly pear plant. Its leaf surface is **greatly decreased** by its leaves being reduced to **protective spines**. Its stem is divided into green lobes that carry out photosynthesis. Each of these portions of stem is fleshy and stores water in **succulent tissues**. Water loss from the stem is kept to a minimum by the **thick, waxy cuticle** that coats its outer surfaces.

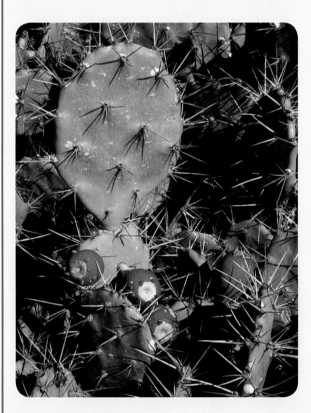

Figure 20.7 Prickly pear plant

Some cacti have **long roots** for reaching supplies of subterranean water. Others possess extensive systems of **superficial roots** that grow parallel to the soil surface. These enable the plant to absorb maximum quantities of water on the rare occasions when rain does fall.

Galapagos finches

Charles Darwin visited the Galapagos Islands in 1835. He found them to be inhabited by many unique life forms including 13 different species of finch. Figure 20.8 shows a few of these finches. They are found to vary greatly in **beak size** and **shape**. These different **adaptations** make each species well suited to its environment by enabling it to exploit a particular ecological niche. For example, the insect-eating 'warbler' finch has a small, sharp, pointed beak that is ideal for picking insects out of narrow crevices in the bark of a tree. The seed-eating finch's large, blunt beak, on the other hand, is well suited to breaking open tough coats surrounding seeds and nuts.

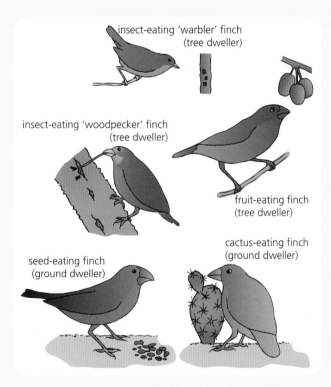

Figure 20.8 Darwin's finches

Plants and specific pollinators

Orchid and moth

The flowers of some plants are **adapted** to be pollinated by a specific animal that also possesses appropriate **adaptations**. For example, the star orchid (*Angreacum*) produces star-like flowers that release perfume at night. The back of the flower (see Figure 20.9) has a **long spur** with a **nectary** at the end of it. The plant's pollinator is a moth that flies by night and is attracted to the perfume. This type of moth has a **long proboscis** that enables it to reach the nectary. During feeding, it brings about pollination.

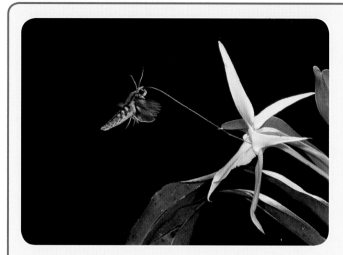

Figure 20.9 Star orchid and moth pollinator

Such a specific relationship is beneficial to both the plant and the animal. The plant gets pollinated without its pollen being wasted on flowers of another species; the animal is guaranteed a food supply unavailable to other animal species.

Acacia and ant

Acacia is a plant commonly found as a shrub or tree in many parts of the world. One type of acacia native to Africa and South America is **adapted** in a way that enables it to benefit from a close relationship with its pollinator as follows.

The swollen-thorn acacia has **large, hollow thorns** that provide a habitat for a type of stinging ant (see Figure 20.10). The tree also supplies the ants with nectar. In return, the ants kill animals such as small herbivores that would attack the acacia plant and they destroy any plants growing close to the acacia that would compete with it for essential resources. The ants patrol their acacia plant 24 hours a day and pollinate its flowers.

Figure 20.10 Swollen-thorn Acacia and acacia ants

Natural selection

Every species of living organism has an enormous **reproductive potential** (see Table 20.1). Its members produce far more offspring than the environment can support and this leads to a **struggle for survival**.

Animal species	Average number of offspring per year
fox	5
red grouse	8
rabbit	24
mouse	30
trout	800
cod	4 000 000
oyster	16 000 000

Table 20.1 Reproductive potential

A simplified example involving rabbits is shown in Figure 20.11. Many offspring die before reaching reproductive age as a result of factors such as:

- competition
- lack of food
- overcrowding
- inability to escape predators
- lack of resistance to disease.

The members of a species are not identical to one another but show phenotypic **variation** in all characteristics (see Figure 20.12). Much of this variation is inherited. It is this inherited variation that is of significance in the process of natural selection.

Survival of the fittest

Those offspring whose phenotypes are **better adapted** to their environment have a better chance of surviving, reaching reproductive age and passing on the genes for the favourable characteristics (that confer some advantage) to their offspring.

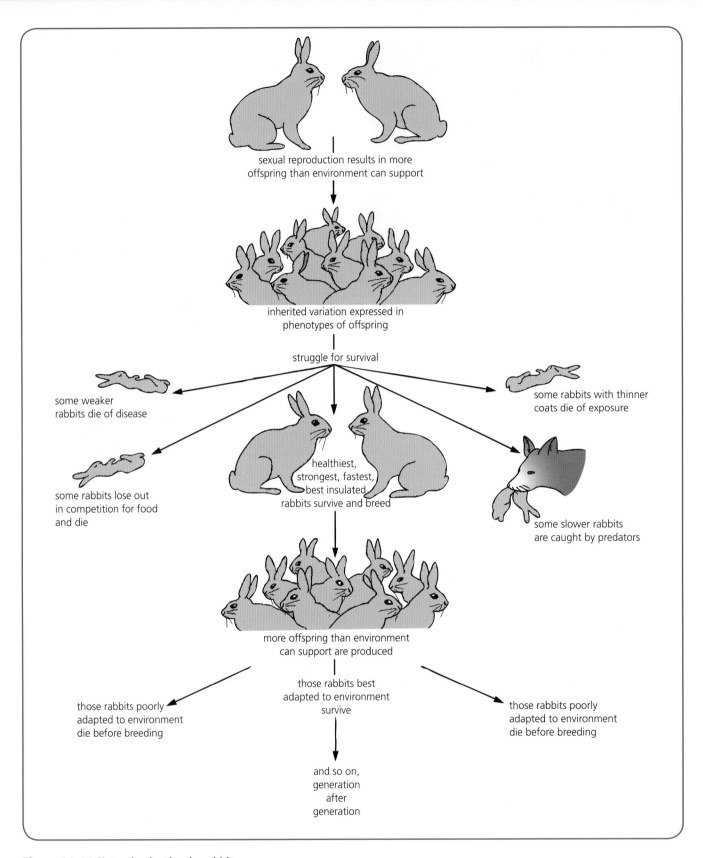

Figure 20.11 Natural selection in rabbits

Figure 20.12 Variation within a population of limpets

Those offspring whose phenotypes are least well suited to their environment die before reaching reproductive age and fail to pass on their genes.

This process is repeated generation after generation and the organisms with the phenotypes best suited to the environment (i.e. the fittest) are 'selected' and predominate in the population. The poorer members are weeded out and die. This process is known as **natural selection**. Charles Darwin first described natural selection in 1858. It is the main factor producing evolutionary change in species over time in response to changing environmental conditions.

| Research Topic | Antibiotics and their over-prescription |

Resistance to antibiotics

Antibiotics have been used in the UK for over 60 years. As each new antibiotic is introduced, it is found to be most effective against bacteria in its early years. Its effectiveness is found to decrease as the number of bacterial strains that are **resistant** to it increase and spread.

Micro-organisms such as bacteria occur in huge numbers. Genetic variation (resulting from spontaneous mutations) exists amongst the members of a population. A mutant bacterium may arise with genetic material that makes it resistant to a certain antibiotic without ever having been in contact with the antibiotic. Some disease-causing bacteria, for example, are able to make the enzyme penicillinase. This enables them to digest and resist penicillin. Figure 20.13 shows how resistant bacteria can spread from person to person.

Over-prescription of antibiotics

Sometimes antibiotics are prescribed for minor bacterial infections that, given time, would have been success-fully dealt with by the body's natural defences alone. This **over-prescription** of antibiotics promotes an increase in the number and spread of bacterial strains resistant to the antibiotics. Antibiotics should only be used to treat bacterial infections that are so severe that they cannot be contained and destroyed by the body's own defences. This is often the case in young children and in the elderly.

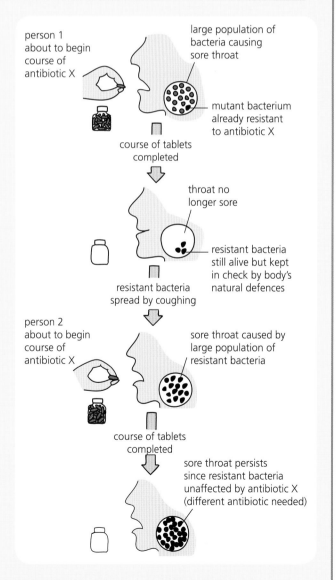

Figure 20.13 Spread of resistant bacteria

Research Topic | Rapid natural selection

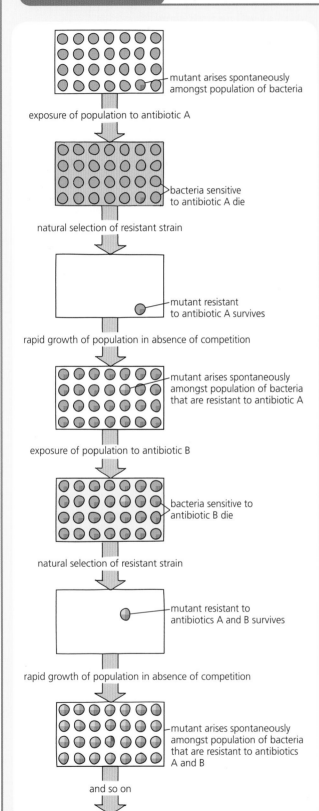

Figure 20.14 Evolution of resistant bacteria

The sequence of events that can lead to the evolution of mutant bacteria resistant to two different antibiotics is shown in Figure 20.14. As the process continues, some strains showing **multiple resistance** may continue to be favoured by this form of **rapid natural selection**. If these bacteria are also disease-causing, they will be difficult to treat.

Exchange of DNA

In addition to the transmission of genes for resistance to antibiotics from one generation of bacteria to the next, it is now known that portions of DNA including genes for antibiotic resistance can be passed from one type of bacterium to another type growing beside it in the same environment.

MRSA

Staphylococcus aureus is a species of bacterium commonly found on the surface of the human skin. It causes one in five of the infections acquired by hospital patients during treatment. In the past it was successfully controlled by a range of antibiotics. However, there now exists a strain of *S. aureus* known as **MRSA** (see Figure 20.15) that is **resistant** to almost all antibiotics.

Figure 20.15 MRSA (methicillin-resistant *Staphylococcus aureus*)

Case Study — Insect resistance to 'built-in' insecticides in GM crops

Pink bollworm

The pink bollworm (see Figure 20.16) is the larval stage of a type of moth. The female adult lays her eggs in a cotton boll. When the eggs hatch, the larvae that emerge feed on and damage the cotton plant. Genetic engineering has been used to produce a transgenic variety of cotton plant containing a gene from a bacterium that makes an insecticide lethal to bollworms. This chemical gives these genetically modified (GM) cotton plants protection against the bollworm pests. However, in some parts of India, a strain of pink bollworm has already been discovered that is resistant to the 'built-in' insecticide present in the GM cotton crop.

European corn borer

The corn borer is also the larval stage of a type of moth. The female lays her eggs on the underside of the leaves of maize ('corn-on-the-cob') plants. When the caterpillars (borers) hatch from their eggs, they damage the cobs and tunnel into the stalks, making the plants fall over. A transgenic variety of maize has been produced that contains a bacterial gene for an insecticide. This toxic chemical is lethal to corn borers, enabling the GM maize crop to protect itself against these pests.

However, it is only a matter of time until a strain of corn borer resistant to the 'built-in' insecticide appears. Already scientists have produced a population of resistant corn borers by repeatedly exposing colonies of the insect to the insecticide in the lab. To try to delay the natural emergence of resistant corn borers on farmland, farmers in the USA who plant GM maize are obliged by law to plant normal, non-transgenic maize nearby. These plants are intended to provide a location to harbour the pests and slow down the evolution of the type resistant to the 'built-in' insecticide.

Figure 20.16 Pink bollworm

Related Topic

Red Queen model of ecology

This evolutionary hypothesis derives its name from Lewis Carroll's *Through the Looking Glass*, in which the Red Queen tells Alice, 'It takes all the running you can do to keep in the same place.'

The **Red Queen hypothesis** proposes that **competition** is the engine of evolutionary change. Variation exists amongst the members of each species in an ecosystem and all the different species living there are co-evolving.

Any species that shows an improved adaptation to a changing environment will have a **selective advantage** over other competing species and will be able to commandeer an increased share of available resources. In order to catch up, a rival species must also show some **improved adaptation** to the changing environment that, in turn, gives it a **competitive edge**. Otherwise it risks being left behind and becoming extinct.

According to the Red Queen theory, in a competitive world of co-evolving species, continuous adaptive change ('running') by a species is essential for the basic survival ('keeping in the same place') of that species.

Speciation

A **species** is a group of living things that are so similar to one another genetically that they are able to inter-breed and produce **fertile** offspring.

Speciation is the formation of **new** species. It occurs when a population becomes **isolated** from the other members of its species for a very long time or permanently. The isolated population finds itself subjected to environmental conditions different from the ones to which it was previously adapted. Under these circumstances, natural selection may take a **new direction** and result in the isolated population eventually becoming a new species.

The simplified version of speciation shown in Figure 20.17 occurs as follows.

1 The members of a large population of a species occupy an environment and **interbreed**, forming fertile offspring.

2 The population becomes split into two completely isolated populations, X and Y, by a **barrier** that prevents interbreeding and exchange of genetic material. This isolating mechanism could, for example, be
 - **geographical** in the form of a river, a desert, a sea or a mountain range
 - **ecological** caused by differences in temperature, humidity or pH.

3 **Mutations** occur at random. Most of the mutations affecting population X are different from those affecting population Y. Any new variation that arises in one group is not shared by the other group. For example, the small mutant that arises in group Y does not occur in group X.

4 The selection pressures acting on each population are different depending on environmental conditions such as type of climate, predators and disease. In this example the isolating barrier has resulted in population Y landing in a region with a warmer climate than the one affecting population X. **Natural selection** affects each population in a different way by favouring those alleles that make the members of that population best at exploiting their environment. For example, small-sized members of population Y will be selected because they are better suited to survival in a warm climate than larger members.

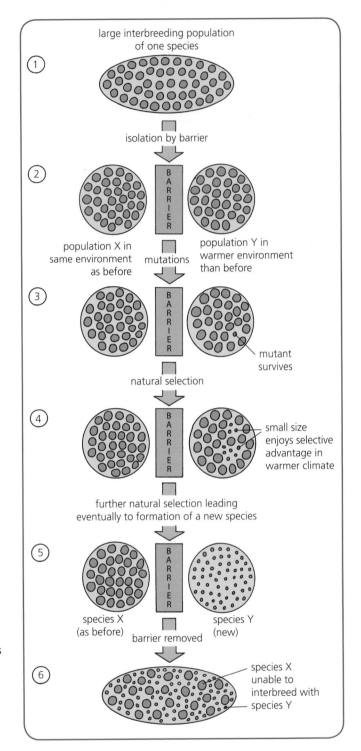

Figure 20.17 Speciation

5 Over a very long period of time, stages 3 and 4 cause the two groups to become **genetically distinct**.

6 If the barrier is removed, they are no longer able to interbreed successfully. **Two distinct species** now exist: species X (similar to the original species) and species Y (a completely new species).

Research Topic	Isolation leading to speciation

Endemic species

When a particular type of organism is found only in a certain region such as an island, it is said to be **endemic** to that region. Endemic species of plants and animals are found to occur on some Scottish islands.

Arran whitebeam

The **mountain ash** is a type of tree commonly found throughout Europe, especially on rocky mountainous soil but not on clay or limestone. The **rock whitebeam** is a shrub (or rarely a small tree) found on crags amongst rocks especially on limestone soil. The **Arran whitebeam** is a small, slender tree, endemic to the island of Arran, where it grows on steep granite banks and mountain slopes. It favours high-altitude environments near the tree line where competition is reduced.

The Arran whitebeam is believed to have arisen as a result of hybridisation between the mountain ash and the rock whitebeam. By growing in habitats different from those favoured by its parents and lacking competitors such as those found on the mainland, the Arran whitebeam has taken its own course of evolution and is a different species from both of its ancestors (see Figure 20.18).

St Kilda wren

St Kilda is a group of tiny islands in the Atlantic Ocean isolated from the Scottish mainland (see Figure 20.19). The type of wren (the **St Kilda wren**) that is endemic to this island environment differs from its mainland relative in several ways. The St Kilda wren:

- is heavier
- has longer wings
- has thicker legs
- is paler and more striped
- lays larger, heavier eggs

mountain ash

rock whitebeam

Arran whitebeam

Figure 20.18 Arran whitebeam and relatives

It is possible that these differences are **adaptive features** that help the bird to survive amongst the rocks in such a wet and windy environment totally lacking in trees. Although **speciation** is well under way, the St Kilda wren has not been isolated from the mainland population for long enough yet to have become a separate species. It is still able to mate with the mainland variety and produce fertile offspring.

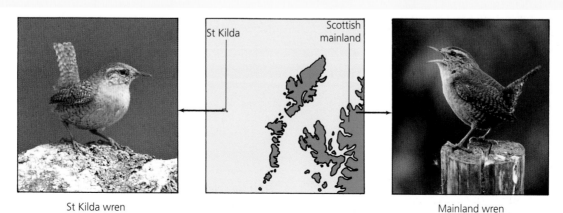

St Kilda wren

Mainland wren

Figure 20.19 Two types of wren

Testing Your Knowledge

1 a) What is meant by the term *mutation*? (1)

b) What is a *mutant*? (1)

c) i) Give an example of a mutagenic agent.

ii) What effect does a mutagenic agent have on an organism's natural mutation rate? (2)

2 a) Table 20.1 on page 181 shows that an oyster has the potential to produce 16 million offspring annually. Give THREE reasons why the seas are not over-populated with oysters. (3)

b) In the struggle for survival, which oysters will:

i) survive and pass on their genes to succeeding generations?

ii) die before reaching reproductive age? (2)

c) What is the name given to this 'weeding out' process that promotes survival of the fittest? (1)

3 a) Explain the difference between the terms *species* and *speciation*. (2)

b) Copy and complete the paragraph below using the following terms: *advantage, isolated, mutations, natural selection, speciation*. (4)

If a population of organisms becomes _____ from the other members of its species, it may undergo _____ and eventually become a new species. This happens if _____ follows a different path in this new environment and some _____ that would have been neutral or disadvantageous before now confer an _____ on the organisms.

4 Decide whether each of the following statements is true or false and use T or F to indicate your choice. Where a statement is false, give the word(s) that should have been used in place of the word(s) in **bold** print. (5)

a) **Adaptation** is the only source of new variation amongst living things.

b) Most mutations confer **an advantage** on the mutant organism.

c) Some mutations are **neutral** and have no effect on the mutant's phenotype.

d) An inherited characteristic that makes an organism well suited to its environment is called an **evolution**.

e) **Natural selection** is the process by which the members of a population best adapted to changing environmental conditions survive and pass their genes on to succeeding generations.

21 Human impact on environment

Population growth

Unlike other species, human beings have managed to overcome most of the environmental factors that normally prevent a population in its natural ecosystem from increasing indefinitely in number. Humans have used their exceptional brainpower to:

- remove the threat of predation
- develop vast areas of land for food production
- improve public health.

As a result, the human population continues to **increase rapidly** and is expected to reach 9 billion by the year 2040 (see Figure 21.1). This continuous increase in population size needs to be matched by an equivalent **increase in food yield**. Attempts to achieve this goal are made by:

- growing vast monocultures of food crops
- employing methods of intensive farming
- developing genetically modified (GM) crops.

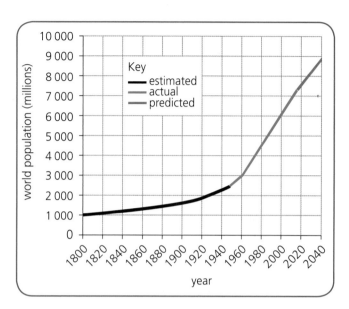

Figure 21.1 Human population growth

Research Topic — Monocultures and intensive farming

Monoculture

A **monoculture** (see Figure 21.2) is a vast cultivated population of one type of crop plant whose members are genetically identical. In order to feed the ever-growing human population, natural ecosystems have been cleared to accommodate vast monocultures of crops such as wheat, maize, rice and potatoes.

In recent years, agriculture has become so efficient that increased levels of food production have generally managed to keep pace with the many millions of new human beings added annually to the world population. Farming in many developed countries is remarkably productive. For example, farmers in the USA, who make up less than 2% of the population, grow the food consumed by the rest of the population *and* produce more than half of the agricultural products exported worldwide. The UK and many other countries also have an impressive record. However, such advances in agriculture using monocultures have been largely dependent on the use of chemicals (see below) and even with their use, increased food yield is now struggling to keep pace with the increase in human population.

Figure 21.2 Monoculture – in this case maize

Intensive farming

Compared with traditional smallholder cultivation of arable farmland, **intensive agriculture** enables farmers to produce more food from the same acreage of land. This has become accepted practice in many countries in

189

order to meet the increasing demand for food. Intensive farming involves:

- growing high-yield crop plants as vast **monocultures** and supplying the plants with large quantities of chemical fertiliser
- making regular use of chemicals such as **herbicides** (to kill weeds that would compete with the crop) and **pesticides** (to remove insects and other pests that would consume the crop)
- rearing farm animals indoors and often confining them to restricted spaces (see Figure 21.3). This so-called 'battery' farming reduces the quantity of energy lost by the animal as heat to the surrounding environment and the energy used by the animal for movement. Therefore it leaves more available for the growth of the animal.

Advantages

A significant **increase in yield** per hectare is achieved. Therefore the food tends to cost less to produce, making it more affordable to the customer.

Disadvantages

Clearing natural ecosystems for cultivation of monocultures and killing weeds and insect communities **reduces biodiversity**. Some of the chemicals may be harmful to humans in the long run. Battery-farmed animals reared in cramped conditions run an increased risk of **suffering disease** and high levels of **stress**. Many people feel that this practice is unethical.

Figure 21.3 Restricted space during 'battery' farming

| **Research Topic** | **Genetically modified (GM) crops** |

Current levels of food production are not expected to meet the projected future demand and already many people in the world lack sufficient food. One way of increasing food production is to develop **genetically modified (GM)** crops. In recent years genetic engineers have managed to do this by inserting a useful gene from some other organism into the cells of a crop plant (see chapter 6). This process has produced:

- maize (see Figure 21.4) containing a bacterial gene for a toxin that makes it resistant to insect pests
- potato that is resistant to fungal blight
- cucumber, courgette and pepper that are resistant to disease-causing viruses
- oilseed rape, sugar beet and soya bean that can tolerate herbicide (weedkiller) while nearby weeds are destroyed
- golden rice that contains a source of vitamin A (see page 45)
- apple and tomato that are slow to ripen (see page 46).

The toxins that some GM crops contain are harmless to humans.

Figure 21.4 GM maize

Most GM crops increase food supply by reducing the quantity of crop that is lost. In addition many of them allow farmers to decrease their reliance on pesticides and herbicides without suffering a decrease in yield. Unfortunately there is no guarantee that a GM plant such as maize resistant to corn borers (see page 185) will remain resistant permanently. Eventually a mutant form of the pest may evolve and overcome the plant's resistance. Then a new strain of the GM crop will be required.

Despite the obvious advantages of GM crops, some people believe that these plants may carry some inherent risk to human health. In addition, they are concerned that genetic material introduced into crops could somehow become incorporated into other species in the ecosystem. This, they argue, could produce new, undesirable strains such as 'super-weeds' resistant to weedkillers.

Fertiliser

The maintenance of a natural balanced ecosystem depends on the repeated **cycling** of chemical nutrients such as **nitrogen** (see page 160). The natural processes of decay and nitrification in the soil **replace nutrients** as fast as they are used by plants.

However, when a crop is grown on cleared land and then harvested and removed, the balance is disturbed. The cycles are broken since almost no dead plant material is returned to the soil for breakdown by micro-organisms. Less nitrate is generated by nitrifying bacteria and the soil becomes **less fertile**. This problem is tackled by adding **fertiliser** to the soil. Fertilisers are chemicals rich in nitrate and other substances (such as phosphate) that are essential for healthy plant growth.

Leaching

If fertiliser from fields **leaches** into a river or loch, it makes the water over-rich in mineral nutrients such as nitrate. This promotes the rapid growth of algae (simple water plants), which form an **algal bloom** (see Figure 21.5).

When the algae die in huge numbers, the bacteria that decompose them undergo a population explosion (see Figure 21.6). Their high rate of respiration uses up the **oxygen** dissolved in the water. This reduction in the water's oxygen level has an adverse effect on the river or loch's animals and many die from lack of oxygen.

Figure 21.5 Algal bloom

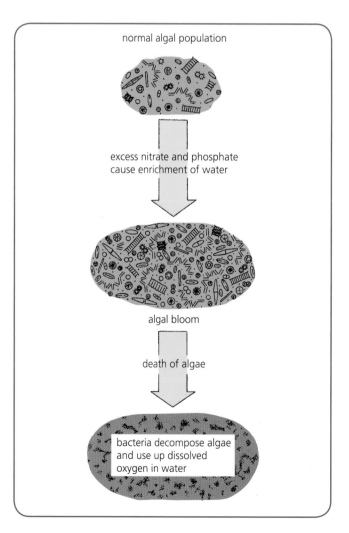

normal algal population

excess nitrate and phosphate cause enrichment of water

algal bloom

death of algae

bacteria decompose algae and use up dissolved oxygen in water

Figure 21.6 Effect of algal bloom on oxygen supply

Investigating the importance of minerals for plant growth

A green plant needs small quantities of several **mineral elements**, such as nitrogen (as nitrate), phosphorus (as phosphate) and magnesium, which are present in fertile soil and absorbed by a plant's root hairs. The importance of each element to a plant is investigated by setting up a series of **water culture experiments** where one element at a time is omitted from the mineral solution. The control experiment contains all the elements necessary for growth.

The glass beaker used in the water culture experiment shown in Figure 21.7 is initially rinsed with concentrated nitric acid to remove all traces of mineral elements. It is surrounded by an opaque cover such as aluminium foil to keep out light and prevent the growth of algae. Their presence would introduce a second variable factor and make the results of the experiment **invalid**. Several seedlings are used in each beaker to improve the **reliability** of the results.

After several weeks' growth, each plant lacking an essential mineral element is found to show certain **deficiency symptoms** when compared with the control (see Figure 21.8). These symptoms often indicate the role played by the mineral element in the plant as summarised in Table 21.1.

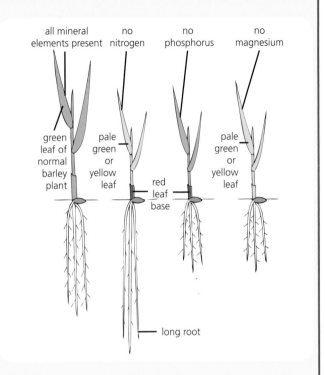

Figure 21.8 Effects of mineral element deficiency in plants

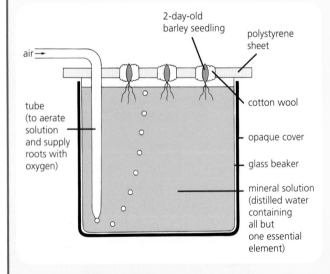

Figure 21.7 Water culture experiment

Element omitted	Symptoms of deficiency	Role of element in plant
nitrogen	overall growth reduced, leaves pale green or yellow, leaf bases red, roots long and thin	needed for production of amino acids, proteins and nucleic acids
phosphorus	overall growth reduced, leaf bases red	needed for production of ATP and nucleic acids
magnesium	overall growth reduced, leaves pale green or yellow	needed for production of chlorophyll

Table 21.1 Role of mineral elements in plants

Pesticides

Importance

It is estimated that without pesticides, cereal crop yield would be reduced by 25% after 1 year and by 45% after 3 years. It is unlikely that wholesome, healthy, unblemished food, sufficient in quantity to feed the world's ever-increasing population, could be produced without the aid of pesticides.

Adverse effects

In addition to having the desired effect, some pesticides also have unintended effects on other populations in the ecosystem. The extent of these disruptive side-effects depends on various factors highlighted by posing the following questions:

- Is the pesticide **specific** in its action or is it poisonous to a wide variety of organisms?
- Is it **biodegradable** or does it persist for a very long time in the environment?
- Is the concentration that is used kept to a **minimum** or is it used in excess?

In the past people often failed to address these issues. This led to the following sequence of events:

- Molecules of toxic, non-biodegradable chemical in pesticides enter and persist in the bodies of producers.
- The toxic molecules are passed along food chains and become more and more concentrated at each level.
- High concentrations of the toxic chemical accumulate in the tissues of the final consumers, which are seriously affected, sometimes fatally.

Indicator species

Some species of living thing only thrive well under certain environmental conditions such as very clean air,

---

| **Research Topic** | **Bioaccumulation of DDT** |

The pesticide **DDT**, which is both **persistent** and highly **toxic**, was widely used in the 1950s and 1960s. It was found to pass easily through food chains with the effect described above. In the example in Figure 21.9, the producer becomes contaminated with a very low concentration of the pesticide blown off neighbouring farmland during the spraying of crops. The concentration increases, however, when plant material is eaten by primary consumers and the DDT persists in their cells.

Progression on up the pyramid of numbers and biomass leads to ever-increasing concentrations of the chemical **accumulating** in living cells. Finally, the few large tertiary consumers at the top suffer severe poisoning.

Thin egg shells

The female birds at the top of this affected pyramid suffer an upset in the balance of the hormones that control the manufacture of strong egg shells. As a result, they lay eggs with **thin shells** that often break during incubation, leading to a significant decrease in reproductive success. The graph in Figure 21.10 shows that as few as 25 parts per million of the pesticide can reduce a shell's thickness by as much as 15%. Once the

Figure 21.9 Accumulation of chemical in a food pyramid

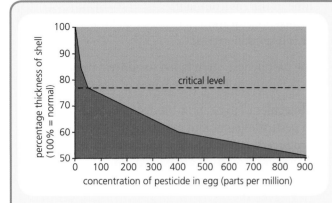

Figure 21.10 Effect of pesticide on thickness of shell

shell is more than 23% thinner than normal, it breaks with disastrous results.

Aquatic ecosystems

Pesticide sprays can also be washed off farmland into local watercourses. If they are non-biodegradable, they similarly increase in concentration amongst the members of the freshwater ecosystem's community. So persistent is DDT that it has found its way into marine ecosystems despite the dilution effect of the sea on polluted river water. Traces of DDT have even been found in the fatty tissue of penguins in the Antarctic.

badly polluted water and so on. Such organisms that indicate the quality of the environment are called **indicator species**. They are important because their presence (especially in large numbers) shows that an ecosystem is affected by a particular set of environmental conditions.

Research Topic   Lichen survey

Lichens (see Figure 21.11) are simple plants composed of a fungus and an alga, often found growing on the bark of trees and on rock surfaces. Different species of lichen vary in their sensitivity to **sulphur dioxide (SO_2)**, a gas that causes atmospheric pollution (see page 144). The variety of lichen species present in an ecosystem decreases as the concentration of SO_2 in the air increases (see Figure 21.12).

The data obtained from a **lichen survey** can be used to construct an air pollution map of an area as shown in Figure 21.13.

Figure 21.11 Lichens

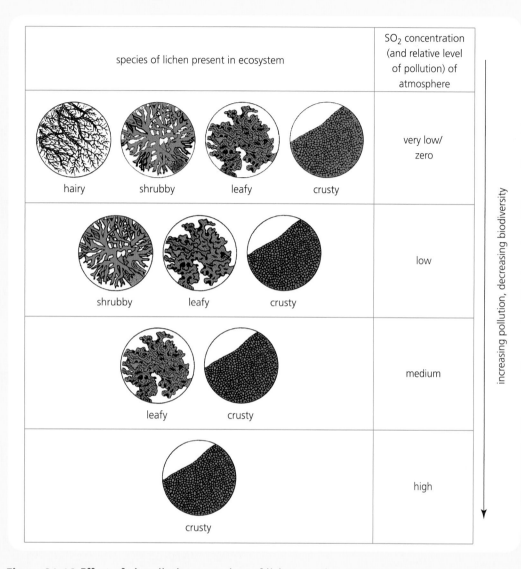

Figure 21.12 Effect of air pollution on variety of lichen species

Key	abundance of lichen types	level of atmospheric pollution indicated
	no lichens or few crusty only	high
	many crusty, few leafy	moderate
	some crusty, many leafy	low
	some crusty, many leafy, some hairy	zero

Figure 21.13 Air pollution map based on lichen survey

Related Topic

Effect of oxygen concentration on freshwater invertebrates

Research into the effects of low oxygen concentration on aquatic animals shows that species differ in their ability to tolerate the **varying oxygen levels** found in a river **polluted** with organic waste (see Figure 21.14). Some animals such as **mayfly** and **stonefly nymphs** are commonly found in clean water rich in oxygen. However, they cannot survive when the river's oxygen content is greatly reduced by the presence of a huge number of decomposer micro-organisms.

If the water becomes extremely polluted and contains almost no oxygen, then the only animals that survive are **rat-tailed maggots** and **sludgeworms**. As the water gradually becomes a little less polluted, animals such as **midge larva ('bloodworms')** and **water louse** are commonly found because they can survive in water of low oxygen concentration.

When pollution eventually decreases to a fairly low level, water plants can survive and produce oxygen by photosynthesis. The oxygen content of the water begins to rise and **freshwater shrimps** and **caddis fly larvae** are now found to become numerous since they can tolerate low levels of pollution. **Mayfly** and **stonefly nymphs** are only found again when the water is very clean and contains plenty of oxygen.

Indicator species

Since each of the above species of invertebrate animal only thrives within a specific range of oxygen concentration, it acts as an **indicator species**. The relationship of these indicator species to oxygen concentration and level of pollution of the water in their ecosystem is summarised in Table 21.2.

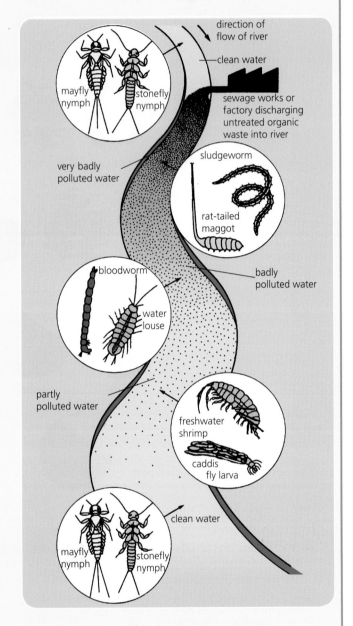

Figure 21.14 Freshwater indicator organisms

Indicator species present	Oxygen concentration of water	Level of water pollution
mayfly nymph stonefly nymph	high	absent or very low
freshwater shrimp caddis fly larva		low/medium
bloodworm water louse		high
rat-tailed maggot sludgeworm	low	very high
no animals present	zero	extreme

Table 21.2 Freshwater indicator species

Combating the harmful effects of intensive farming

The significant increase in yield achieved by intensive farming may be accompanied by **harmful effects** such as:

- destruction of natural ecosystems and loss of biodiversity
- pollution of the environment by pesticides
- death of helpful, as well as harmful, insects due to pesticides
- bioaccumulation of pesticides along food chains.

One way of trying to redress the balance is to use **GM crops** such as maize that produce their own 'built-in' toxin. These GM crops are able to resist pests and do not need to be sprayed with pesticide. A further alternative practice used to mitigate the effects of intensive farming is **biological control**. This is the reduction of a pest population by the deliberate introduction of one of its natural enemies such as a predator or a parasite. The use of ladybirds to clear greenfly from plants is an example of biological control. The natural enemy acts as the control agent and specifically targets the pest. No environmental pollution occurs and no chemicals persist and accumulate in food chains.

Related Activity

Investigating biological control

Use of ladybirds

Ladybirds (or more correctly ladybird beetles) prey on **scale insects** and **aphids** (see Figure 21.15). Ladybirds are active from spring to autumn and can consume a large number of aphids such as greenfly in one day. Ladybirds are used by some horticulturists to act as a means of **biological control** to keep their crop of tomatoes or cucumbers in a glasshouse free of aphids. Some gardeners purchase cultures of ladybirds from suppliers to release in their garden (for example, on rose bushes infested with greenfly) in preference to using an insecticide spray.

Figure 21.15 Ladybird and aphids

Use of virus

Myxomatosis is a disease that was first discovered in South America. It is caused by a **virus** and affects the South American cottontail **rabbit** (*Sylvilagus*), which suffers a relatively harmless form of the disease.

Many years ago, the European rabbit (*Oryctolagus*) was introduced into Australia. It lacked competitors and became so successful that by 1950 its numbers had reached 600 million. It was regarded as a serious pest and the myxomatosis virus from South America was deliberately introduced into the rabbit population as a means of **biological control**.

The disease developed by the European rabbit involves swelling of mucous membranes, formation of skin tumours, blindness, fever, pneumonia and death. It had a devastating effect and reduced the rabbit numbers in Australia to 100 million in two years. The rabbits that survived were naturally resistant to the disease and gradually the population recovered. A further attempt at biological control was carried out in 1996 using a second virus (rabbit calcivirus).

Use of cactus moth

The **cactus moth** (*Cactoblastis*) is a native of South America. Its larvae feed on a type of **cactus** whose scientific name is *Opuntia*. In South America, both organisms are members of a balanced ecosystem where their population numbers are held in check naturally.

Prickly pear cactus is a type of *Opuntia*. It was introduced to Australia in 1840. In the absence of its natural enemies and competitors, the cactus flourished. Within a few years it was spreading at a rate of almost half a million hectares a year and rendering vast areas of potential farmland unsuitable for cultivation or grazing.

In 1925 the cactus moth from Argentina was introduced to Australia to act as an agent of **biological control**. The larvae (see Figure 21.16) bored into the prickly pear cactus and spent many months living inside the plant and feeding on it. Once the plant was destroyed, the larvae pupated in the debris on the ground and later emerged as adult moths. This form of biological control was repeated generation after generation and eventually the prickly pear cactus in Australia was brought under control.

The same procedure was tried in other countries with mixed results. For example, in South Africa it proved to be problematic because the cactus moth larvae destroyed much of the population of spineless *Opuntia* that had traditionally been used as animal fodder. The cactus moth has now spread worldwide and is regarded as a pest by the ornamental cactus-growing industry in the USA.

Figure 21.16 Larvae of cactus moth and *Opuntia*

Testing Your Knowledge

1 a) Briefly explain why, unlike other animals, the human population continues to increase rapidly. (2)

   b) Name TWO ways in which attempts are being made to increase food yield. (2)

2 a) Explain why fertiliser needs to be added to land where a crop is repeatedly grown, harvested and removed. (2)

   b) What events lead to the formation of an algal bloom? (2)

   c) Why does an algal bloom lead to a reduction in oxygen content of the water in the affected ecosystem? (2)

3 a) In general, what is the purpose of a pesticide? (1)

   b) Identify a possible adverse effect of the bioaccumulation of molecules of a non-biodegradable pesticide along a food chain. (1)

4 a) Define the term *indicator species* and give ONE named example in your answer. (2)

   b) Define the term *biological control* and give ONE named example in your answer. (3)

What You Should Know Chapters 20–21

adaptation	fittest	offspring
adapted	genetic	oxygen
advantage	increase	quality
alleles	indicator	radiation
bacteria	intensive	random
biological	isolation	selection
bloom	mutagenic	speciation
disadvantage	mutation	toxicity
enemies	natural	yield
fatal	non-biodegrad-	
fertiliser	able	

1 A _____ is a change in the structure or composition of an organism's _____ material. It may confer an advantage or a _____ on the organism or be neutral and not affect it.

2 Mutations occur spontaneously and at _____ but rarely. They are the only source of new _____.

3 Rate of mutation can be increased by _____ agents such as _____ and certain chemicals.

4 An inherited characteristic that makes an organism well suited to survive in its environment is called an _____.

5 The members of a species produce far more _____ than the environment can support. This leads to a struggle where only the _____ survive.

6 Those individuals best _____ to a changing environment pass on the genes that confer a selective _____ to their offspring. The less well adapted members die. This weeding out process is called _____ selection.

7 _____ occurs when a population becomes isolated for a very long time and natural _____ takes a new direction. Gradually the group becomes adapted to environmental conditions that differ from those that affected it before _____.

8 The human population continues to _____ rapidly and this needs to be matched by an increase in food _____.

9 When _____ from farmland leaches into watercourses or lochs it may over-enrich the water and cause formation of an algal _____. When the algae die, the decomposer _____ that act on them undergo a population explosion and use up the water's dissolved _____ supply during respiration.

10 Molecules of pesticides that are _____ can accumulate in the bodies of organisms. This leads to an increase of _____ along food chains, which may be _____ to the final consumers.

11 A species that by its presence indicates the _____ of the environment is called an _____ species.

12 Attempts are made to balance the adverse effects of _____ farming by using GM crops and employing _____ control as alternatives to the use of pesticides. Biological control is the reduction of a pest population by the introduction of one of its natural _____.

Applying Your Knowledge and Skills Chapters 17–21

1 The information in Table KS3.1 was collected by studying eight different species of snail present in six Scottish lochs. (+ = snails present) (ppm = parts per million)

Loch	Species of snail								Concentration of calcium (ppm) in loch water
	A	B	C	D	E	F	G	H	
1	+	+		+	+	+	+	+	19.9
2		+	+		+	+	+	+	17.8
3			+	+	+		+	+	15.3
4				+		+	+	+	9.5
5							+	+	7.1
6								+	5.2

Table KS3.1

a) What concentration of calcium was present in loch 5? (1)

b) Which loch contained 9.5 ppm of calcium in its water? (1)

c) Which species of snail was found in every loch? (1)

d) Which loch possessed only five different species of snail? (1)

e) How many different species of snail were found in loch 2? (1)

f) i) What relationship seems to exist between the number of species of snail present and the concentration of calcium in the water?

ii) Give a possible explanation for this relationship based on the fact that one of the components of a snail's shell is calcium. (2)

2 Figure KS3.1 shows a form of atmospheric pollution. Match the numbered boxes in the diagram with the following lettered descriptions to show the correct sequence of events. (1)

A acid rain falls on land and water environments

B fossil fuels burned by industry, power stations and motor vehicles

C acid gases form acid rain clouds

D trees suffer dieback and fish die

E acid gases released into the atmosphere

3 Figure KS3.2 shows the number of units of energy (in kilojoules/m²/year) that are transferred from organism to organism in a pond food chain.

a) What percentage of sunlight is successfully captured by the phytoplankton? (1)

Figure KS3.1

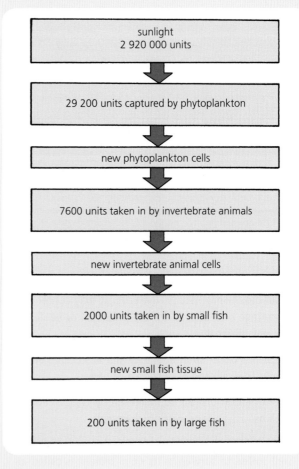

Figure KS3.2

b) What percentage of energy is lost between intake of energy by small fish and intake of energy by large fish? (1)

c) How many units of energy are lost when small fish feed on invertebrate animals? (1)

4 a) Copy and complete Table KS3.2, which refers to some of the design features that apply to the cress seed investigation on page 163. (4)

Feature of experimental design	Reason
equal mass of cotton wool and equal volume of water added to each carton	
yoghurt cartons are encased in black paper or painted black	
only recently purchased cress seeds are used	
experiment is repeated many times and results are pooled	

Table KS3.2

b) It could be argued that the water was lost by the evaporation from the two cartons at different rates and that this introduced a second variable factor. Suggest an improvement that could be made to the design to overcome this problem. (1)

5 Figure KS3.3 shows the results from an investigation into the numbers of two closely related species of spider, X and Y, living on a climbing ivy plant. The size of the circle at each sample site indicates the relative size of the total population of spiders found there. The black portion indicates species X and the blue portion species Y.

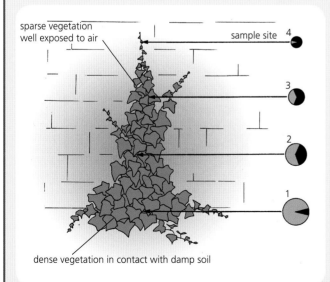

Figure KS3.3

a) What relationship exists between the *total* number of spiders and the distance from the ground? (1)
b) Which species is more numerous at ground level? (1)
c) Describe the trend in relative numbers of the two species of spider that occurs from site 1 to site 4. (1)
d) i) Predict what will happen when equal numbers of the two species of spider are placed in the plastic tube shown in Figure KS3.4.
   ii) Explain your answer. (2)

Figure KS3.4

6 The information in Figure KS3.5 and the key of paired statements below refer to eight different fish.

Figure KS3.5

KEY

1

body with large scales .... go to **2**

body with tiny scales.................................... go to **5**

2

one dorsal fin present................................... go to **3**

two dorsal fins present, the first with
spiny rays .... go to **4**

3

dark spot behind head .... **shad**

dorsal fin placed far back on body .... **pike**

4

dark spots on first dorsal fin forming bands...... **zander**

dark spot on rear end of first dorsal fin........... **perch**

5

two or more barbels around the mouth.....go to **6**

no barbels present ....go to **7**

6

one long barbel on lower jaw, two barbels
at nostrils...**burbot**

two long barbels on upper lip ....**catfish**

7

one long dorsal fin present....................**blenny**

two dorsal fins present, the first with
spiny rays ....**miller's thumb**

    a) Identify fishes W and X shown in Figure KS3.6. (2)

Figure KS3.6

    b) Give TWO characteristics of a burbot. (2)
    c) Name TWO features shared by a zander and a perch. (2)
    d) Identify fishes Y and Z from the following descriptions:
      i) Fish Y has two dorsal fins, the first with spiny rays. It has a fairly broad head with the eyes on the top of it. It is a small fish and has neither barbels nor large scales.
      ii) Fish Z lacks a lateral line but does have one black spot behind its head and one dorsal fin. It has large scales and those on its belly form a sharp toothed edge. (2)
    e) State TWO differences between a pike and a miller's thumb. (2)

7 The graph in Figure KS3.7 refers to an investigation into the effect of increasing radiation on the percentage number of X chromosomes showing a lethal (deadly) mutation. The animal used was the fruit fly (*Drosophila melanogaster*). The results are plotted as points with the line of best fit drawn through them.

Figure KS3.7

    a) What was the one variable factor altered by the experimenter in this investigation? (1)
    b) How many conditions of this factor were used? (1)
    c) Name TWO other factors that would have to be kept constant to make the experiment valid. (2)
    d) What conclusion can be drawn from the above results? (1)
    e) Explain why it is acceptable that a hospital patient with a suspected fractured limb be exposed to X-rays yet the radiographer must remain behind a lead screen to avoid exposure. (1)

8 Figure KS3.8 refers to three subspecies of the European wren.

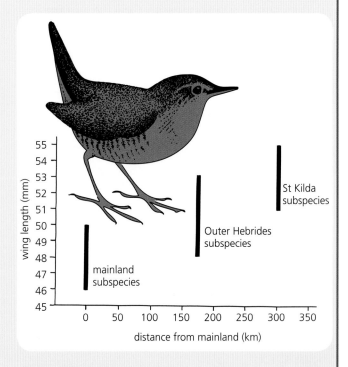

Figure KS3.8

a) What is the range of wing lengths found amongst the St Kilda wrens? (1)

b) How many of the three subspecies contain birds with a wing length of:
   i)   47 mm?
   ii) 49 mm?
   iii) 52 mm?
   iv) 54 mm? (4)

c) What relationship exists between wing length and distance of the bird's habitat from the mainland? (1)

d) Identify the barrier that isolates the three subspecies of wren. (1)

e) By what means could scientists find out if the three subspecies have become distinct species? (1)

9 The apparatus shown in Figure KS3.9 was one of a set of water cultures used to investigate the requirement by cuttings of *Tradescantia* (wandering sailor) for certain chemical elements. Each of the gas jars was thoroughly cleaned in hot, soapy water and rinsed under the tap before use.

Figure KS3.9

a) i) Identify TWO sources of error contained in the procedure adopted during the setting up of this investigation.
   ii) Explain your answers. (4)

b) Assume that the two sources of error have been eliminated in an improved version of the experiment.

i) Compare Figure KS3.9 with Figure 21.7 on page 192 and state which set-up would be likely to give more reliable results.

ii) Justify your answer. (2)

c) After 6 weeks, the *Tradescantia* plants in an improved version of the experiment were examined for deficiency symptoms.
   i)   What is meant by the term *deficiency symptom*?
   ii) Which leaves would be most likely to show them?
   iii) Explain your answer to ii). (3)

d) i) Predict what would have happened to a *Tradescantia* plant if distilled water had been used in the gas jar instead of mineral solution.
   ii) Explain your answer. (2)

10 Figure KS3.10 shows the concentration of the pesticide DDT in parts per million (ppm) found in the cells of the members of a loch community.

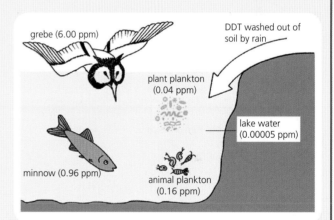

Figure KS3.10

a) Construct a food chain that includes the four types of organism shown in the diagram. (1)

b) Construct a table to show the concentration of DDT found in the cells of each type of organism with the information arranged in increasing order. (2)

c) i) By how many times did the concentration of pesticide increase between loch water and plant plankton?
   ii) Between which two organisms did the pesticide concentration increase by exactly six times? (2)

d) i) Which animal do you think was found to suffer most and often die as a result of DDT poisoning?
   ii) Explain your choice of answer. (2)

e) Suggest why the use of DDT is now banned in Britain. (1)

Appendix 1

Units of measurement

Quantity	Standard unit	Symbol	Relationship between units
length	**metre**	m	
	other useful units:		
	centimetre	cm	1 cm = 1/100th of a metre = 10^{-2} m
	millimetre	mm	1 mm = 1/1000th of a metre = 10^{-3} m
	micrometre	µm	1 µm = 1/1000th of a millimetre = 10^{-3} mm
			1 µm = 1/1000 000th of a metre = 10^{-6} m
area	**square metre**	m^2	
volume	**cubic metre**	m^3	
	other useful units:		
	cubic decimetre (litre)	dm^3 (l)	1 dm^3 = 1/1000th of a cubic metre
	cubic centimetre	cm^3	1 cm^3 = 1/1000th of a cubic decimetre (litre)
mass	**kilogram**	kg	
	other useful units:		
	gram	g	1 g = 1/1000th of a kilogram
	tonne	t	1 t = 1000 kg
energy	**joule**	J	
	other useful unit:		
	kilojoule	kJ	1 kJ = 1000 J
time	**second**	s	
	other useful units:		
	minute	min	1 min = 60 s
	hour	h	1 h = 60 min = 3600 s
temperature	**degree Celsius**	°C	

Table Ap 1.1

Appendix 2

pH scale

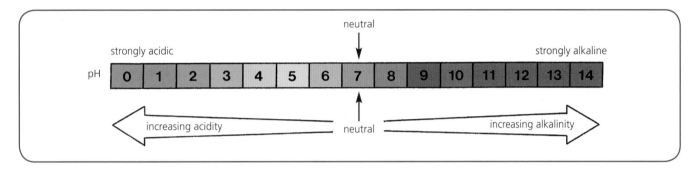

Figure Ap 2.1

Appendix 3

Size scale of plants and micro-organisms

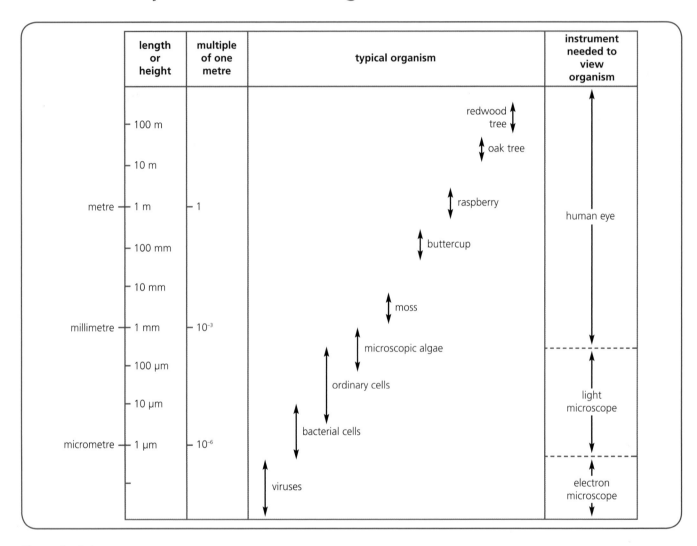

Figure Ap 3.1

Appendix 4

Variable factors

Each of the pots shown in Figure Ap 4.1 contains the same **number** of seeds planted at the same **soil depth**. These words in bold print refer to factors that are constant in Figure Ap 4.1 but that could be varied. These are therefore called **variable factors**.

In a scientific investigation, a test is **valid** if it deals with **one variable factor** at a time, as shown in Figures Ap 4.2 and Ap 4.3. However, if the parts of an experiment differ from each other by more than one variable factor, the test is unfair and therefore invalid. In Figure Ap 4.4, the pots differ from one another in two ways:

- seed number
- depth of planting.

This is an invalid test because it will be impossible to say whether the seeds that grow best have done so due to their number or their depth of planting.

Figure Ap 4.2 Seed number as variable factor

Figure Ap 4.3 Depth of planting as variable factor

Figure Ap 4.4 An invalid test

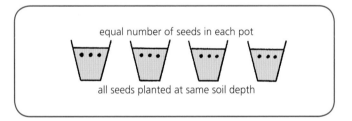

equal number of seeds in each pot

all seeds planted at same soil depth

Figure Ap 4.1 Variable factors kept constant

A

abiotic factors 144–9, 152–3, 173–4

absorption 127

abundance (of plant types) 169

acacia 181

acid rain 148

active sites 35, 36

active transport 15–17

adaptation 179–81

additive effect 105

adenosine triphosphate (ATP) 48, 51

adrenal glands 88, 89

advantageous mutation 178, 179

aerobic respiration 51, 52, 54

agar 25

air pollution 144, 194–5

airborne micro-organisms 24–5

albumin 41

alcohol 131–2

algal bloom 191

alimentary canal 125–6

alleles 104

alveoli 124–5

amino acids 32, 35

ammonium compounds 160, 161

Amoeba 13, 19

amylase 39

anaemia 133

anaerobic respiration 52, 54

animal cells 3, 4, 19, 52, 54

anthers 96

antibiotics 183

antibodies 36

ants 181

anus 126

aorta 120

aphids 197–8

appendix 126

aquatic biomes 149

aquatic ecosystems 194

arctic tundra 150, 151

Arran whitebeam 187

arteries 121–3

aseptic techniques 25–6

atmospheric nitrogen 161

atmospheric pollution 194–5

ATP (adenosine triphosphate) 48, 51

atrium 120

autoclaves 25

axon fibres 85

B

bacteria

    cell structure 2, 3, 4

    chromosomal material 43

    nitrogen cycle 160, 161

    resistant 183–4

bacterial

    culture 27

bar graphs 100

'battery' farming 190

beetroot cells 6

belt (line) transects 174

bile duct 126

biodiversity 144, 190

biological catalysts 36–8

biological control 197–8

biomass 158–9

biomes 149–51

biotic factors 144–9, 166–70

blight resistance 46

blood clots 132, 133

blood glucose regulation 90–1

blood groups (bar graph) 100–1

blood pressure 129

blood vessels 74, 120, 121–3

bloodworms (midge larvae) 152, 196, 197

bone marrow transplantation 79

bracken 155

brain 83, 84

brain damage 132

breathing rate 52

bronchi 124–5

bronchioles 124–5

brown trout 162

bubble potometer 114, 115

C

cacti 180

cactus moth 198

caddis fly larvae 152, 196, 197

cadmium 133

Caledonian forest ecosystem 152–3

Canadian pondweed 152

cancer 132, 134, 177

capercaillie 152, 153

capillaries 122, 123, 125

carbohydrates 56, 58–61

carbon dioxide 60, 63

carbon fixation 58

carbon monoxide 7–8, 130, 133–4

carrier molecules 15

cartilage 124

catalase 37, 40

catalysts 36–8

cats see wild cats

cell culture 24–8

cell division 19, 82

cell membranes

    diffusion 7–9

    role 8–9

    structure 3, 4, 6–7

cell models

    osmosis 11

cell walls 2, 3, 4, 14

cells

    multicellular organisms 74

    and osmosis 12–14

    size 4–5

    structure 2–4

central nervous system (CNS) 83, 85

centromeres 22

cerebellum 84

cerebrum 84

Chargaff's rules 31

cheek epithelium 74

chemical analysis

    DNA 31

chemical energy 48

chemical mutagens 177

Chernobyl 177

chlorophyll 56, 60

chloroplasts 2, 3, 4, 56, 116

chromatids 22

chromosome complement 19–20

chromosomes 2, 19–20, 43

cilia 124

ciliated epithelium 74, 75

circular chromosomes 2, 3, 4

circulatory system 77, 120–5

cirrhosis 132

climograph 149

CNS (central nervous system) 83, 85

columnar cell 74

communities 152

companion cells 76, 117–18

competition

    in ecosystems 162–5

    Red Queen hypothesis 185

complementary base pairs 30–3

concentration gradient 7

coniferous forest 150

continuous variation 98–101

contractile vacuole 13

controls 36

cornea repair 79–80

coronary artery 122–3

cress seedlings 163

crossbills see Scottish crossbills

cultures 25

cystic fibrosis 109, 178

cytoplasm 3, 19, 117–18

cytoplasmic strands 75

D

daisies

    distribution 174

    petals 100

data presentation 100–1

DDT 193–4

deciduous forest 150

decomposition 160, 161

deforestation 144, 145

denaturation 40

denitrification 160, 161

deoxyribonucleic acid (DNA) see DNA (deoxyribonucleic acid)

desalination (osmosis) 15

desert biomes 149, 150, 151

desert mammals 179–80

desert plants 180

desertification 145–6

diabetes 91–2, 132

diffusion 7–9, 111

digestive system 77, 125–6

diploid cells 94, 95, 97

diploid chromosome complement 20, 22

disadvantageous mutation 178, 179

discrete variation 98

DNA (deoxyribonucleic acid) 30–3, 184

dominant characteristics 103

double helix 30

dragonflies 152

dyes 2, 17

E

ear types 99

ecological niches 154–6

ecosystems

    competition 162–5

    composition 152–3

    definition 144

    practical investigation 166–76

effectors 84

egg white 41

eggs
    human reproduction 94–5
    osmosis experiment 10
electron microscope 2–3
Elodea bubbler experiment 61–4
Elodea leaf cells 2, 3
embryonic stem cells 78–81
endemic species 187
endocrine glands 88
energy 48, 49
energy flows (food chains) 157–60
environment
    and health 133–4
    and polygenic inheritance 108
environmental hazards 176
enzymes 35, 36–41
epidermal cells 75, 76
epidermal growth factor 45
epidermis 75, 76, 117
epithelial cells 75
equator 22
Escherichia coli 3
ethics
    intensive farming 190
    stem cell research 80–1
European corn borer 185
evolutionary adaptations 179–81
exchange vessels 122
excretory system 77
exercise
    lack of 129
    and pulse rate 131
exhaust emissions 133–4

F
family trees 108–9
farming, intensive 189–90, 197
fats and proteins 58
fatty deposits
    in blood vessels 132
fermentation 52, 54
fermenters 28
fertilisation 95, 97
fertilisers 161, 191–2
fingerprint types 99
fish species
    and pH 148, 149
flaming process 26
flowering plants
    gamete formation 96–7
    organs 76
flowers 76, 96–7
fluid mosaic model 7

food calorimeters 49
food chains 157–60
food transport system 125–8
food yield 189–90
foods
    energy content 49
    salt content 130
foxes *see* red foxes
freshwater ecosystem 152
freshwater shrimps 196, 197
frog tadpoles 152
frogbit 152
fruit flies 20, 33
fungal culture 27
fungi 3, 4

G
Galapagos finches 180
gall bladder 126
gametes (sex cells) 94, 104
gaseous exchange 124–5
gastric band surgery 135
genes 30, 104–5
genetic code 31
genetic engineering 43–5
genetic material
    transfer 43
genetics
    and variation 101
genotypes 104–5
glucagon 90, 91
glucose 48, 51, 58–61, 90, 91
glycogen 90
GM (genetically modified) crops
    190–1, 197
GM (genetically modified)
    organisms 43, 185
goblet cell 74
golden rice 45
gonads 94
grain colour 107
grasshoppers 162
grazing 147
grey squirrels 162
grouse *see* red grouse
grouse-shooting 153
growth 19, 22–3
growth curves 22–3
growth medium 27
guard cells 76, 116, 117

H
habitats 144
haemoglobin 123, 133

hair colour 108–9
haploid cells 20, 94, 95, 97
heart 76, 120–1
heart attacks 122, 132
heart valves 121
heather moorland ecosystem 153
height (histogram) 100–1
hepatitis B antigens 45
herbicides 190
heterozygous genotypes 104–5
HGH (human growth hormone) 45
high-fat diet 129
high-salt diet 129
histograms 100–1
homozygous genotypes 104–5
hormones 35, 88–92
hornwort 152
human beings
    cells 74
    chromosomes 20
    diffusion 8
    embryos 78
    growth curves 23
    organs 76
    polygenic inheritance 105, 108–9
    sexual reproduction 94–5
    tissue 74
human cheek epithelium 3
human growth hormone (HGH) 45
human population growth 189–90
human serum albumin 45
humidity 114
hydrogen carbonate indicator 50
hydrogen peroxide
    and catalysts 37

I
ice (terrestrial biome) 150
identification of organisms 170–2
indicator species 193–7
inheritance 101–3
inoculating loops 26
insect resistance 185
insecticides 185
insulin 45, 90, 91
intensive farming 189–90, 197
interspecific competition 162
intraspecific competition 162–5
iodine solution 2, 16–17
ionising radiation 177
iron 45, 133
islets of Langerhans 89
ivy plants 176

K
kangaroo rats 179–80
keys (identification) 170–2
knee jerk reflex actions 87–8

L
lacteal 127
lactic acid 52
ladybird beetles 197–8
large central vacuole 3, 4
large intestine 126
leaching 191
lead 133
leaf structure 116, 117
leaves 76
leeches 152
lichens 194–5
lifestyle choices
    effects of 129–35
light-dependent stage
    photosynthesis 57–8
light energy 56
light intensity
    effect on daisies 174
    measuring 173
    photosynthesis 61–2, 63
light/moisture meters 173
lignin 117–18
limiting factors 62, 63, 64
limpet shells 100, 183
line (belt) transects 174
lipid molecules 6–7
liver 90, 91, 126, 127
lung cancer 130–1
lungs 76, 124–5

M
maize 190
mammalian circulatory system
    120–5
mayflies 152, 196, 197
measurement units 204
medical applications
    genetic engineering 45
medulla 84
Mendel, Gregor 105–6
meristems 81–2
mesophyll 76, 114, 117
messenger RNA (mRNA) 32
micro-organisms
    genetic engineering 43
midge larvae (bloodworms) 196, 197
minerals
    and plant growth 192

mitochondria 2, 3, 4, 51
mitosis 21–2, 82
molecular model
    osmosis 11
monoculture 189, 190
moths 180–1
motor fibre 74
motor neuron 74
mountain ash 187
mouth 126
mRNA (messenger RNA) 32
MRSA 184
mucus 74, 124
multicellular animals 8
multicellular GM organisms 44
multicellular organisms
    transport systems 111
mustard gas 177
mutagenic agents 176–7
mutants 176
mutations 176–9, 186
myxomatosis 198

N
National Health Service (NHS) 135
natural selection 162, 179, 181–5,
    186
nectary 96
nerves 74, 83, 84
nervous system 83–8
neurons 84–5
neutral mutation 178
NHS (National Health Service) 135
niches 154–6
nicotine 130
nitrates 160, 161
nitrification 160, 161
nitrites 160, 161
nitrogen cycle 160–1
nitrogen fixation 160, 161
nitrogenous waste 161
nuclear bombs 177
nuclear power stations 177
nuclear transfer technique 80–1
nuclei 2, 3, 4
nutrient agar 25, 26, 27

O
oak trees 163
obesity 129, 131, 132
oesophagus 74, 126
onion leaf cells 2
optimum pH 41
optimum temperature 38, 40

organelles 2, 74
organisms
    identification of 170–2
    as integrated whole 77
organs
    flowering plants 76
    gaseous exchange 124–5
    humans 76
osmoregulation 90
osmosis 9–15, 113, 114
osmotic imbalance 91
ovaries 88, 89, 94–5, 96
ovulation 95
owl pellets 147–8
oxygen
    and algal bloom 191
    diffusion 7–8
    gas exchange 125
oxygen debt 52, 54
oxygen levels 196
oxyhaemoglobin 123

P
pain receptors 86
palisade mesophyll 76
pancreas 88, 89, 90, 91, 126
pea plants 102, 103, 105–6
pepsin 41
peristalsis 125–6
pesticides 190, 193
Petri dishes 25–6
pH
    and bacterial growth 28
    and enzymes 40–1
    and fish species 148, 149
    measuring 173
pH scale 205
phenotype 101–2
phenotype ratio 103
phloem
    comparison with xylem 117–18
    structure 75, 76
    water transport experiment 112
photosynthesis
    biochemistry of 57–61
    light-dependent stage 57–8
    process 56–7
    rate 61–4
pine martens 154, 155
pink bollworms 185
pitfall traps 166–7
pituitary 88, 89
plant cells

cell division 19
    fermentation 54
    meristematic 81–2
    osmosis 12, 14
    structure 2, 3, 4, 75, 76
plant growth
    and minerals 192
plant tissues 75
plant transport systems 111–18
plants
    gamete formation 96–7
    organs 76
plasmids 2, 3, 4, 43
plasmolysed cells 14
platelets 74
pollen grains 96
pollen tubes 96–7
pollination 96–7, 180–1
pollution 133, 144, 148–9, 194–6
polygenic inheritance 105–9
polyploids 178
pond animals 172
pond netting 169–70
pond shrimps 152
pond skaters 152
pond snails 152
pooters 170
population growth 189–90
potato cells 10
potatoes 46, 59
power generation (osmosis) 15
practical investigation
    ecosystems 166–76
predation 147–8
proteins 6, 35
ptarmigan 155–6
pulmonary artery 120
pulmonary vein 120, 122
pulse rate
    and exercise 131
pumps 16
pyramid of biomass 158–9
pyramid of energy 159–60
pyramid of numbers 158
pyruvate 51, 52

Q
quadrats 167–8
quantitative techniques 166–70

R
rabbits 147, 182, 198
radiation 134, 176–7
rainbow trout 162

rapid natural selection 184
rat-tailed maggots 152, 196, 197
receptors 84
recessive characteristics 103
rectum 126
red blood cells 12–13, 74, 123–4
red dye experiment 112
red foxes 154
red grouse 164–5
red onion cells 14
Red Queen hypothesis 185
red squirrels 162
reeds 152
reflex actions 86–8
reflex arcs 85
replication 22
reproductive organs 94–5
reproductive potential 181
reproductive system 77
resistant bacteria 183–4, 190–1
respiration 7–8, 48–54
respiratory system 77, 124–5
reverse osmosis 15
ribosomes 2, 3, 4, 32
rickets 134
river pollution 196
robins 164
rock whitebeam 187
root epidermis 75, 76
root hair cells 76
root hairs 75, 113–14
root nodules 161
root tip meristems 81–2
roots 75, 76

S
salivary glands 126
salt content 130
sampling (organisms) 166–70
savanna 150
Scotland
    biodiversity 144
Scottish crossbills 152, 154–5
scrubland 150
sensory fibres 85
sex cells (gametes) 94
sexual reproduction
    flowering plants 96–7
    genetic significance 101
    multicellular animals 94–5
sheep 147
sieve tubes 76, 117–18
single gene inheritance 102–3

size scale
  plants and micro-organisms 206
skin 76
skin cancer 134, 177
skin grafts 79
sludgeworms 196, 197
small intestine 126, 127–8
smoking 130–1
smooth muscle cells 74
sodium chloride 130
sodium/potassium pump 16
soil animals 171
soil ecosystem 167
soil moisture content 173
speciation 186–7
species 186
sperm 94–5
spinal cord 74, 83
spindle fibres 22
spongy mesophyll 76
squamous cell 74
squirrels 162
St Kilda wren 187
stains 2
star orchids 180–1
starch 58–61
stem cells 78–81
stems 75, 76
sterile conditions 25–6
sticklebacks 152
stigma 96, 97
stoma 117

stomach 76, 126
stomata 114, 115–16
stomatal mechanism 116
stonefly nymphs 196, 197
stress 132
strokes 132
structural proteins 35
sugar transport 116–18
sulphur dioxide 194
surface area to volume ratio 111–12
survival of the fittest 181–3
symbols 104
synapses 85
systems 74

T
target tissues 88
temperate grassland 150, 151
temperature
  and bacterial growth 28
  and enzymes 38–40, 41
  measuring 173
  and photosynthesis 64
  and thermal pollution 148–9
terrestrial biomes 149, 150
territorial behaviour 164–5
testes 88, 94–5
thermal pollution 148–9
threadlike chromosomes 2
thyroid 88, 89
tissue 74
tissue stem cells 78, 81

tobacco 130–1
tomatoes 46
toxic heavy metals 133
trachea 74, 124–5
transpiration 114–16
transport systems
  food 125–8
  plants 111–18
  water 111–15
tree beating 170
tropical rainforests 145, 149, 150, 151
trout 162
true-breeding strains 102
true pyramids 159–60
Tullgren funnels 169

U
ultrastructure 2
ultraviolet radiation 177
ultraviolet rays 134
unicellular animals 13
unicellular fungi 3, 4
unicellular organisms 7–8
units of measurement 204
UV light 134, 177

V
valves 121, 122
variable factors 38, 207
variation 98–101, 181, 183
veins 117, 121–3
vena cava 120
ventricle 120, 121

villi 127
vitamin A 45
vitamin D 134

W
water beetles 152
water boatmen 152
water concentration gradient 9–10
water culture experiments 192
water lice 196, 197
water pollution 196
water spiders 152
water transport
  plants 111–15
waterlouse 152
waxy cuticle 117
weight gain 129, 131
white blood cells 74
wild cats 154

X
X-ray crystallography
  DNA 31
X-rays 177
xylem
  comparison with phloem 117–18
  structure 75, 76
  water transport 112, 114

Y
yeast 3, 17, 53

Z
zygote 78, 95, 97